ROCKING
TOWARD A
FREE WORLD

ROCKING
TOWARD A
FREE WORLD

WHEN THE STRATOCASTER BEAT THE KALASHNIKOV

ANDRÁS SIMONYI

GRAND CENTRAL
PUBLISHING

NEW YORK   BOSTON

Grand Central Publishing
Hachette Book Group
1290 Avenue of the Americas, New York, NY 10104
grandcentralpublishing.com
twitter.com/grandcentralpub

First edition: June 2019

Grand Central Publishing is a division of Hachette Book Group, Inc. The
Grand Central Publishing name and logo is a trademark of Hachette Book
Group, Inc.

The publisher is not responsible for websites (or their content) that are not
owned by the publisher.

The Hachette Speakers Bureau provides a wide range of authors for
speaking events. To find out more, go to www.hachettespeakersbureau.com
or call (866) 376-6591.

Library of Congress Cataloging-in-Publication Data has been applied for.

ISBNs: 978-1-5387-6221-9 (hardcover), 978-1-5387-6223-3 (ebook)

Printed in the United States of America

LSC-C

10 9 8 7 6 5 4 3 2 1

For my grandchildren, Olivia, Jens, Ben, and Nico

CONTENTS

Note to the Reader ix
Introduction xi

Chapter One 1
Chapter Two 8
Chapter Three 15
Chapter Four 22
Chapter Five 27
Chapter Six 33
Chapter Seven 41
Chapter Eight 52
Chapter Nine 60
Chapter Ten 76
Chapter Eleven 79
Chapter Twelve 86
Chapter Thirteen 94
Chapter Fourteen 99
Chapter Fifteen 105
Chapter Sixteen 112
Chapter Seventeen 114
Chapter Eighteen 120
Chapter Nineteen 129

CONTENTS

Chapter Twenty 138
Chapter Twenty-One 144
Chapter Twenty-Two 150
Chapter Twenty-Three 156
Chapter Twenty-Four 161
Chapter Twenty-Five 167
Chapter Twenty-Six 173
Chapter Twenty-Seven 178
Chapter Twenty-Eight 185
Chapter Twenty-Nine 196
Chapter Thirty 201
Chapter Thirty-One 213
Chapter Thirty-Two 226
Chapter Thirty-Three 233
Chapter Thirty-Four 240
Chapter Thirty-Five 251
Chapter Thirty-Six 257
Chapter Thirty-Seven 266
Chapter Thirty-Eight 272
Chapter Thirty-Nine 281
Chapter Forty 288
Chapter Forty-One 295
Chapter Forty-Two 299
Chapter Forty-Three 311
Chapter Forty-Four 314

Acknowledgments 319
About the Author 321

NOTE TO THE READER

It has been seventy-plus years since the Cold War ripped the world apart, fifty-plus years since the events in this book took place. The divide between the liberal West and the authoritarian East was absolute. It seemed nothing could bring these two sides together. Certainly not politics or diplomacy. And yet, an unseen force was emerging, propelled by youth, optimism, and a burning desire to buck the status quo. This great power was rock and roll, and it swept through the world, breaking down barriers and infiltrating the Soviet bloc, of which my country, Hungary, was part. I was among the few who had experienced the communist East and the democratic West, having spent my formative years in both Hungary and the Kingdom of Denmark. It was in Denmark that I learned the meaning of freedom and democracy. And it was in Denmark that I was introduced to rock and roll.

When my family returned to Hungary, my most prized possessions were my electric guitar and a deep attachment to rock music. It's that connection I'm writing about here. I'm not attempting to provide a history of rock and roll or a treatise on the political might of the Soviet Union, but to explain the hard-hitting impact of this incredible musical and cultural phenomenon. I'm writing as an individual, as part of a generation who grew up behind the Iron Curtain, a generation that, against stern repercussions and strict limitations, appropriated this force and made it our own.

This book is a testament to the formidable power of rock and roll. It chronicles the longing for freedom of thought and expression to show how we, the youth of the Eastern bloc, used rock and roll to connect with our peers in the West. Listening to our favorite bands gave us precious moments of autonomy. Performing rock and roll—despite the many barriers presented by the authorities—gave us the ultimate freedom.

I've done my best to represent the events of my life as faithfully as memory allows. In addition to relying on my own recall, I have reviewed diaries, notes, and letters made at the time and have asked family and friends to help fill in the gaps. Where available, I have consulted original sources such as books, newspapers, and magazines. In some instances, I have taken creative liberty to construct scenes and dialogues out of my own true stories. I have used real names in most cases, occasionally protecting a person behind a pseudonym. However, all the characters are real people, and some of them, sadly, are gone. I have tried my best to give them the justice they deserve.

INTRODUCTION

G rowing up in Hungary in the second half of the twentieth century meant growing up in a strange gray zone of isolation. An Iron Curtain had descended between us and the free world. After fighting on the wrong side in World War II, Hungarians had lived through a few hopeful years in which they could almost believe in the possibility of a democracy. But in 1948 the country was thrust mercilessly into the Soviet orbit. It would take forty years to pry loose the oppressive hand that was the Russian occupation; forty years in which the Hungarian people were forced to contend with a ruthless and oppressive Soviet system, in which liberty was denied and individuality threatened. Advances toward democracy were quashed, and Hungary was forced to pull back from the democratic ideology it had been leaning toward. Still, for all that we were separated from the free world, we were never totally disconnected from the West and the breadth of opportunity it represented.

Admittedly, I had a privileged childhood. My family

had a comfortable home with hot and cold running water. We had food on the table and books on our shelves. A working record player with American records. My brother, sister, and I were loved and cherished. My parents made sure that we received a good education and gave us everything they possibly could. They even gave us a taste of freedom.

If you've always lived in freedom, it might be hard to imagine how potent a concept it is. Let me put it into context. Imagine New York after a devastating war. Imagine that people with blue eyes and red hair, good people who have long since proved their allegiance to the country, are rounded up, herded into cattle cars, and transported to concentration camps where they will be executed. Men with curly hair are next, followed by women with brown eyes.

After that comes occupation by a foreign power. All banks and privately owned businesses are nationalized, and their owners, pushed to the fringes of society, are transported to a camp on Staten Island. Times Square, once spectacular, is now dimly lit and covered in drab ads—approved, of course, by the Party. When not hawking inferior products manufactured by state-owned factories, the ads proclaim the great deeds of the Party, of which there is only one. Picture the once grand apartments on Fifth Avenue now confiscated by the city council, sliced up into small flats, the marble cracked, the furniture broken. The concierge of each building watches everyone who goes in and everything that goes on; he reports all activity to the secret police.

Imagine that most of the theaters on Broadway have been shut down and the few that remain open are told which acts can perform. Imagine that blue jeans can only be obtained on the black market; that rock and roll is broadcast by pirate radio stations operating offshore, and by Radio Free New York in Connecticut. The First Amendment is suspended "in the name of the people," and New Yorkers require a permit to visit New Jersey. The wait for a passport is two, possibly three years.

Now imagine that even in the face of such tyranny, the people of New York never really surrender. With resilience and resourcefulness they form friendships, find love and passion, create and nurture families. Even under the harsh restraints of a callous dictatorship, they find ways to live as best they can. And if they happen to be a boy like me, they join the rock-and-roll revolution that is taking over the world. Because a boy who dreams of freedom from a crude regime understands the power in guitar riffs and drum solos; in the raw vocals that refute the status quo. He knows instinctively that rock and roll means power. And he never loses hope that one day, things will be different.

CHAPTER ONE

Even at the worst of times, we always had chocolate.
Dutch Droste cocoa powder, to be exact. This sweet
pleasure was anything but a staple in Hungarian house-
holds, but we were lucky. We had relatives in Holland and
Belgium who would send us brown paper packages from
the West, where all nice things came from. My older
brother Gyuri, my younger sister Zsuzsi, and I would sit
around the dining table when the packages arrived and
watch in awe as our parents held up each item in turn:
blue jeans for Gyuri and me; a tartan skirt for Zsuzsi;
Chanel No. 5 for my mother. And the small metal box of
Dutch Droste cocoa.

There was something beautiful about that box: a nurse
standing with a tray of steaming hot chocolate on one
side, and gleaming gold medals on the other, proof of
the quality cocoa tucked inside. It was so different from
the dull packaging found in Budapest stores, colorless
packets that told of the poor quality of the goods inside.
Maybe that's why our breakfast ritual of *kakao* felt so

bourgeois. Every morning my mother would get up and prepare it in exactly the same way: pour five teacups of water into a bowl, add a mix of granulated sugar and cocoa powder, bring it to a boil on the gas stove. When the liquid started to bubble, turning that beautiful shade of brownish blue, she'd pour fresh milk in the bowl. And there it was. The most comforting drink in all the world. The ritual that started the day.

As a child I was curious about the place where our cocoa came from—the forbidden West where people suffered under the yoke of capitalism, where the fat, cigar-smoking banker squeezed blood out of the poor, miserable worker. Not at all like Hungary, which of course was a workers' paradise. That was the Party line, but it wasn't what most Hungarians thought. Hungarians had an almost mythical view of the West, especially America, which we regarded as a world of abundance where people dressed in beautiful clothes, drove around in nice cars, and had the freedom to travel wherever and whenever they wanted.

Hungarians fantasized about the West, and would pass around contraband glossy magazines some wily person had managed to procure, a Sears or Quelle catalog, just to look at a world that was closed to us. What must life be like in that suit, with that radio or that bike. The West was where we exercised our imaginations and let our dreams roam free. In private we talked about the West with longing. It was a different matter in public, where everyone would suggest that they were content with their life and lot, where, with a straight face, they'd criticize the West and praise communism. My parents and their friends never said anything bad about the West. They expressed only fondness when talking about Antwerp and London, Paris and Rome—and always with a note of desire. They'd go to great lengths to find an Italian silk tie or a Western publication, both of which were considered tremendous social assets. The people who lived in the countryside weren't as sophisticated as their comrades in the city. They didn't have access to the goods or the information that we did. Consequently, they were more accepting of what the Party told them, and more antagonistic to the West.

The Party turned a blind eye to small infractions: a little contraband in the form of American cigarettes, nylon stockings, Chiclets chewing gum. Occasionally, however, just to make a point, officials would harass someone for making a public statement that deviated too far from the official line. It could be as innocuous as saying "Oh, to be *suffering* in Vienna," or "I wonder if they have to line up to get into the stores in London?" Any comparison in which the East was made to look inferior was met with retaliation. When Stalin was alive, such a transgression could mean death. Later, when the Party softened, a public humiliation or demotion would do. Still later, as the Party felt secure in its grip on power—and perhaps to ward off popular discontent—there was a deal in place: pretend to accept Party rule and the authorities will pretend you're devoted to the system. They even went so far as to amend the Party slogan from the infamous "Those who are not with us are against us" to "Those who are not against us are with us." That was fine with my father and his colleagues in foreign trade. They knew how to make this system work for themselves and their families.

Foreign trade was Hungary's lifeline to the outside

world. Our factories produced a large quantity of goods, many of which were intended for consumption at home and by other communist countries. But these products were mostly shabby and of poor quality—a missing part here, a broken knob there. Then there were the products intended for the West. "For export" items were made of the best materials by the best craftsmen—wool suits, a racing bike, a handwoven rug—and were used to secure dollars, pounds, kroner, guldens, and deutsche marks, the hard currency the government depended on.

My father's profession was a blessing. A textile engineer who grew up in Vienna and spoke German like a native—not to mention a number of other languages—he was given advantages others didn't have. The regime needed him. It was that simple. The Ministry of Foreign Trade assembled skilled professionals for jobs related to the export market. Men like my father who spoke German, French, or English were in high demand, dispatched to what was referred to cynically as the *damned world of the West* to deal with the *dirty capitalists*. Which was how I got my first taste of freedom.

When my father told us he was to head the Hungarian commercial office in Copenhagen, I didn't know what to make of it. My experience of the outside world was limited to the colorful maps in my geography textbook and the postcards Father would send from his trips. And of course those brown paper packages. My brother, sister, and I had a lot of questions:

"Where is Denmark?"

"What do you call the people who live there?"

"Do they speak English?"

"Do they drive Mercedeses and Jaguars?"

In the months before our departure, we prepared. Diligently. Father showed us Copenhagen on the map.

"Here," he said. "This is where we are, in Hungary. What countries are next to us?"

I listed them. "The Soviet Union, Romania, and Yugoslavia. Here is Austria, where you grew up, Father. Here is Czechoslovakia, where Mari Blaskovics's family comes from. The capital is Prague."

"That's right, Andris, and look," my father continued. "Right up here, past Czechoslovakia, is East Germany. Past East Germany, across this blue line that is the sea, that's Denmark. That's where we're going."

Our mother watched.

"We will fly by airplane. You will have to behave nicely—no quarreling."

As the day of our departure grew near, Father brought home the View-Master. This 3-D picture viewer—from America, of course—was a little miracle of its own, offering "stereo pictures" of Denmark from its "Nations of the World" collection. Those little white disks were a type of crude and wondrous virtual reality that made you think you really were seeing Hamlet's castle, a herring smokehouse, the changing of the guard.

Palace guards. Strong young men wearing bearskin headdresses and light-blue jackets with gold buttons, black trousers with white stripes running down the sides. A shiny silver sword hanging from their belts. These guards wore serious expressions as they stood outside the Danish Royal Palace, and yet they still seemed friendly to me. Father explained that they were there to protect King Frederik IX and Queen Ingrid.

"Maybe you'll even meet them," he told me.

I held to this thought in the days before we left. We were going to live in a country with a king. A king who would be my king.

Our Soviet-made Ilyushin Il-14 left Budapest on a gray September morning. This was 1961, long before flip-flops and T-shirts were acceptable travel wear. Flying on an airplane was a special occasion for us, and we dressed accordingly: Father in a suit and tie, Mother in her best outfit. I wore blue short pants and a crisp white shirt. My carry-on bag was stuffed with important things: an inflatable fox made of rubber; the *Essential English* textbook; and my pocketknife. We were on our way to the West. But first we had to refuel in East Berlin.

The Wall had been erected just a few days before, on August 15, and when we touched down at Berlin's Schönefeld Airport our little plane was surrounded by military. Tanks, jeeps, and soldiers with machine guns made sure we didn't leave. They needn't have worried: we were anxious to get to Denmark and wanted nothing more than to wait safely in our seats. We tried hard to close our ears to the angry shouts coming from outside the plane.

"Niemand verlässt dieses Flugzeug. Verstanden?"

"Alle Pässe kontrollieren. Aber schnell!"

"Auch die Kindern!"

We couldn't ignore the East German officers who boarded the aircraft. They filed down the rows in silence, glaring at us with cold eyes. Hard men secure in their authority, so sure of their ability to intimidate, these soldiers could do anything to anyone and get away with it. They knew it and we knew it. Father sat straight-backed in his seat, his eyes alert and watchful. Mother gripped Zsuzsi's hand, while Gyuri and I exchanged glances. We didn't understand the escalating tensions of the East-West confrontation, but we knew enough to be terrified.

Just a few days before, the citizens of Berlin could come and go as they pleased. Families may have been scattered between East and West, but those who lived in the Soviet-controlled part of the city could mix freely with those who lived under Allied jurisdiction. Yet while we were packing for Copenhagen, planning our move to this important country with its own king and queen, East German soldiers were unfurling the barbed wire that would become the Berlin Wall.

I've always felt that there was something fateful about our family leaving the Iron Curtain at a time when things were getting worse for those trapped behind it, when other families were being rent in two.

But I was a small boy in the midst of something big in my own life, and I only knew that everything was about to change. I had felt secure in my world, protected by loving parents, comforted by a familiar routine. I had friends with whom I had grown up, and a teacher, Auntie Ancie, whom I loved. I knew all our neighbors and I could tell from the click on the lock who was entering or leaving our building. I was a sheltered child, the perils of the world mostly unknown to me. I understood on one level that things were bad, but it was too much to take in. Besides, I was nine years old and on an airplane with my family. Soon I would see the Round Tower, the red rooftops of Copenhagen, and the brand-new airport terminal at Kastrup. Soon I would arrive in the free world.

CHAPTER TWO

My first impression of Copenhagen was the smell of salt water and the closeness of the sea. As we made our way down the boulevard named after Hans Christian Andersen, past city hall—the very building I had seen on the View-Master—I could feel things opening up before me. I knew I'd be happy here in this wonderful place with fine people and their colorful clothes. Looking out the car window, I was thinking that maybe we would come back to town soon. I wanted Father and Mother to buy us new toys. I wanted a bright-yellow raincoat like the ones I saw Danish children wearing, and a bicycle with hand brakes. I wanted to touch the sea. I wanted this to never end.

Our temporary accommodations were small, but I didn't care. To me—*to us*—the apartment was beautiful. Our ground-floor lodgings had unusually large windows that let in a great deal of light. The bedrooms, each with its own balcony, overlooked a big grass field. I'd never seen so much green. As for the kitchen, which I knew from my mother was the most important room in any house, this was not like a Hungarian kitchen. The cabinets were mounted on the walls, the countertop ran from one end of the room to the other, and there was even a stainless-steel sink. Yet for all these modern conveniences, it was the furniture that caught my eye. The sofa, the tables and chairs—everything was light and contemporary, made of a lustrous brown wood I had never seen before.

"Denmark is famous for its furniture," Father explained. "This," he said, knocking on a table, "is called teak."

Teak. A new word. Solid, exotic, and warm, just like the wood.

"I can't wait to prepare the *kakao* tomorrow in this pretty kitchen," Mother added, smiling. She was like all of us, I guess, eager for this new adventure to begin.

I didn't object to going to bed early. It had been the longest of days and I was tired. Mother sat down by my bedside, tucked the duvet under me. She turned to Gyuri and Zsuzsi, snug in their own little beds.

"Did you notice how nice they were at the airport?" she asked. We weren't used to such consideration.

Zsuzsi, ever the precocious one, nodded. "Mama," she said. "This Danish is such a funny language. The words they say...do they make it up as they go along?"

"No, dear, it just sounds funny to you because it's a new language. Now get some sleep. But first, here is something for each of you." She handed out the little toys she had found in the boxes of Tide laundry soap. "*Jó éjszakát,*" she said. Good night.

Gyuri, Zsuzsi, and I woke early the next day. After breakfast we ventured out to explore our new neighborhood, where I took in the smallest discoveries with great enthusiasm. Close by our apartment, a wide bridge spanned the construction of a new highway. I stood there for a while watching the heavy machinery moving up and down, the steamroller smoothing the surface. I had never seen a highway before, and here, just a short walk from our new apartment, a road was being built with lanes so wide two cars could move in each direction. I imagined four streams of colorful cars, gleaming bright in the sunshine. I could hardly believe it.

Crossing the bridge, I saw modern shops with large welcoming windows. I peered inside one and saw orderly shelves full of goods you wouldn't see in Budapest: stacks of oranges and bananas, dark-brown bread, and odd black sticks, which I later learned were licorice. The man behind the counter was handsome and blond. Everyone here was blond!

An ambulance turned the corner, speeding. It was cherry red and white, with a bright-blue light on top. A Chevrolet, like the ones I'd seen in magazines and occasionally in Budapest with Viennese license plates.

I kept exploring. I was puzzled by a strip of asphalt beside the road, until I saw a man ride by on a bicycle, shortly followed by another, and another. A road *just for bicycles*. How could this be?

"*Davs!*" a man said as he passed me, which I guessed meant "hello." A stranger would rarely greet me like that in Hungary.

The houses, too, were so unlike the ones in Budapest. At home the buildings were covered with plaster—mostly gray—and many were stippled with bullet holes. Sometimes the plaster was missing. More often it was damaged, like a chipped tooth. The houses in Copenhagen were beautiful, so colorful and inviting it seemed that there should be a different word to describe them—just plain *house* felt lacking, somehow. That would become a familiar feeling in those early days in Denmark, the desire for a new vocabulary to express this new experience.

Thank goodness for English and for Aunt Julia, the lady with the British husband who had taught us English at home in Budapest. Looking back, I wondered how long Father had been planning our relocation. Was his posting here really just "the luck of the draw," as he had said, or was there something more to it? I knew of no one else who had learned English, which the Party referred to as "the language of the imperialists." No one else my age could speak English to the milkman. There was so much I didn't know.

Mother was so impressed with my language skills that she asked me to run an errand. She wanted a big ballpoint pen. She had used a ballpoint before. We all had, of course: the inventor, László Bíró, was Hungarian. But now that she was in the capitalist West, it seemed Mother wanted a *big* pen. I was happy to oblige.

I walked boldly into the paper store.

"*God morgen, kan jeg hjælpe dem med noget?*" the lady behind the counter asked.

"I speak English," I said, "and I would like please to buy a big pen." She reached into a box and pulled out a pen.

"Take this one. It's the biggest I have," she responded in a kind of singsong voice, which I would later realize was typical of the Danes.

"Yes, this is good. I would like to be buying it."

The dark-blue pen had a large barrel chamber and felt heavy in my hand. I had never seen a pen so big. Mission accomplished, I paid and dashed home.

"Here you are, Mother!" I felt good. Self-satisfied. Prouder than Jack with his beanstalk.

"What is this?" she asked.

"It's what you asked for. A big ballpoint pen," I boasted. "The biggest."

"A big pen? Oh, no!" Mother was laughing now, laughing so hard she couldn't speak. She left the room and returned with a glossy magazine. "This is what I want," she said, pointing to an ad. "The *Bic* pen. Look—it will not leak or clog. It can write for over a mile and a quarter. That is the pen for me."

Authorities in Budapest believed that children of officials posted abroad should attend Soviet embassy schools. How else to avoid the corrosive influence of the dirty capitalists? But Gyuri, Zsuzsi, and I were fortunate. We didn't have to go to a Soviet school where our every move would be watched, with a curriculum devised to further communist ideology. My parents defied the authorities and enrolled us in the best international school in Copenhagen, named after the Swedish Count Bernadotte. I never did find out how we managed to get away with it. But one thing I did know: when it came to family, my father had his ways.

I was nervous that first day of school. Maybe even a little scared. I had no idea what to expect. Would I like my teachers? Would I make friends? I needn't have worried. At Bernadotte, students were encouraged to cooperate and to accept each other's differences. I hadn't known what Father meant when he told me that the school had an "international spirit" and that it fostered a "mutual understanding." But when I recognized in my classmates the qualities of kindness and respect—virtues I treasure to this day—I knew that everything was going to be okay. My new friends didn't care that I came from behind the Iron Curtain. Even Bruce, whose father was an American colonel, couldn't have cared less that I had grown up in "enemy territory." I was simply András, the new boy.

Those first days and weeks were exhilarating. There was so much to do, so much to take in. It was a joy to arrive at school every day. I loved the fun exchanges before class, picking up new words and expressions in English. I especially loved the diversity: Americans, Scots, Finns, Israelis, Danes, and Norwegians all shared stories of their respective countries, their lives so different from my own. An American told me about his father in the air force. An Israeli boasted about growing oranges in the Negev desert. I was in awe of these boys and wanted to join in. I saw my chance when a Scottish boy talked about the secrets of the kilt. "My sister has Scottish skirt," I told him. I had wanted to establish that I knew about the tartan, but when I said, "Skirts not for men. That's funny!" he got red in the face.

"It is not funny," he said. "It's tradition. Shows how much you know."

I tried to apologize for hurting his feelings, but he continued, quieter now: "There's a big secret. Only real Scots know what men wear under their kilts...if they wear anything at all. You're not a Scot, so you're not allowed to know."

I tried so hard to match his story, to come up with

something I could tell him in return, something that only Hungarians knew. Later I thought I should have told him that we once had one of the world's largest collections of books—the Bibliotheca Corviniana—all belonging to the court of King Mátyás. Or that we had built the first underground transit system on the Continent. But I could think of nothing in the moment. Besides, I felt that the conversation was already heroic, given how far I had pushed the boundaries of my limited English.

CHAPTER THREE

Almost everyone at Bernadotte was from somewhere else. How different it was from Budapest's Lehel Street Primary School, where every child spoke Hungarian and wore the same dark-blue robe and starched white collar. That was the "national school dress" worn by every Hungarian schoolchild, and it was intended to project the notion of equality and uniformity. But of course it didn't. Some children—and I was one of them—were fortunate to have a new uniform each fall, while many others wore threadbare hand-me-downs that told of years of use by older brothers and sisters. Even as children we knew there was no such thing as "equality." Now here I was, a world away in this international school with its privileged and liberal ideas, voluntarily adopting its dress code: Blue jeans. *American* blue jeans. Levi's, Wranglers, and Lee.

My parents encouraged me to be like "Danish" boys, to wear what they did, to do the same things they did. I played baseball, even though I had no idea what I was doing. I developed an interest in toy cars and saved up my money to buy a Corgi—a yellow Mark II Jaguar, the most beautiful car in the world. That was fun, as was singing Danish songs that I didn't particularly understand. My parents got us bicycles so we could ride with our friends. We would never dream of letting Father's driver take us to school. We took public transportation, like our friends. It wasn't that we were trying to blend in, to pretend that we weren't Hungarian. When we ate the smørrebrød from our lunch box—the thin slices of dark bread with chocolate or cheese—we were just accepting that we were in another country. It was new. It was fun. Mostly, it was easy.

"Come, sit down. I want to talk to you," my father said to me a few months after we'd arrived. "You like it here? How's school?"

"It's good. I have now a few friends!"

"Who?"

"David and Michi. An American—Bruce. And Allan, he plays the clarinet."

"Any Danes?"

"Yes, there is one I like. Her name is Mette. She is from the Danish section in another building. But we meet in the lunch breaks and play dodgeball." Franey, Zsuzsi's friendly and wonderful teacher, would occasionally pull me into her class where there were more Danes.

"If I were you I would use every minute to be with those new friends. I hope you will get to be friends for a long time. And now that you speak English, you must learn Danish as well."

"But that's hard!"

"Yes, but that's what they speak here. I am learning it and I am not that young anymore. For you it will be easy. You never know..."

And so I learned Danish. At nine years old I picked up new languages quickly. The notion of democracy, however, wasn't so easy to decipher. It was Father who introduced the concept to me. I had come home from school one day with the news that one of my teachers was a card-carrying communist. Father thought it was a little unusual to find a Party member in Denmark, but he told me that was just the true nature of democracy.

I asked him what that word meant—*democracy*.

"When someone is allowed to have an opinion that differs from that of the government, without being punished, that is democracy. When there are as many newspapers as there are views, that is democracy. When you are allowed to hang out with Americans at school, that is democracy."

"Is Hungary a democracy?" I asked.

He paused for a second. "Denmark is a democracy," he replied.

I was a small boy, determined to make myself visible among my new friends—those tall Americans, Danes, and Argentinians. I learned to argue and to express my opinions. That was new to me. In Hungary I had been taught that authority was everything. No questions. No discussion. Just obey authority. Follow the curriculum. Do as you are told. Now in Denmark I was encouraged to ask questions, have my own point of view, and discover my own interests—which soon included comic books.

I remember what a shocking experience it was to first see an American comic. It was Bruce, the American boy, who introduced them to me. He pulled an issue out of his bag while asking if I knew who Superman was. I had no idea—such things weren't available in Hungary. But after paging through one comic, I was hooked.

I asked Bruce if he could bring more, and over the next days and weeks he brought in Batman, Spider-Man, and Flash. The covers of those shiny little books were a phenomenon in themselves: powerful and bold, every drawing suggesting movement and strength, the fight for justice, right over wrong. The comic books matched my vision of America as an exceptional place populated with heroes who were out to save the world. It didn't take much effort, even at the age of nine, to understand that Brainiac, the Joker, the Penguin, or Doctor Alchemy were based on the real-life enemies of the United States. Although who those enemies were I couldn't really say.

The stories were simple and captured my imagination. It was all about the fight between good and evil. Good always won. To be precise, America always won. That only encouraged my admiration for all things American, and soon I learned everything I could about my heroes. I knew about Bruce Wayne's family history and Clark Kent's relationship with Lois Lane. I understood the impact of kryptonite on Superman, and for a while I used the word as if it were my own. If I didn't like a vegetable or a song on the radio, it was kryptonite to me. I loved Superman, but Flash was my favorite. I had detailed knowledge about how fast he could run and how he stored his impact-resistant suit in his ring. I even got myself a Flash T-shirt, which I wore with pride.

Not everyone shared my love of comics. My teacher, Ted—an American, himself—thought they were a waste of time, that I'd become a stupid boy if I read them. Worse, he told me that if he ever caught me with a comic book in class, he'd tear it up in front of me. Unfortunately, I didn't take him seriously.

"What's that you have there?" Ted asked one day.

"Nothing," I said—the favorite form of denial of children everywhere. I tried to push the comic under my desk. But it was no use. I handed him the contraband, stealing a sidelong look at Bruce, who had turned pale. It was his comic book and he'd made me swear I wouldn't lose it. This was worse than losing it, however. This was humiliation. This was destruction. And it was a special issue, where Batman almost got killed by the Joker. I had barely made my way through half of it when this tragedy struck.

I had never seen Ted so angry. "I told you that if I ever caught you with one of these stupid comic books, I would tear it into pieces." He looked around at his terrified audience and, with a theatrical flourish, tore the comic book in half and threw it into the wastebasket. I could hardly believe my eyes. I sure couldn't look at Bruce.

After school had finished for the day, I crept back into the classroom to rescue Batman from the trash. I used three rolls of Scotch tape to put the comic book back together, and still it was ruined. Those comic books had transported me to America, to a world I didn't know but wanted to. A different world in which anything could happen. Anything but this.

Ted was my coolest teacher and he insisted his students call him by his first name. He was Mr. America at school, but tearing up this comic book was as anti-American as you could get. I didn't understand. The closest I came was thinking about what Father had told me about democracy, and how it encouraged people to have different opinions. In the end I decided to chalk it up to that, even if Ted's action was anything but democratic.

America seemed like the kind of place where opportunity was everywhere, where anything could happen. I was always impressed by American self-confidence and informality. We were an optimistic bunch at the international school, and like children the world over, we enjoyed imagining the power and majesty of our adult lives. Our dreams were influenced by comic books and movie plots, a family legacy, or even just a casual remark. And we all had an answer to the question, "What do you want to be when you grow up?"

My future was settled. I was going to be a cabinet minister. I'd known this for a while now, as our neighbor in Budapest kept telling me so.

"You'll be a cabinet minister one day, András. Just you wait and see." Perhaps if Dr. Robert Tarján had told me I was going to be a barber, I wouldn't have been so inclined to believe him, but a cabinet minister: that was all right with me. I didn't know exactly what a cabinet minister did, but I understood prestige. I'd make a lot of money as a cabinet minister. I'd drive around in a big car with a special license plate, and I'd have a lot of people working for me—people who would call me sir. That was all right with me.

Then, in my first year at Bernadotte, the class went on an outing to Svaneke on Bornholm, the small Danish island in the Baltic Sea. Just the sort of educational excursion the teachers thought would enrich our young minds. How could they have known that we would meet a local performer who would change the course of my life?

We had just eaten dinner and were being treated to an

evening's entertainment. The tables in the dining room had been pushed to one side and the chairs set up in a circle. Then a man showed up carrying a box the shape and size of a big violin. Casually, yet with great care, he opened the case and pulled out an acoustic guitar, which he strapped over his shoulder. The guitar was perfect. Dark at the sides and lighter toward the sound hole, it had a burnished wood neck and mother-of-pearl inlay on the headstock. This was the first time I had seen a guitar so close-up. I was taken by its raw beauty and power.

The musician himself was a tall, thin man who wore a floppy felt hat. He looked to me to be about thirty-five years old, but who knows. I was almost ten, and the differences between twenty, thirty, and forty were all but indistinguishable to me. I sat quietly as he tuned his instrument. He looked happy, as if he were lost—not in thought, but in anticipation of the music to come. Then he started to play.

Our teachers had expected us to be impressed by the clifftop ruins of the medieval castle of Hammershus, the herring smokehouse at Gudhjem, and the round church of Østerlars. But here I was mesmerized by a humble guitar. I couldn't understand how an instrument and a voice could become one, and how it could fill the room like an orchestra.

As I listened to the man sing—"My Bonnie," a simple but beautiful song—I gave up the big car with the special license plate. I wished my staff good luck in their new endeavors, and resigned my esteemed position as future cabinet minister.

From that moment on I was determined to be András Simonyi, guitar-man.

CHAPTER FOUR

R ock and roll was in the air. It blasted from radios, from passing cars, from the tape recorders that neighborhood boys had received for their birthdays. When a record came out in England, it was in stores in Copenhagen the next day. When a glossy beat magazine hit the stands with news about the British and American bands, Gyuri and I fought over who would get to read it first. My friends called it the rock scene, and I wanted desperately to be part of it.

It wasn't my first exposure to rock and roll. Father had taken us to see *The Three Musketeers* at the Danube cinema in Budapest. The film was enjoyable enough—I thought d'Artagnan a fine fellow—but it was the news-reel that really caught my attention. Typically newsreels were short, black-and-white informational films designed to highlight national achievements and promote the Party line. The subjects were varied, but predictable: Hungary's "close friendship" with the Soviet Union; the opening of a new factory; happy families enjoying an afternoon in the countryside—"recreating," as we liked to say.

Sometimes, however, they were truly interesting, like that afternoon at the Danube. After the clip showing happy workers going about their tasks on the factory floor, the screen blasted with noise as a group of young people appeared. They were American teenagers, the announcer said, and they were caught up in a dangerous craze that was sweeping the nation: *rock and roll.* I watched, rapt, as these young people twisted and jumped, legs jerking, arms akimbo. Some boys even threw girls over their heads and across their backs. They moved like they were possessed. If I was to believe the commentator, I wasn't supposed to like what I saw. The voice, which disrupted the music, said that this rock and roll was making young people sick. It was degeneration. It was American culture at its worst and these poor boys and girls were sure to be damaged by it. Words like *debauched, libidinous,* and *depraved* were used, language I couldn't begin to understand.

I sat in my seat, my legs dangling, too short to reach the floor, and all I could think of was how much I liked what I was seeing and hearing. The beat was irresistible, and the kids were having a great time. Then the camera panned to a small band comprising a singer, a guitarist, a stand-up bass, and a drummer. The singer was moving his body in what even I knew to be a provocative way. The announcer reserved his greatest condemnation for the young man, "this Elvis Presley," who worked the kids up into such a frenzy that it could only result in an orgy.

Elvis Presley. I remembered his name and his dark quiff, the blaze of energy when he played his guitar. When I recalled these things later that night in my room, I knew I wanted more than anything to be like him—commanding the stage, playing my guitar like he played his. The screaming girls didn't appeal to me. Not then, anyway. But I wanted to be with those boys and girls in America, moving to the beat, getting lost in the world of rock and roll. I was spellbound, and a little sad, too. I had a feeling that adults might not like the music as much as I did. I didn't really understand what the commentator said, but I knew that at some level it was supposed to be bad, and I knew that this corrupt music was out of my reach. It would take some doing if I was to listen to it again.

I remember talking about it to Father. "You enjoy the movie?" he asked me as we were walking home.

"Yes, I did. I liked that American guy, Elvis Presley, from the newsreel."

"Oh, yes, I saw that you liked him. America is far away, you know."

"I know. But I like this American music and the way the kids dance to it." I made a clumsy twist.

We stayed on the subject for a while, with my father explaining the notion of popular music. He told me that Elvis was not popular in Hungary, that people preferred songs such as "Dabbling Little Girl." Then I asked my father if I could play the guitar instead of the piano. I was testing the waters.

"No, Andris," he said. "I like to listen to you play the piano, and Aunt Martha is a great teacher. But perhaps I can get you a record from this Presley one day."

"One day." I held those two words close to my heart.

*   *   *

Two years had gone by since we arrived in Denmark. So many new things. So many new experiences. Yet nothing compared to the first time I heard the Beatles. It was a Saturday-afternoon party in the Bernadotte school gym, a small space that was barely lit and a little austere. It was crowded that day, though, thanks to a record player and a set of sturdy loudspeakers.

Some older boys were hanging around the stack of records discussing music—what else?

"I love Buddy Holly," Allan, the American boy, raved.

"Have you guys ever heard of Chubby Checker? He has a song called 'Let's Twist Again.'"

"Yes, but listen to this one. The Beatles. This is p-h-e-n-o-m-e-n-a-l." I didn't know the word, but I was sure it meant something important, the way Bob stretched it out as he pulled the record out of its sleeve, which had a photo of four guys with identical mushroom haircuts. He put the little forty-five on the turntable, lifted the record player's arm, and put the needle down on the Bakelite disk with studied nonchalance.

"P-h-e-n-o-m-e-n-a-l," he repeated.

The Beatles started singing. Really loud.

I lost my breath.

That singing. That drumming. That guitar solo…

This was a new and unexpected sound. I had never heard anything like it before, but it was strangely familiar. It made sense to me musically and I didn't know why. This *phenomenal* record reached me in a way no other music had reached me before. Not Elvis Presley. Not *West Side Story*. Nothing. It touched my heart as much as it touched my musical senses.

These Beatles understood who I was.

I stood next to the turntable blocking anyone who wanted to change the record. I played "All My Loving" again and again and again.

"You seem to like this," Bob said.

"This is crazy!" I said.

Seeing the look on my face, Bob put on the entire *Please Please Me* album: "Love Me Do," "I Saw Her Standing There," "Twist and Shout" . . .

This was the music of my generation.

This was my music.

This was who I was.

CHAPTER FIVE

Gyuri, Zsuzsi, and I returned to Hungary in the summer months, and for good reason. Our Danish education wasn't recognized by the Hungarian authorities. If we were to return to Hungary for good—always a possibility—our years in Danish schools would have been lost, forcing the three of us back to whichever level we had completed when we had left. I guess that was why, as much as our parents wanted us to enjoy our new life in the West, they made sure we didn't forget our roots. We read a great deal in our mother tongue and reviewed the Hungarian school material, almost daily, to prepare for our annual return to Budapest, where we would take our national exams. These exercises were a necessary discipline, like our daily dose of cod liver oil, which I also hated. I thought it was all a big waste of time. Father had made sure we didn't have to enroll in one of the Soviet embassy schools. He even got us into one of the best schools in Denmark. Yet here I was, back at my old school in Budapest's Thirteenth District, where my former classmates greeted me with a strange mix of curiosity and respect.

"András, how is Denmark?"

"How can I get there?"

"Will you invite me?"

"How is the food?

"Are you rich?"

Auntie Ancie, from my old class, was happy to see me, but most of the teachers clearly did not like me at all. They regarded me as a foreigner. Of course they did. I looked foreign. I felt foreign.

More than anything I wanted to to go back to Denmark. Budapest was a grim reminder of what my brother and sister and I had left behind. This great city—this Paris of the East—was still recovering from the devastation of the last months of the war, when Hitler's armies retreated from advancing Soviet troops. Eighty percent of the city's buildings had been destroyed or damaged. The seven bridges traversing the Danube were wiped out. A mere decade later the city suffered further devastation in the ill-fated uprising of 1956. That vain attempt to break away from the Soviet empire scarred the people of Hungary just as the bullets and mortar shells had disfigured the once grand buildings.

Yet life went on much as it always had. Fathers went to work and mothers cared for their children. Buses ran according to schedule. And because small things matter in times of hardship, people made friends at the vegetable stand or did a favor for the local electrician, anything to ensure fresh produce for Sunday's lunch or to get that frayed wire replaced before it sparked a fire. People did what they could to make life more livable, to ensure that unhappy circumstances didn't lead to an unhappy life.

It's doubtful that outsiders would have had the sense that Hungary was thriving, but they might get the impression things were okay, that people had enough, maybe even a little more than enough to get by. But anyone who cared to look closely would understand that Hungary was not what it pretended to be. It wasn't an efficient modern society, and it wasn't an industrialized nation with a traditional economy based on supply and demand. Far from it. After the war in Hungary everything—production, distribution, prices, and wages—was regulated down to the smallest detail. Factories were nationalized; the market was suppressed. This was a *planned economy*, Soviet-style.

The state owned almost everything, so almost everyone was employed by the state. It would be an exaggeration, however, to say that everyone with a job was gainfully employed, that they were all engaged in work that was useful or productive. Workers labored hard, but the drive for quantity over quality resulted in shabby products of such low quality that they often had to be discarded. There were no real consequences for careless work. Better work did not necessarily result in better pay. No one was ever fired. Morale among workers was low with no incentive to improve it.

"They pretend to pay us and we pretend to work," the joke went those days. If you wanted to make more money, you had to moonlight—what we called *fusi*—which meant using state assets to produce your own profit. If you were employed by a state-owned garment factory, for example, you might use the sewing machines and materials there to make something nice for a special order and pocket the money. That was *fusi*, and if it wasn't a common practice, it wasn't uncommon, either.

Everyone was enrolled in the trade unions, though they were not the same organizations whose members had once banded together for fair wages and better working conditions. My grandmother, who had been an early trade unionist and a suffragette in the 1920s, wouldn't have recognized the membership of the early 1960s. With Hungary now the happy land of workers, what need was there for organizations whose purpose was to fight against the exploitations of capitalism?

So the trade unions took over less urgent tasks like organizing International Women's Day celebrations and running recreational homes for their members. Once owned by aristocrats and the bourgeoisie, these recreational homes were mansions that had been confiscated by the government after the war and were located in some of the most beautiful spots in the country: Lake Balaton, the Mecsek Mountains in the south, or the North Hungarian Mountains by the Czechoslovak border. This was one of the Party's better ideas. These recreational homes provided wonderful holidays for many working families. And because they were paid for by the trade unions, they were practically free.

During one summer back in Hungary, my parents decided to send Gyuri and me to a recreational facility for children. We didn't want to go away to more strangers and a strange place, but any appeals to our father were in vain. He was busy making the arrangements.

Father was a worldly man who knew how things worked. To be precise, he knew that adding a carton of Kent Goldens to his application to the textile workers union would secure a placement for us in one of the best recreational facilities. It was an "act of generosity" designed to smooth the process. In other words, corruption. Perhaps not the more nefarious type of corruption that allowed a director to put his laborers to work building a summer home instead of the metro construction they had contracted for. This was petty corruption, really, nothing compared with the standards of today. But it was corruption nonetheless. Father didn't think of it as such, however; you'd be hard-pressed to find a decent Hungarian who did. This was a simple transaction—unremarkable considering the context—the Cold War equivalent of tipping your waiter.

American cigarettes were a scarcity in those days. One of many, along with pantyhose, quality soap, and shampoo. The carton of Kent Goldens that Father gave to the program administrator was merely a gesture, a token of his appreciation; he expected only a small favor in return. Mrs. Szabó would not smoke the cigarettes herself and certainly she would not allow Mr. Szabó to smoke them. She might use them to smooth the process of obtaining a new TV set, a transaction that would otherwise take years. The director of the electrical appliance store would not smoke the cigarettes, either, because he might need them to obtain a driver's license, or perhaps secure better treatment at the hospital should he require care for some ailment or disease. Who knows where the cigarettes ended up? Certainly not in the ashtray.

So it was that Mrs. Szabó let my father choose the time and place of our holiday. He chose a beautiful spot down by Lake Balaton, about eighty miles from Budapest. It was a great location—maybe the best—and it had an added appeal: Before the war one of our relatives had a holiday home at Lake Balaton. Father loved the place, which he would visit often with his cousins. In fact, Father had inherited a nice property near the lake after the war. Alas, he quickly got rid of it because he was afraid of being branded bourgeois. This would turn out to be one of his greatest regrets. So I imagine securing a holiday at Balaton was his attempt to give his sons something that he had cherished in his youth. In a way, he was sending us to the family property. Or so he would have had us believe.

CHAPTER SIX

I 'd always loved trains. Gyuri and I had a big set of Märklin model trains, complete with passenger carriages, cattle cars, and cooler wagons. We loved to play with them, imagining the glorious places we'd travel, the fascinating people we'd meet. So my brother and I had high hopes when we saw the steam engine waiting for us at Budapest's Southern Station. A magnificent black beast with a wide red stripe running down the side, the MÁV locomotive made us think that perhaps our trip to Balatonszemes might be better than we had anticipated. Then we entered the train and were clobbered by the fetid smell of the toilet.

Gyuri and I dashed down the crowded corridor, dodging suitcases and backpacks as we tried to get far and fast away from the odor. The train was filled to capacity, and men and women stood outside their compartments smoking. We didn't know anything about secondhand smoke back then; we were just glad that the tobacco fumes helped smother the stench.

We found two window seats in a compartment with a well-fed family from the countryside—a father, mother, and their three children. Most of the passengers were casually dressed, the men in cotton trousers and muscle shirts, the women wearing lightweight dresses in anticipation of their arrival at Lake Balaton. Not this family. The man, corpulent and red-faced, had on knee-high boots despite the summer heat. He wore heavy black pants and a shirt of white broadcloth, as did his two sons. The mother and her daughter were dressed in a similar fashion, with skirts instead of trousers. This would have been their festive dress, reserved for big holidays such as Easter or Christmas. Or, in this case, a rare trip to the capital.

Gyuri and I had talked about our trip on our way to the station—about how we wanted to pull down the windows and feel the locomotive smoke on our faces. It seemed like a fanciful thing to do, something you'd read about in an adventure story. One look at the man we presumed to be the father told us it was no use. He wasn't the type to allow such an indulgence. He was a rule follower, buttoned up tight, with his arms folded across his chest and his feet planted firmly on the floor. The boys mimicked their father's pose as they sized up the two city dwellers who had annexed their compartment. They stared at our suitcases, which were decked out with attractive stickers from London and Paris. They also stared at our hair. Slightly overgrown, but neatly slicked back on the sides and carefully arranged in the front into a deliberate messiness, all held in place by a greasy substance. My hair wasn't as good as Gyuri's—his was a masterpiece.

"Why do you wear your hair like that?" the father asked.

"We like Tony Curtis, the actor," I responded.

"How do you manage to keep it in place?"

"It's called Brylcreem," Gyuri said. The marvelous English hairstyling formula, introduced to us by our cousin Georges in Belgium, was the foundation of our daily grooming.

"My children will never wear their hair like that! Right?"

The two boys, whose own hair was cut like the monks I had seen in Father's books, nodded.

"Never!" the youngest proclaimed.

Their little sister just stared. Their mother occupied herself by steadying a wooden crate between her legs.

"Did you visit the agriculture museum next to Heroes' Square?" Gyuri asked—his brave attempt to find some sort of connection with this clearly unfriendly person.

"Yes," the father responded as he shifted uncomfortably in his seat.

"And did you go to the Zoo and the Amusement Park?" Gyuri continued.

"Yes," he said, clearing his throat. "The Zoo. The Amusement Park with the crazy roller coaster and the hall of horrors and the dodgem." *Dodgem* was the Hungarian name for "bumper cars."

"Did you visit the National Museum?"

"No."

Mother and Father had always taught us that there was an art to conversation. *Be polite to others*, we were told. *Show interest and ask questions. That's how you get to know people. That's how you make friends.* Mother had also told us to be sure and let the other person do the talking so as not to monopolize the conversation. But Mother had never met our red-faced farmer and his one-word answers.

"Where are you going?" I tried.

"Home," he said.

"That's nice," I said, trying a little bit harder. "Where is home?"

"Lengyeltóti. Do you know where it is?"

"Yes," Gyuri lied.

I had no idea.

"Where are you from?" asked the father.

"Angyalföld," Gyuri said. He winked at me and I knew I had to shut up. Two years my senior, my brother was smart enough not to tell this man that we lived in Denmark.

Angyalföld—Hungarian for "Angel's Land"—was a Budapest workers' district on the eastern, Pest side, close to the Danube River. It contained the district of New Leopold Town, which was where we lived. Like everything in Budapest, New Leopold Town had a rich and tragic history. It was once a thriving Jewish enclave, home to prosperous bank directors, engineers, merchants, and writers. Then came the war, when most of the residents were rounded up by the Nazis. When the communists took over, they folded the area into the workers' district.

Gyuri was smart to name Angyalföld that afternoon. It did the trick. The man warmed to us and his family followed suit. His wife even offered us some very good sheep's cheese and a slice of fresh bread.

I enjoyed the four-hour journey, looking out the window and seeing the villages and wide-open pastures. I saw the combines working the fields, leaving a cloud of dust behind. There were trucks, and here and there a horse-drawn cart loaded with melons or hay. Every so often the train would stop in the middle of nowhere, either to pick up passengers or for some other reason unknown to us. We'd wait for long minutes, wondering what was going on. An accident, possibly. Maybe the engine had broken down. Eventually the train would start moving again and put an end to our speculations.

At every terminal, we watched as the station chief gave command, waving his signal disk—red on one side, green on the other—while the train blew its whistle. We were on the move again. It didn't matter that our companions were not the exciting people we had imagined. They were humble folk leading decent lives. Surely this father wanted what my father had wanted—to give his children the best, to help them grow up to be strong and good. Still, I couldn't help feeling sorry for the boys and their sister, who might never leave the country. What was in store for them?

The train worked its magic. With each mile we traveled, I found myself looking forward to adventures to come—exploring the countryside, swimming in the Balaton, making new friends. But I was a little bit afraid, too. It wasn't anything I could explain. I wasn't scared of meeting strangers and I wasn't afraid of new places. Mostly, I was afraid that someone would steal the little yellow Jaguar I had hidden in my pocket. It was the Mark II model, and nobody had one like it. Maybe I should have left it behind, but it was a custom in our family to carry something from home wherever we went. That Jaguar was one of my best-loved possessions, and given my other options—the new building bricks they called LEGO and the Solingen stag-horn hunting knife—it was the better choice to bring with me.

We arrived at the little village of Balatonszemes, half a mile away from the lakeside camp where we'd be staying. The town had a picture-postcard quality: tidy streets, lots of trees, and gorgeous villas with their shutters closed tight against the heat. It was all very pretty. Had I been older, I might have appreciated it more. But I was growing aware of the opposite sex, so what really caught my eye were the four young women waiting to meet us. Supervisors, not schoolgirls, these women had that strict, self-protective attitude Hungarians have when meeting strangers. Age encourages a hierarchy when you're young, and these girls—several years older than we were—looked at Gyuri and me with something close to contempt, as if they had had the good sense to grow up and we, alas, had not.

They studied us as we got off the train. I studied them. They stood tall and poised in their white cotton robes, usually worn by kindergarten teachers. It wasn't really a dress, but these girls wore it like one, belted tight with the two top buttons left open. One had pinned a pretty brooch to her tunic. Another had embroidered hers with flowers. Like so many young women, they had made the uniforms their own.

"Get on the bus," one of them ordered.

There was no courtesy extended. No *please* or *thank you*. No *welcome to Balaton*. I recalled our arrival in Copenhagen and how hospitable everyone had been. I thought of Dorothy in *The Wizard of Oz*, which I had seen some years before at the Danube theater, and all I could think of was how much I was like her, after the tornado swept her away from home. I certainly wasn't in Denmark anymore.

We were ushered onto the bus, a brand-new Ikarus with its ducklike tail engine. The bus was gray, typical of Hungarian-made vehicles in those days, so different from the striking red London buses that I saw in magazines or the yellow ones in Copenhagen. Still, I was fascinated by its beauty, by the machine and the driver standing proudly beside it in his blue uniform and matching chauffeur's cap. The bus was impressive—robust and strong—and when the engine roared to life it signaled the adventure to come.

"My name is Aunt Maria," said one of the supervisors, standing in the front of the bus and speaking into a microphone, "and this is Aunt Ildikó. You can sing a song if you want to. But sit properly. No messing around." Aunt Maria walked to the back of the bus—presumably to get a better view of our bad behavior. Aunt Ildikó stayed up front, behind the driver. Soon we arrived at camp, a sprawling constellation of brick structures, some old, some new. The older buildings were mansions once owned by wealthy families, and they showcased the intricate architecture that was popular before the war—slate roofs, columns, grand wooden staircases. Some even had the original porcelain bath fixtures.

The new buildings were plain—austere, even. There was something appealing about the simple design, but the materials were of poor quality and the execution shabby. I likely wouldn't have noticed had I not been privileged to have spent time in Copenhagen, where I was exposed to their architectural opposites. Now all I could think of was how sad these dwellings were, how they stood out wanting and apologetic, like poor relatives.

The bright-yellow villa where Gyuri and I were holed up may have been nice at one time, but it was a standard dormitory now, a stern one at that. There were maybe ten or twelve bunk beds in our dorm, but when I look back on that first day at Balaton, I can't recall seeing anyone besides Gyuri and me. That doesn't seem likely—if there was one thing the trade unions knew, it was how to pack a room—so maybe this was just a trick of memory, a way to remember how safe and happy I felt with my big brother. He could be a jerk sometimes, but he always took care of me.

We fell asleep that first night whispering across the space between our beds.

"Which girl did you like?" Gyuri asked.

"You mean among the kids?"

"No, you idiot. The women."

"I liked the one with the short brown hair."

"She is pretty, isn't she?"

"She sure is."

Ildikó stood out to me with her cropped hair, her big brown eyes, and her very pretty face. Something about her promised mischief. I hoped—really hoped—that she would be our supervisor.

"Do you think she will like us?" I asked.

"Who can tell?" he responded with all the wisdom of an older brother. "When it comes to girls, you never really know what they're thinking."

CHAPTER SEVEN

It was Ildikó who woke us that first morning. She was surprised to see us dressed and ready to go at seven, but we had always been early risers, sitting down to breakfast every morning at seven fifteen. My stomach was a Swiss watch.

"So you are ready for the day?" Ildikó asked.

"Yes, thank you, I am!" I said, hoping to impress her with my enthusiasm and good manners.

"Good," she said. "We have a lot planned."

"Ildikó, where do you live?" I asked. I loved her voice. I could have listened to her all day.

"I am from Budapest," she said while she helped fix the bedcovers and fold our clothes, which we had been struggling with. "But for now I study at the teachers' college in Pécs, like the others."

"We are from Budapest as well," I said, thrilled to find that we were connected in some way.

"Ah, we are neighbors!" With that she took a comb to my hair, fixing my bed head.

"Th...thank you," I said, blushing.

"Follow me," she said as she put the comb in her pocket. "We'll line up with the others downstairs and walk over to the dining room together."

Everything about Ildikó was appealing. She was tall and graceful and walked with a long stride like the models who worked with Father at the textile company. But Ildikó was in my orbit, not Father's, and that made her all the more exciting.

"Psst, Gyuri," I whispered in English. "That Ildikó sure is sexy."

I had always thought that "sex" and "sexy" were English words. I had no idea they were part of a universal vocabulary, that everyone, everywhere, knew what they meant. Not until the moment Ildikó snapped, "I heard that!" and threw me a dirty look. I was crushed.

"Oh, I...I'm—" I sputtered.

"I bet you don't even know what sex is," she asked.

"Well, I...um—"

Hearing Ildikó talk this way was thrilling. I was a kid and I still played with model cars, but I was aware of the power women possessed, and I knew that there was nothing sexier than an attractive woman who was proud and comfortable in her own skin—like Ildikó.

"And what do you know about sexy?" I saw a smile break through at the corners of her mouth. She was only pretending to be cross.

"Well, I—"

"Come back a few years from now and we can have a conversation about it," she said, laughing.

"Will you wait for me?" I asked.

"I sure will," she replied.

We both knew that wouldn't happen, but it didn't matter. Ildikó and I were friends from then on—despite her being an older woman of nineteen.

I became a child again when I got to the dining room and lined up with the other boys and girls. It was like a scene out of *Oliver Twist*: a gloomy space with long tables covered in hideous yellow oilcloth that smelled of rancid food and body odor. Old women—solid and gray—were busy plunking down trays loaded with slices of buttered bread streaked with apricot marmalade. Large pitchers had already been placed on the tables, cheerful polka-dot jugs that made the thin tea feel like some kind of trick.

I sat down next to a boy a year or two older than me.

"Hello," I said. "My name is András."

"Zsolt," he responded while eyeing me up. "What kind of car do you have in your pocket?" He must have seen me play with it on the bus.

"It's a Jaguar Mark II. It's called the little Jaguar. A Corgi car. Diecast," I added, proud of my treasure.

"Show it to me." I pulled the little car from my pocket. "This is a good thing to have," he said. "Where did you get it?"

"Copenhagen." I don't think Zsolt cared about where I got the Jaguar. It was the toy he was interested in.

"I want to borrow it," he said. It wasn't really a question.

"I am not sure. I'd like to hold on to it," I responded.

"You don't want to let me play with it?"

I tried to explain. "It's my favorite, and it's from home."

Zsolt frowned and called me a jerk. I thought that was the end of it. I felt bad, but I wasn't inclined to share on command like that. My parents had taught us to let others play with our toys and to take good care of what was ours. But I didn't trust this kid. My instincts were proved right when, a few days later, I discovered that the Jaguar had disappeared from my bag. I was positive Zsolt had taken it, but I couldn't prove a thing.

The days were filled with the usual camp activities: Ping-Pong, group gymnastics, and soccer, which I hated. I never saw the point of chasing a ball across a field, and I couldn't stand the way the bigger boys pushed me around. Thank goodness Ildikó took Gyuri and me under her wing. She brought us to the staff dormitory, to the kitchen, where we'd hang out gossiping, and to the boathouse, where young men and women gathered after work. One day she took us to the camp across the street.

"You'd better behave," she cautioned us. "Otherwise we won't ever be allowed back. This is a big deal, guys. Something really hip, okay?"

"Don't worry, I can handle myself," I said. I had no idea if I could, but it felt like the right thing to say.

"What makes this camp so different from ours?" Gyuri asked.

"Just you wait and see!" Ildikó said.

The two camps were divided by a narrow country road, lined with tall poplars. As we walked across the street, a grand estate with wrought-iron gates came into view. Ildikó led us through the gates to a movie theater. A *real* movie theater, with a large canvas screen and an actual stage. I expected to see uniformed schoolchildren like Gyuri and me reciting poems from the youth movement, or rapt young faces watching a Soviet children's film like *Timur and His Gang*, but this was different. A few people were milling around inside the theater, two sharply dressed boys among them. Ildikó introduced us.

"Tibor and Laci Gesztenye are the sons of someone important in the Party," she said. "They live in Moscow."

We knew these kids were important because they didn't wear the blue shorts, white shirt, and red scarf that were the uniforn of the Young Pioneers—the communist version of the Boy Scouts. Nor did they wear the ugly blue sweat suits that we called the "teddy-bear." They wore blue jeans and shirts made of cloth like the cowboys wore in American westerns. They wore ankle boots like the ones John, Paul, George, and Ringo wore onstage.

The little princes didn't say hello to us when we entered. They were arranging tables and chairs onstage, looking very important themselves, as if they were getting ready for a performance. They made it clear that they had privileges, and one of those privileges included not having to acknowledge the likes of Gyuri and me. In fact, every time we tried to ask them something, to engage them in polite conversation as we had been taught, they looked away from us and turned their attention to their Soviet-made Pobeda wristwatches.

We found out why an hour later when their father's driver arrived from Budapest in a shiny new car. Now they wanted to show off. I couldn't really blame them. Any American car was a rarity in Hungary, but this one—a 1959 Chevrolet Biscayne with sleek tail fins and a duo-tone paint job in olive and white—was the coolest car in the world. I recall it had license plates with the letter *A*, which suggested the importance of the driver. All the important license plates started with an *A*. The size of the car and the license plate spoke for themselves.

Comrade Driver was a well-built man who never removed his jacket. His tie, which was brown, didn't match his suit, which was black. His belt didn't match his shoes. A gun stuck out of his back pocket. It matched everything.

"Do you see what I see?" Gyuri asked. "You know who wears a gun, don't you?"

"Shush," I silenced him. I knew from the moment Comrade Driver pulled up that he wasn't an ordinary chauffeur. An ordinary chauffeur would have been driving a Soviet-made car like a Volga, a Pobeda, or maybe a big black Tchäika with the back windows curtained. I didn't realize he was part of the secret police until I saw the gun.

The secret police were everywhere, or so the authorities would have us believe. Certainly, as far as perception went, they were omnipresent. They were the faces hiding behind newspapers, the footsteps you'd hear late at night. But as often happened in that strange gray zone in which we lived, the myth of these agents had outgrown the reality.

The secret police were part of the Ministry of the Interior, which was why they were called, simply, interiors. I had first heard of them from a third-grade classmate.

"Do you know what an interior is?" Gyuszi Klein asked. A group of us had been hanging out in the second-floor corridor at the Lehel Street Primary School. We became Gyuszi's captive audience the moment he asked the question. "An interior is secret police. He carries a gun and is an important man," he told us. "There is an interior in our house and he has a gun. I have seen it with my own eyes."

There were murmurs of "Wow, really?" and "*Hű-ha.*"

"But nobody is supposed to know he is an interior because he is one of the men who kills people." This was said with more reverence than fear. "He takes them away and kills them." We were silent now, rapt. We looked at Gyuszi with a new appreciation, as if he were the interior. "My father said that they are everywhere," he concluded.

"Everywhere?"

"Everywhere."

I looked over my shoulder for a long time after that. The secret police couldn't be everywhere, not in the numbers we imagined, anyway. That was the insidious nature of it all. Fear and suspicion spread among us like a drop of ink on blotting paper. You watched what you said. You wondered who your friends were. That was the whole point.

Comrade Driver seemed like a nice man. As I would learn later in life, people like him always seem like nice men. He was friendly and even let us sit in the driver's seat of the Chevrolet, one by one. But I was under no illusion. Get in his way and he'd squash you like a bug.

As we jockeyed for position in the Biscayne, Comrade Driver took a reel-to-reel tape recorder, record player, and loudspeakers from the trunk and set them up on a table in the cinema room, next to a stack of records and tape reels. There was only a handful of boys and girls there, and it was a privilege to be included. This was one of those small advantages we all were on the lookout for, the little gestures and opportunities that separated you from everyone else and made you feel a little better about who you were.

As Comrade Driver helped the boys set up the equipment, a charge of excitement moved through the theater. When everything was in place, when a knob was twisted and a green light illuminated on the tape recorder, one of the brothers—maybe Laci—pressed the button on the tape recorder with a theatrical flourish. The combined sound of an electric guitar, drums, and bass rushed to life with an incredible power.

"Who's playing?" I asked Tibor, somewhat timidly, my attempt at building rapport. "Who is this?"

I felt a hard fist of anger seizing my chest when Tibor didn't respond. Whether I was angry at him or at myself, I couldn't tell. Being the same age and stuck together in the same place should have been enough for some sort of camaraderie, if not friendship. Tibor was being incredibly rude. But there was more to it than that. I wanted him to appreciate me, to recognize my knowledge of music and let me into this scene. I didn't want him to own the experience alone. As much as I hated to admit it, I felt a kinship with these little princes and their music. I wanted them to see it, too.

Of course I knew exactly who was playing. It was the Rolling Stones, the ones who had even longer hair than the Beatles. I tried again, a different approach.

"Oh, right," I said. "These are the Rolling Stones, that English group."

"Pretty good," Tibor responded reluctantly.

"This is great, where did you get this?" I went on, emboldened.

"None of your business," he said. He could have shut me down again, but perhaps he thought he could impress us with his musical knowledge. "Let's see if you know this one." He looked in a little notebook, where all the locations of the songs were written down, then fast-forwarded the tape until the counter showed 278. "You Really Got Me" blasted from the speakers.

"That's Ray Davies and the Kinks," I said nonchalantly. "His brother Dave plays rhythm. The bassist is Pete Quaife and Mick Avory is the drummer."

"Hey, that was good. So you really know them. We have all their songs at home in Moscow, if you really want to know." Tibor lingered on the word *Moscow* as if it were some kind of sweet. Now he was the one who wanted to impress me. Tibor positioned the West German–made BASF reel to play "Poison Ivy." Gyuri and I had mainly been listening to the Beatles, the very best as far as we were concerned, and had grossly neglected this other band, these Rolling Stones. Everybody, I thought, had to take a position. You were either with the Beatles or with the Stones. There was no contest as far as I was concerned. The Beatles were much more than just a group: they were the ones who started it all.

The Rolling Stones were a great band, but they were nothing like the Beatles. They were the original sinners, the ones who created a revolution and, to me, the ones who invented the rock band. All those other bands, including the Rolling Stones and the Kinks, were great, but first love is first love. The Beatles were the ones who drove the older generation crazy *first*. They were the ones who drew thousands to a concert *first*. They were the ones who made young girls faint, who started a mania—Beatlemania.

So although we had heard the Stones before, they had never come across as powerfully as they did on this afternoon. The music seemed different now, in this unlikely setting. It was harsh and intense. Mesmerizing. Ildikó liked the music, too, dancing in place to the beat. I could tell that she didn't like Tibor or Laci from the way she stood at the corner of the stage, arms folded.

Later that evening, on the way back to our own compound, Ildikó spoke seriously to Gyuri and me. She treated us like grown-ups now.

"These guys, they come from God knows where, they show off their stuff and behave like they are better than we are. Just because their father has powers and connections, just because they are where they are, just because they think they are *special*," Ildikó said. "Your father is also an important man, but the two of you never talk like that."

Father had repeatedly warned us that he would punish us if we ever bragged about our good fortune. He drilled it into us that the things we enjoyed and the opportunities we had were not the result of our own hard work or our abilities. He told us to be aware that we had access to many things that were unavailable, even off-limits, to others, and that we should never look down on anyone because they didn't have the same advantages.

"Once you have finished your studies and you get a good job and have a career, maybe then you'll have earned your bragging rights," he told us. "But as long as you are *special* as a result of what Mother and I give you, because of our good circumstances, I don't ever want to hear you doing that. Understood?"

We understood.

Ildikó spoke with an irony in her voice when she referred to *connections*, which were obviously a metaphor for something.

"But the music is great, you know," she continued. "I have heard the Rolling Stones a few times before, mainly on Radio Free Europe, and I've seen pictures of them. There is the one who is really cute; I think his name is Breean. They're not as cute as the Beatles, of course, especially Paul." She looked like she was dreaming of being in London and being invited to meet Breean—Brian Jones, of course—or Paul, as in McCartney. Just like me, just like the Gesztenye brothers, this beguiling girl from the teachers' college had fallen hard for rock and roll.

Years later I saw Laci Gesztenye on the streets of Budapest. He looked a little shabby—the jeans and Beatle-boots gone. We never really knew what his father did in Moscow, but I had heard that he had fallen from grace. Comrade Driver, I was told by a friend, had reported on the family's excessive interests in Western culture. He had been spying on them all those years, even on that lovely day at the camp. "They are like the bourgeoisie," he might have said, which to the Party meant "alien to our socialist culture." The family lost the Chevrolet and the big apartment, neither of which they ever owned. Gyuri said that they were lucky to have moved back to Budapest and not to have ended up in Siberia. This was the first but not the last time I saw betrayal like this. Comrade Driver might have been a decent man, deep down. He might have had a family to support. Perhaps this was his way of distancing himself from a disgraced family. In the end everything would come down to survival.

CHAPTER EIGHT

It was hard to say goodbye to Ildikó and my friends in Budapest, but it wasn't hard to return to Denmark. It wasn't just that Copenhagen was beautiful or that the sun was shining all the time. Now that I was back in the West, it was like I could breathe freely again. I could feel the air of prosperity and, with that, a sense of optimism and forward thinking. I had turned eleven in May of that year, and was beginning to make sense of the world around me. I could make out the differences between a democracy and a dictatorship. I understood what it meant to have a diversity of ideas—the freedom to speak your mind, the liberty to travel. We didn't have such liberties in Budapest, and they made all the difference.

My family flourished in Denmark. Mother thrived. She had experienced deep poverty as a child and now she found great satisfaction in sticking to a budget. Saving a krone delighted her. She never took a taxi and even avoided public transportation when she could. She sewed her own dresses, knit her own sweaters, and grew her own vegetables. "Money in the bank is better than money wasted," she liked to say.

Father dug into work, and he enjoyed the colorful political debates on Danish television, where people addressed each other politely, but argued passionately. He learned Danish just to follow along.

"This could never happen in Hungary," he repeatedly told me.

"Why not?" I asked.

"Because here they appreciate different views. In Hungary they don't," he said. "You will learn that when you are a bit older."

I was at the age when everyone told me things I would understand when I was older.

"You see this man with the big fat cigar?" he continued, pointing at a picture in his newspaper. "He is someone I know. Per Hækkerup is the foreign minister. He is a Social Democrat, like your grandmother and I used to be before the war. He is a good man." I was impressed that my father knew someone whose picture was printed in the newspaper. "And look," my father continued. "Here he is having dinner with his adversary from the Conservative Party. They are different, and yet they sit and have a nice meal together. I like that."

By this time, our family had moved from our small apartment to Hellerup, the finest neighborhood in Copenhagen. My parents had found a jewel of a house with two floors and every modern convenience. Not only was there a garden, but at long last, I had my own room to decorate as I liked. I put up pictures of the Beatles (of course!), the Swiss actress Ursula Andress, and the silver Aston Martin from the James Bond movies.

Our landlord, Mr. Koch, had been a pirate in his youth—a real pirate, who roamed the seas and stole other people's cargo. I couldn't believe my luck. I remember visiting Mr. Koch at his own house way up north, where he told us tales of sailing to Asia and showed us some of his "found" treasures. Ivory carvings, paintings, framed pictures, and exotic knives covered every inch of wall space. He named them all for me. Katanas from Japan. Kris from India. Weapons that had once belonged to warriors. I asked him about the faded photograph of a steamboat. "That's me and my men," he said. "Vikings."

I knew all about the Vikings. They were a tough people, and they had been feared just as the Hungarians once were. It was easy to forget that we, too, had been a powerful people. The best riders with the strongest and fastest horses, Hungarians were feared in both the East and the West. We were once one of the most modern empires; three seas washed our shores. No wonder we gave the world hussars. Like the Danes with their Vikings, we were a proud nation with a glorious, storied past.

If the more recent past had been less triumphant, Hungarians took this as proof that our somber nature was deserved, earned even. Hungarians are gloomy. A nation of pessimists. Even in the best of times, we are never totally content with life or with ourselves. I might never have realized this part of our national character had I not become close friends with an American boy, Billy Hanson.

Billy was small and skinny like me. He had his own record collection and shared my passion for rock and roll. To me Billy *was* America. He was more than a good friend; he was my entry to a bright and shiny new world that otherwise would have been inaccessible.

I liked Americans. I liked being around such positive people. What a contrast with us Hungarians. Ask an American, "How are you?" and the worst you'll hear is, "I'm okay." Ask a Hungarian, "How are you?" and you'll get an in-depth response that includes the smallest detail of how his mother-in-law has been creating problems and that just this morning he found a cigarette hole in his best suit, which really was his only suit since the other one had been appropriated by his brother, and oh, tomorrow he has to go and have his cough checked out by the doctor and it's probably something very bad, perhaps even fatal. He will end with, "I am worse than I was yesterday, but better than I will be tomorrow."

After three years in Denmark, Gyuri and I were moved to a different school called Old Hellerup. Old-fashioned and conservative, Old Hellerup was about as different from my liberal alma mater as you could get. Likely my parents thought I needed a little more discipline—and a little more math—a curriculum that more closely resembled the schools in Hungary. It was a smooth transition, made almost seamless because of Ida, a neighborhood girl I'd long had a crush on.

And my friend Billy Hanson went there, too.

Billy's father was the pastor of the small American community in Copenhagen, and he seemed keen to get Gyuri and me to attend. We weren't religious, but that didn't seem to matter to Billy.

"I sing in the choir," he said. "You guys should come."

"We don't go to church," Gyuri responded.

"You don't go to church?" he replied, somewhat surprised.

"We're not really religious," I said.

"Maybe you are and you just don't know it yet." Well, that was a new one. He continued: "Have you ever sung in a choir?"

"In Budapest, yes. Every day at school."

"Then you should come."

Just like that we became churchgoers.

It wasn't a crime to be religious in Hungary in those days. Not quite. But it wasn't without its ramifications, either. Religious people were discriminated against, chastised, stigmatized. They were frequently bypassed for promotions, sidestepped in favor of Party members. Attending church—even worse, an American church—would have damaged my father's career had the authorities in Budapest become aware of it.

Mother grew up Catholic, so she knew about Jesus and the Virgin Mary, about all the stories in the Bible. We celebrated Christmas like most other families in Hungary.

For my brother, sister, and me, the "Little Jesus" who arrived after sunset on December 24 did not have any job other than delivering the gifts. The job was performed by Santa Claus in some hard-core communist families—not ours. It didn't matter that our father was Jewish. When he was a boy his family had put up a Christmas tree, like their Christian neighbors did. For them, it was a demonstration of being Hungarian. Mother, whose own mother was a strict Catholic, grew up celebrating Christmas. It was for many the most important family holiday of the year. The communists didn't dare mess with it, even though it was clearly about Christianity. Father once told us, "Jesus was a Jew." With that he cut the Gordian knot between Christians and Jews. The two-thousand-year conflict between them was easily resolved. Jew or Catholic, it didn't matter.

So when we came to Mother with the idea of going to church with Billy, she didn't blink. "Billy is a good boy. You can go. But be careful that no one at the embassy finds out. They wouldn't like this at all. Oh, and keep it from Father. He might get worried."

This was a time of open secrets. Father knew that every Sunday morning at eight thirty, we climbed into the Hansons' black Ford Zodiac and drove downtown to church. We knew that he was aware of our role as choirboys, even though we pretended he wasn't.

It wasn't really about church. I just liked hanging out with my friend. When Pastor Hanson read from the Bible, my mind would wander and I'd think about a trip to the amusement park or buying a guitar. I jumped up and sang my part when it was time for the choir to sing, though; I just had no idea what I was singing about. As for Jesus...he seemed like a nice enough guy. I liked that he had long hair and I thought that if he hung a guitar around his neck he would have looked like a rock star. I felt sorry for him when I read about how Judas betrayed him.

Billy was a bit older than I was. He went to the local Danish school, which meant that not only was he much better connected to the Danish boys in the neighborhood, but he also had access to local "business opportunities." Billy had an after-school job at the local hardware store, and he would tell me about the work he was doing and the money he was making. Gyuri was working for the local milkman. I was the only one without a job.

I knew money was important. I already had a savings

account where I stashed every krone I got for washing cars and selling wildflowers on the street, but I needed real money if I was to buy the things I wanted, especially a guitar. I needed a job. Billy had just the thing.

"You know the baker, Bruselius Hansen? The one on the corner of Hellerup Street?" Billy asked me when I told him my goal.

"Yes, I do. He is nasty."

"I heard he is looking to hire a couple of kids who can handle a delivery bike."

"What's the job?"

"We would deliver bread. You would have a route and I would have a route."

"How much will he pay?"

"Forty-five. A week."

"That's not bad. What's the catch?" I asked. I was trying to think like a capitalist.

"We start at five thirty. Every day."

"Every day?"

"Every day!"

I arrived at the bakery each morning at five thirty and loaded up my Long John bicycle with bread and morning cakes, which I then delivered to the wealthy people of Copenhagen. Wealthy people, I soon found out, loved to give you advice. Like A. P. Møller, an old man who would come to the door in a bathrobe and slippers to thank me for doing a good job. "Continue this good work, young man, and you, too, will own a big house like mine one day." He gave me advice, but no tip. Lesson learned.

Besides being a delivery boy, I also helped out cleaning the large metal baking plates, scrubbing off the greasy remains with a knifelike tool. No water, just this tool. It was a tough, dirty job and I'd come home tired, my hands raw. Sometimes baker Bruselius Hansen would check the plates and, if he wasn't satisfied, would make me go through the whole lot again. He could be nasty, that was for sure, but I had to show him that I was as good as any of his apprentices.

Perhaps I was taken advantage of, but I made good money and learned the virtue of hard work. Every Saturday I was paid exactly forty-five kroner, which I would take to the *Sparekassen*—the savings bank. It was a big moment, opening up that big brass door, handing over my money and the little yellow bankbook. After a few transactions the lady at the counter recognized me.

"You are saving nicely," she said.

"Thank you. Forty-five every week."

"Keep it here, you will get good interest. If you keep it here a whole year, you will receive a lot more than you have put in."

Mother, Gyuri, and I had been calculating my gains. I knew exactly what the interest was. And I knew exactly what I was going to spend it on—my very own guitar.

CHAPTER NINE

I was enjoying the capitalist life, working hard and saving for something I wanted. I was enjoying Denmark, too, which felt very much like home. But now, in our fifth year, something seemed to have shifted within our family. My parents had always been close, despite their different backgrounds. Father, a Hungarian Jew who grew up in Vienna, lost most of his family in the Holocaust. It was this, the Holocaust and the devastation it wreaked, that made me a Jew. Mother was born into a good middle-class Catholic family, the daughter of a well-respected prison warden. My grandfather had a big job, but when a communist escaped from under his watch in the early thirties, he was stripped of his rank and imprisoned, and the family fell into poverty. Mother started work at age twelve but still finished school despite the hardships. They were a good match, the smart Jewish man and the stalwart Catholic woman—a team of fighters, a gang of survivors.

All my young life, my parents had only been kind and courteous to each other. Solicitous, even. They tried to please each other in many ways, and I had never heard either of them raise their voice, even when they disagreed on things. Father brought home flowers on many occasions, and Mother would cook my father's favorite meals. Now my parents were quarreling a lot, bickering over small things that never would have bothered them before. Only with hindsight did I suspect that their fights were over one issue: whether to return to Hungary or not. Many years later Father told me that the years in Denmark were the best six years of his life. Perhaps it was Mother, who made most of our family's important decisions, who insisted on our return. I never found out for sure. I never will.

In September 1965, my parents sent Gyuri back to Budapest to start high school. I was lonely. My friend Billy was also gone, having returned to the United States with his family. I missed my brother. I missed my best friend. I felt all alone. The only thing that kept me going was the thought that soon I would own my own guitar.

I was a teenager now, and no longer content to simply listen to music. I was dying to play it for myself. Every chance I got I would take my bike to the Apollon music store on the boulevard by the sea and spend hours looking at the guitars in the shop window. It was an old-fashioned store, with two large display windows in which electric guitars were lined up one after the other. The Fender Stratocasters and Telecasters—sunburst, red, and blue—the Gibsons, the Rickenbackers, the Framuses. I stood there analyzing each and every one: the number of pickups, the scratch plates, the shape of the pegheads, the tremolo arms. I knew that one day I would own one of those beautiful instruments.

When I wasn't looking longingly into shop windows, I was poring over the catalogs Father brought home. I especially loved the Framus brochure, with its lush pictures and detailed English descriptions. This one had a modern "painting" on the cover: a man and two women, dancing in colorful elegant clothes, musicians in suits in the background. I imagined I was the man with the guitar, as I always did.

It was the Golden Framus that caught my eye, one that looked like the Fender Jaguar. "Highly modern, technically sophisticated electric guitars with vibrato, organ effect, and six or twelve strings," the description said. Lots of buttons and a tremolo. The organ effect was a special feature no other guitar had. The scratch plate had a tiger-skin-like design, and there was a gilded plate underneath the volume and tone knobs. I knew I'd just discovered the guitar I wanted.

There were hundreds of other guitars out there, but you know when you see The One. I hoped Father would go along—and he did. The Golden Strato was expensive, around six or seven hundred kroner, which would have been around two hundred dollars—a lot of money in the 1960s. I had saved almost a whole year to get my half together. Father kept his promise to pay the other half and we placed the order. All that was left was the agonizing wait for the instrument to arrive.

The big day arrived a few weeks before Christmas when Father called to make sure I'd be home when he got in from work. I stood at my window as his car rolled in, watching as he got out and opened the trunk. My heart raced as he pulled out one box, then another. It was here! My guitar had finally arrived! I rushed down the stairs and ran to the car to help Father carry the precious goods into the house. We opened the boxes together and put first the guitar case on the dining room table, then the Dynacord amp, then the AKG microphone and the cables.

When I opened the brown leather case, I saw that the guitar was even more beautiful than I had imagined. I waited for minutes before I lifted it out, hardly able to believe my good fortune. I held the guitar tight. At last it was mine. After a few minutes I was able to put the guitar down long enough to pick up the instructions to the amp, which I slowly read. I connected the cables, turned on the Dynacord, waited for the power tubes to glow golden yellow, hung the strap around my neck, stood up, and strummed the Golden Strato. I was in heaven.

I spent all my spare time playing the guitar, but every evening when I put my Golden Strato back in its case, I wished I could share the moment with my brother. Thinking of him, I was filled with a terrible sense of dread knowing that I, too, would soon return to Hungary. The thought of being separated from my parents for such a long time triggered an overwhelming anxiety. The letters from Gyuri did nothing to make me feel better. After briefly telling me of a new friend he'd met or a soccer game he'd been to, he'd ask me to send this or that from Denmark: chewing gum, pop magazines, and porn, which he advised me to hide under boxes of chocolate. He missed the life that I was living. Soon I would miss it, too.

My last year in Denmark was like being on death row, knowing that the day would come when life as I knew it would end. I stocked up on everything precious to me as if I were preparing to leave for a different planet, which in a way I was. Getting ready for life on the other side, as I thought of it, I hoarded useful and useless things. Books, magazines, pictures of rock bands, plenty of guitar cables, picks and strings, lots and lots of chewing gum, clothes, plenty of licorice, a Swiss knife, and bottles of Coca-Cola. I was terrified of what lay ahead.

I thought of the stern faces of the teachers in Hungary. I thought of the gray streets and the old cars. And what of my connection to rock and roll? Were my Levi's to be replaced by a somber school uniform? I thought I knew the answer to all those questions. No wonder I was fearful as the date of my departure approached.

Denmark had been my home. My formative years had been spent in one of the most liberal places in the world. For five happy years I had been surrounded by acceptance, by friendship. I had no idea what to expect of my real motherland, the country I knew little about and understood even less. I had only one hope: maybe rock and roll would save me.

In September 1966, I joined Gyuri in Budapest. Only the lucky Zsuzsi stayed behind with my parents in Denmark. For your own good, my mother had said. It's the right thing to do, she told us. I knew that my parents loved us beyond anything, but this felt like a punishment.

I was a precocious fourteen-year-old, was keenly aware that I had seen more of the world in five years than most Hungarians would see in a lifetime. I spoke three languages fluently and believed I understood the world around me better than most. I thought I was smart. I didn't realize I was vulnerable.

Five years before I had boarded a plane with a rubber fox, a pocketknife, and a copy of an English-language primer. Now I was stepping off the train in Budapest with an electric guitar and a copy of George Orwell's *Animal Farm.*

All around me were reminders that I had moved from a rich country to a poor one, from democracy to communism. The roads were congested with homely cars from the Soviet Union, Poland, and East Germany. The few Western cars—a red Mini Cooper, a green Ford Anglia—stood out like pretty girls. The citizens of Budapest were dressed in stark uniformity, mostly gray. Men or women, young or old—it didn't matter. Only a few ambitious citizens tried to make themselves more interesting with a bright scarf or Western-style tie. I longed for the cheerful colors of Copenhagen—for my room, my job at the bakery, my friends. But longing was for fools. Even I knew that.

Gyuri and I moved in with relatives from my father's side: Uncle István and Aunt Anni, and our cousins, János, Miki, András, and Matyi. Their enormous apartment on Dózsa György Street was close to Heroes' Square in the Sixth District, a prime location. But the once grand building was in decay. I wasn't surprised by the peeling paint, the fractured woodwork, or the lone bare bulb dangling in the hallway. Such things, I soon realized, were just part of the communist ecosystem. But when I saw the stained-glass windows, I felt something splinter within me. The luscious colors and intricate patterns of Miksa Róth were unmistakable—the leaves were still a verdant green, the flowers rich violets and plums—but where the glass had been broken, crude attempts at repair had been made.

Ham-fisted efforts that seemed to mock the original accomplishment, as if to suggest that great artistry could be achieved with a paint-by-numbers kit.

Uncle's building on Dózsa György Street had been designed with a sense of purpose and an aesthetic that was meant to enrich the lives of the families who lived there. The original apartments had been more than beautiful. Their large windows, spacious rooms, and high ceilings conveyed a spirit of generosity and optimism that now seemed out of place. What's more, those old homes had a certain intuition about them. There was a natural order to things, a logical path where every element seemed to contribute to the greater motive of the space. Enter a room and you knew instinctively where to turn. Where there was a wall, there was a reason for a wall. Where there was a door or a nook or a window—there was a reason for that, too.

But in 1966 the apartments were sad remnants of once great homes. Having been cut in half—sometimes in thirds—these poorly thought-out units had only one purpose: to squeeze in as many people as possible. Certainly, many more than were originally intended. These make-do constructions weren't designed with living in mind. A kitchen might lead on to a bathroom. A bedroom might be carved out of a hallway. The work was slipshod and the materials coarse. You'd be hard-pressed to find any optimism in these small spaces—austerity had taken its place.

Of course, the housing shortage after the war necessitated some of these adjustments—but only some. Most of these refurbishments were prompted by the communist belief that a large home was bourgeois. For most, that is. Some people, like my uncle, still occupied one of the grand, intact apartments on the upper floors.

An English garden had once beautified the back of the house. The flowers were gone now—the marble fountain was dry and broken. The space had been relegated to a dusty old soccer field, where the boys from the building would kick the ball and each other's shins every now and then, two makeshift garages serving as goalposts.

Sándor was the janitor. He was an older man who used to work for the ÁVO, the dreaded communist secret police during the 1950s. His wife, Annus, had an unpleasantly high-pitched voice, which she used to abuse people whom she thought behaved improperly. Like all janitors, Sándor and Annus followed the happenings in the house day in and day out and took notes on the tenants' activities.

The tenants in the house were especially nice to this powerful couple who could make their lives miserable if they wanted to. Sándor and Annus were given the task of observing other people's lives: their relationships, their friends and visitors. It was an assignment they took seriously, and this husband and wife team would regularly report infractions to their superiors, even when they never actually happened. I was well aware that we were not supposed to pick a fight with Sándor or Annus. The superintendents and concierges had always had real power in Hungary. This was a country of caretakers.

Uncle István was strict. He would have been in his fifties then, younger than I am today, but he seemed a lot older—perhaps because he was always angry. A former government big shot, Uncle had earned his reputation in the

Party before the war. This was during a time when communists were in illegality and were persecuted by the Fascist regime. But my uncle never let this stop him. As a young doctor he treated poor workers and their families for free. When the war came he fought in the resistance, braving the Nazis. But by 1966 there were few traces of that idealistic man left. Uncle was by then a university professor at the medical faculty. He carried himself with the air of intimidation expected of the head of an important health facility.

Gyuri and I were afraid of Uncle. When he was at home, not a sound was to be made. Unfortunately, with five boys in the house—János had already moved out—noise was inevitable. Until he left for work in the morning, we would all have to be very still. Dinner was always conducted in cemetery-like silence. The rules were strict, but with so many boys around, perhaps it was necessary. It was a tough regime.

Aunt Anni was a smart woman, herself a university professor in philosophy. She was the first line of defense, a family manager and go-between always trying to smooth things over. Aunt Anni ran the family with love and affection, as well as discipline. She made sure we stayed out of harm's way when Uncle came home angry; if they had a dispute, she would usher him into their bedroom, out of hearing range. Or sometimes she would say to him, "Don't be angry, they have problems of their own"—referring to us being away from our parents.

She could be strict, but Father was important to her. They were first cousins, and were among the very few in the family who had survived the Holocaust. Maybe that's why she was so protective of us.

We loved our aunt, but her family adhered to an old-fashioned setup where there was no doubt that a woman, even a woman as smart as Aunt Anni, came second to the man of the house. This was so different from my family, where Father and Mother were clearly equals.

My cousins were smart and talented, two of them great mathematicians. János, the oldest, was a good boy with a great heart, a bit of a loner, perhaps because he had suffered more than his fair share during the war. Miki, the second oldest, was already married to Emmi, whom I loved. Miki had become a professor of mathematics at a young age and was now an assistant to Pál Erdös, the great mathematician. András, the second youngest, also a mathematician, lectured us constantly, throwing out obscure questions about Gaussian functions and the like. Matyi was just a kid, much younger than me.

Gyuri and I did what we could to keep in Uncle's good graces. The electric guitar was a problem, however. It wasn't just about the noise, although that was part of it. To Uncle it was a symbol of something dangerous, a reminder of the awful yeah-yeah-yeah racket that all the young people were listening to. So I was forced to part with my Golden Framus—for a while, anyway. I stowed it with a neighbor who didn't mind the noise.

Our family in Budapest treated us like sons and brothers. They were happy to take us in and were willing to share everything they had. Unfortunately, they had nothing we wanted. No beat magazines or American comic books. No records or tapes—just some Tchaikovsky, Mozart, and Beethoven. Nothing I wanted to play.

"How do you listen to rock-and-roll music?" I remember asking András.

"We don't."

"Don't you like the Beatles?"

"We don't!"

No Beatles? No rock and roll? This was bad. It wasn't even like we could spend our time watching TV, because that, too, was forbidden. The best televisions in Eastern Europe were being made by the Orion factory in Hungary, but Uncle had declared that there would be no TV in his house. There was to be no distraction from our studies. Period.

My only real source of happiness was the Bakelite Crown transistor radio. Boys who owned such a radio would be very popular indeed. A real Japanese transistor radio was a status symbol because it could receive all the Western stations on short and medium wave. At that time Gyuri's Bakelite radio was definitely something to brag about. And we did. At the request of his schoolmates, Gyuri had to take the radio on collective class outings to the hills of Buda, where they could tune in to all the foreign stations. The reception was better there, with less jamming by the authorities. As a rule, Radio Free Europe, the BBC, and Voice of America were banned in Hungary as in all the other Eastern European countries, and so the signals were jammed. But listening to these and other Western radio stations was a regular pastime for us. We shared tricks to circumvent the jamming, like attaching a wire to the antenna and connecting it to a radiator, and discovering new wavelengths in places where reception was reasonably good.

Radio in hand, Gyuri would take to the hills almost every weekend. He took me, too. Amazingly, while there were thirty-eight boys and girls in his class, not one of them ever reported us for listening to banned channels. Not just banned; listening to Radio Free Europe or the Voice of America was a crime. Get caught listening and the penalties could be severe, even for a teenager. We were engaged in an ideological war with the West, and these stations were the voice of the enemy. As teenagers, we didn't quite understand what this ideological warfare was, or why we should hate the West. What we did know was that according to the authorities the West was bad; rock and roll and a free press and Coca-Cola were enemies of the people.

Citizens of the West were the imperialists—the exploiters. Those in the Peace Camp—as the Soviet Union and the captive nations of Eastern Europe were called—were good. They were the liberators who had freed us from the oppression of the capitalists. But this dogma rarely confused anyone. Even those preaching communist ideology hardly believed in its "superiority" as was proclaimed.

With the experience in Denmark under our belt, Gyuri and I knew very well that most of it was a lie. But we kept this to ourselves. I frequently remembered what Ildikó had told me: Teenagers are smart. They know when they're being lied to.

Gyuri and I were given a room with a balcony and large windows that overlooked the English garden. It was generous of Aunt Anni to give us those accommodations—decisions such as who slept where fell under her jurisdiction. This particular room had no connection to the bedroom where our aunt and uncle slept, so it seemed like a safe place. Our Bakelite radio was wrapped in a velvet cloth and kept securely in its case. At nine o'clock each night we unpacked it and turned it on.

Radio Luxembourg was everyone's favorite because it was mostly music with not much talk. The pirate radio station transmitted from Luxembourg every night, broadcasting rock and pop exclusively. I can only remember the name of one of the disc jockeys—Paul Burnett—but as far as I recall the DJs were all Brits. This was where tens of millions of young people—East and West—heard British and American hits for the first time.

When I listened to that station, it was as if I had once again become one with my friends in the West. I closed my eyes and the border disappeared. I was in Copenhagen or Amsterdam, London or Detroit. I was like any boy my age, connected to the world by rock and roll. All by the grace of Radio Luxembourg.

Turning on the radio was an important moment for Gyuri and me. We'd lie in bed and listen to the good vibrations that cheered us. The Beatles and the Rolling Stones, Steve Winwood and Stevie Wonder, Bob Dylan and Donovan, the Beach Boys and Sonny & Cher, Manfred Mann and the Who, the Hollies, the Four Tops and the Supremes, the Kinks. The list was long and our spirits were high.

At home in Denmark, what we thought of as our real home, all of this was a natural thing to do. Here it was different. We knew that and were careful. When we tuned in to Luxembourg, we turned the dial so low that we could barely hear the music or understand which band the DJ was talking about. We were well aware that not everybody was as fond as we were of Western radio stations and the music we loved; that it was illegal to listen to it in the first place. Gyuri and I felt safe enough in the confines of our room, but even so we were always listening for the opening of a door or the sound of footfalls down the corridor.

What's that old line: *Just because you're paranoid doesn't mean they're not out to get you?* This was Hungary in the 1960s. We should have known that *everyone* was out to get us. To this day I wonder if we had become complacent, if we'd turned the radio up a little too loud or gotten carried away singing along. All I know is that one night our entertainment was interrupted by the sound of footsteps in the hallway, footsteps that grew louder and louder until they were threateningly close.

"Turn it off, quick!" Gyuri hissed at me.

I fumbled for the dial, but it was too late.

Uncle burst into our room with a bang, pushing the door open and turning on the light.

"Damnit, you boys. What is this noise?" he roared.

"Uncle, we...we...we are so sorry," I said. "We were just listening to some music. I'm sorry if we woke you."

I turned to Gyuri for backup. Some big brother—he had pulled the covers over his head.

"*Music?* You call that music?" His face stretched with anger until he looked like Batman's nemesis Two-Face. "Give that damn thing to me." He snatched the radio from my hand and left as he had entered—in a rage.

Gyuri and I should have known better. We should have obeyed the rules of the house. At least we should have waited until Uncle was out before we turned on the radio. We knew how much he hated noise. We blamed ourselves. What a disaster it would be if we couldn't get the radio back. How were we supposed to show our faces in front of the other boys and girls without a radio? We could think of nothing but the next weekend's excursion to the hills of Buda. What would our friends say?

"I promised everyone I'd bring the radio," Gyuri said. I'd never seen him so close to tears. "How will we be able to catch up with what's going on in the land of rock and roll?"

The situation looked bad.

The next morning we spoke to Aunt Anni as if she were our union representative.

"Uncle took our radio last night," Gyuri said. I stood right behind him.

"I know, and Uncle is angry," Aunt Anni responded.

"Please tell Uncle we did not want to do anything wrong, and that we would like to have the radio back," Gyuri continued.

Anni was usually willing to help, but this time she didn't seem very encouraging. In fact, she was angry, too. She left it to Uncle to give the verdict.

We knocked weakly on the door to Uncle's study, entering only after hearing his gruff "Come in." Uncle was distant. He was sitting at the far end of the spacious room, which had large windows on two sides. He sat quietly in the green velvet armchair by the inlaid round coffee table, with a small doily. He didn't bother to look up from the book he was reading. He meant to intimidate us. He was successful.

I spoke first. "Uncle, we want to apologize for the noise last night. We are very sorry."

"Yes," Gyuri joined in. "It will not happen again, Uncle. We promise."

Silence.

I tried to be the brave one. "Can we have the radio back please?"

He suddenly looked up.

"You want your radio back?"

This was good. At least he was talking. But the look on his face didn't encourage us. He was cold, firm, and totally in control of himself. He did not look tense; just authoritarian. No emotions. That was scary.

"No!" he said. Never had there been a more brutal word. Uncle continued. "It wasn't the noise. You boys are not supposed to listen to *that* music on *those* radio stations. Not in this house. Not under my roof. The radio will stay locked away." And with that, he returned to his book.

Welcome to communist Hungary.

CHAPTER TEN

Our school in Budapest was named after Stephen I, the first king of Hungary, crowned in the year 1000 and declared a saint. The word *Saint* was removed from his name after the war as part of the concerted efforts by the communists to get rid of religion altogether, in effect to rewrite history. When I enrolled, it was simply called Stephen I. Built in 1910, the school was an enormous brick building, spared from destruction during the war and the subsequent revolutions. The interior corridors, classrooms, and even the chemistry and physics labs were all painted a nauseous olive green up to about six feet; the rest was whitewashed. Sparsely decorated, the place felt empty of everything but despair. A few plants hung in clay pots from the classroom walls. The window frames were painted in the same olive green, which was peeling off in strips. Pictures of great moments of revolutions through the centuries were affixed to the walls, mostly bad prints of events that had nothing to do with the lives of the students. Like a reproduction of an original painting that showed an angry Lenin giving a speech from a balcony, or a scene from the Great October Revolution, or the storming of the Winter Palace in St. Petersburg in 1917—a painting based on a "true historic event" that actually never happened.

The lavatory was the meeting place for the bad boys, kids who would smoke in defiance of the strict rules. Smoking was in; only sissies didn't smoke. I tried and it only made me sick. The big boys had a trick: they would wet the tip of the cigarette butt and send it flying upward with their thumb. If they were good, it would stick to the whitewashed ceiling. A few months into the school year, the ceiling was nicely decorated with cigarette butts, which prompted angry raids by the gym teacher. But the toilet was the safe space where we spoke about the relationship between the physics teacher and the history teacher. Or looked at pinups. Or shared cheat sheets, folded so small that even a Soviet counterspy couldn't have found one.

The teachers were strict. They didn't hang out with the students after class the way teachers in Copenhagen did. It was *Yes Mr. This, No Mrs. That.* Yet, according to my mother, Aunt Anni had gone to a lot of trouble to get us into this particular school. I wasn't sure what "gone to a lot of trouble" meant, but I knew that I was expected to appreciate her efforts. Like children everywhere, I was told to be grateful. And just like children everywhere, I wasn't. Yes, Gyuri and I always appreciated what we had; we knew our father's position brought us privilege. But being told to be grateful to our aunt Anni for arranging such a "great" school—this was new. This was different.

Every morning I'd get up, wash, get dressed, pack my lunch box, and put something to show my classmates—a magazine, a record sleeve, a guitar catalog—in my leather bag. Gyuri and I would always leave the house together, taking the trolley bus that stopped outside the building or, if the weather was nice, walking the mile. It wasn't long before my body felt an aversion toward the school: as we approached the big wooden double gate, I'd get a cramp in my stomach. It would follow me through the day, as I walked the stairs and corridors and lined up with my classmates to walk into class. I'd settle into my desk and hope I wouldn't be called on.

My classmates were a diverse group, if not by nationality, then by socioeconomic background. There were three distinguishable groups: First were the "bourgeois" kids like my brother and me, those with successful parents who had big careers, most of whom owned cars. Then there were the working-class boys whose parents held jobs at one of the factories in town. They were visibly poor, but they displayed a certain dignity, no doubt instilled in them by their parents. Then there were the kids from the countryside who traveled long distances every day, some of them even taking the train.

My classmates knew about my background, that I was different and a "rich boy," but I never felt I was the object of envy. Thanks to my parents, I always had the ability to fit in, to find common ground and common language when talking to people.

"You meet a minister, talk to him like a minister. You meet a street vendor, talk to him like a street vendor. You meet a professor, talk to him like a professor," my mother had told us. "People will appreciate that. People appreciate it when you talk to them with respect, even though you might be of a different status. You must demand that people do the same to you."

An important lesson, then. It made all the difference now.

CHAPTER ELEVEN

There was plenty of officially sanctioned music at school—classical music, that is. Some of the more radical or younger teachers brought Hungarian beat music into class (the Hungarian term for "rock and roll"), but they were always careful not to overstep the line. In general it wasn't a great idea to tout your encyclopedic knowledge of rock or run around with magazines in front of the teachers.

But outside the view of these teachers, the school was a stock exchange for rock and roll. Reels of tapes were passed around. Sometimes even real vinyl records made it to school, although rarely, as the danger of these being confiscated was high. We traded West German magazines like the colorful *Bravo*, the *New Musical Express* from England, and sometimes even *Billboard* like Americans traded baseball cards. Some of us managed to get hold of these from friends and relatives in Vienna and Frankfurt, and even from faraway places like San Francisco or Copenhagen. One boy in Gyuri's class, Tamás, had an uncle in the United States who regularly sent him magazines that miraculously made it past the vigilant customs enforcers. Tamás even had a pair of Lee jeans, which he of course wore to school under the blue uniform, much to the envy of the other students.

Occasionally a teacher would seize a magazine, but that just made the risk of reading them that much sweeter. The teachers never did destroy them—not like Ted and the Batman comic—and I suspected they might have taken them home for their own children. Perhaps even the teachers themselves were not immune to the pull of rock and roll.

Every now and then someone would make an attempt to brighten up the classroom by taping up a torn-out photo of a rock band from a magazine. I once hung a huge poster of the Kinks, looking like eighteenth-century nobility in their red velvet stage garb and ruffled white shirts. They were really big by then, and I was a huge fan of Ray Davies. It was beautiful, I thought, to see their picture next to the portraits of Lenin, Marx, and Engels, the great thinkers of communism, but it was a risky move on my part. The class giggled as our teacher Mr. Pálffy entered the classroom, sat down behind his desk, and spotted the poster only after he'd finished paging through his notes. The Kinks, unsurprisingly, failed to impress him. The poster was summarily removed.

My classmates found different ways to claim rock music as their own. The names of songs were inventively translit-erated and transformed into Hungarian. The Spencer Davis Group became Spencer, and their hit "Gimme

Some Loving" was *Kiviszem a Lavórt,* which then became *Giv-e-sema-lovaurt,* meaning, quite literally, "take out the bathwater." "(I Can't Get No) Satisfaction" by the Rolling Stones was "Get No." The Rolling Stones—called the Stones all over the world—were called simply Rolling by their Hungarian fans. Everything got a little twist. Perhaps Hungarians just can't live without giving a little twist to things. We can get into the revolving door after you and get out before you. It's a scientifically proven fact.

Every day we compared notes about the charts, the latest hit songs, and the newest releases. Decca, Parlophone, Atlantic, and Motown were all household names. We knew about these labels like a carpenter knows his tools. We meticulously debated each new song, picking apart every riff and solo.

"Did you all hear Eric Clapton play 'N.S.U.'?"

"Yeah, Cream."

"Sure did. He plays a red Gibson semi-acoustic. He plays that solo faster than anyone."

"That's what they said on Radio Luxembourg: he is the fastest player in the world right now."

"Faster than Pete Townshend?"

"That's what they said."

"Does anyone have it taped?"

"I got it down. It's not perfect, but you can copy it if you want to."

And so it went.

Later I would smuggle in my Philips cassette recorder so we could listen to songs between classes. This was something new. The cassette recorder was small and delivered a reasonably good sound. It was nothing short of a miracle. Unlike the heavy reel-to-reel tape recorders, it could be carried anywhere. It ran on batteries. It was light. The cassettes fit in your pocket, they were robust, and they could be reused. If you removed a little protective piece of plastic on the side, it would prevent it from being erased, which was especially useful when you didn't want to lose a treasured song.

We'd rewind and reuse those cassette tapes a hundred times, until they were almost inaudible. In breaks between classes, I would stand in the corridor with the Philips in my hand, and boys and girls from the other classes would stand around me in silence and listen to the songs I played. I got a lot of friendly looks and a great deal of street cred for owning a Philips and, perhaps more important, for sharing.

One favorite pastime was ranking the world's best rock musicians. The competition among the guitarists was fierce, with Eric Clapton and Chuck Berry taking the lead. The drummer category was a no-brainer: no one was better than Ginger Baker from Cream. Steve Winwood was the undisputed winner in the vocal and keyboard categories. Janis Joplin would soon be known as the best female singer.

The Party didn't like to see young people aping the rock musicians from England and America, as it went against everything they thought was decent and civilized. It didn't reflect the "socialist" character that young people were supposed to possess. By 1967 the authorities understood the threat and power of rock, and they got scared. Rock and roll was to them Western decadence. To fight it was to fight Western influence. Young people with long hair were considered weirdos and subversives, sexually rebellious and inappropriate, all because they listened to this crazy music. But instead of a total ban, the authorities aimed at total control.

Sometimes I would talk about my years in Denmark, what I had seen. Sometimes my classmates believed me; sometimes not. When I told my friends that I would ride my bike into town to a place called the Stork Fountain and sit there listening to a man playing music, that Donovan had once sat there and played, they were suspicious. When I told them that a friend of my father drove around in a big Jaguar and that he owned a factory that made the electrical switches for all of Denmark, they were incredulous. Not everyone liked to hear my stories about "the other side"—like Mr. Müller, our Hungarian teacher who also taught us German. A short, heavyset man, Mr. Müller reminded me of Švejk, a famously clumsy soldier in the Austro-Hungarian army, immortalized by the Czech writer Jaroslav Hašek in his book *The Good Soldier Švejk.*

On one occasion Mr. Müller decided to humiliate me in front of the whole class while he was handing out marks for composition. "Simonyi, stand up."

"Yes, Mr. Teacher."

"Perhaps your choice of subject was not the best."

"My choice of subject, sir?"

"I can't even give you a two. I have to mark this as a one." School grades were on a scale of one to five, with five indicating excellence and one indicating failure.

"But sir, you told us to write about a subject of our choice. Something we really liked." I tried to be respectful, while holding my ground.

"I didn't ask you for comments, Simonyi. This…" Mr. Müller couldn't even say *rock and roll.* He waved my paper in the air as if trying to rid himself of a nasty odor. "This silly thing is unworthy of our school." With that he ordered me to sit down.

I was innocent—and stupid. I thought that writing an essay on the topic of my choice meant exactly that—*my choice.* I should have known better than to write about a rock concert I had attended in Copenhagen. By focusing on the famous Carousel Club with Dave Dee, Dozy, Beaky, Mick & Tich—a British band—I had lauded the West.

"This club is the best club in all of Copenhagen. Even the Rolling Stones have played there," I wrote. I recalled how I was standing and screaming in the first row throughout the concert, right below the stage, and how my brother and I were among the youngest to be allowed there. It was an amazing night, a one-of-a-kind experience. DDDBMT were huge those days with their hits like "Hideaway" and "Hold Tight." They weren't the greatest band, but they were certainly one of the most colorful. It was an honor and a privilege to see them live.

Now that I was back in Budapest, that concert seemed like a dream to me. The concert was so distant, so different, as if it had happened on a faraway planet. Perhaps the way I had written about the evening made me sound a bit crazy. I should have been less enthusiastic. I should have known that bragging about my Western experience was a bad idea.

I wrote about how Dave Dee had made the crowd happy by singing "Hideaway," "Bend It," and "Hold Tight," and about the Union Jack bell-bottoms he wore. Then came the best part, about how I'd staked out the band outside the club for hours after the show, waiting for them to show up so I could shake hands with Dave Dee and of course Tich the guitarist, and why it meant so much to me. I concluded by saying I wished they would come to Budapest.

The teacher had no idea what I was talking about. What's more, he didn't care. He did not want Dave Dee, Dozy, Beaky, or Mick & Tich to come to Hungary, nor did he want his students to be influenced by that kind of music. He clearly did not understand me. I had just wanted to share my experience with the world. What a fool I had been.

CHAPTER TWELVE

I had no business being in Hungary, but I had no choice. I was fourteen and my parents wanted me to attend high school in Budapest. I had to accept it; what else could I have done? So, I kept my head down and my feelings to myself as I trudged through this no-man's-land. Father had told me all about World War I, about the strip of territory between the trenches of the two opposing armies and how, one Christmas Day early in the war, the German and Allied armies put down their guns and played a friendly game of soccer. It was supposed to be a pleasant story of good cheer and camaraderie, but all I could think about was the next day, when the men resumed fighting and it was gunfire, not a soccer ball, that traveled over no-man's-land.

These were my thoughts as I tried to climb back into life in Budapest. There were moments when I thought maybe it would have been better never to have seen *the other side*. But that was stupid. In the end my experience wasn't first and foremost a source of desperation, but of hope. Yet, here I was, caught somewhere in between, neither here nor there—neither friend nor foe. I wasn't a child, but I wasn't an adult. I wasn't a Hungarian, but neither was I a Dane. It wasn't so much about Denmark versus Hungary—I didn't feel an opposition in that way. Despite Mother telling me to live like a Danish boy, I always knew I was Hungarian, as much as I knew that my friend Billy was American. I dreamed and thought in Hungarian. It was my mother tongue and I didn't have a trace of a foreign accent. But something was missing, something I couldn't put a name to other than recognizing it as longing. Whether it was a longing for something I had lost or for something I had yet to experience, I couldn't say.

Denmark was more than just a place for me; it was a symbol. Yes, I missed certain things: I missed my friends, and the safety of my room. I missed the bicycle path and the record store and the tiny boutiques that sold stuff we didn't need, but loved to look at. I even missed the baker Bruselius Hansen and his nasty wife.

At fourteen, I just wasn't comfortable being back in Budapest. I didn't feel secure. For the first time in my life, I thought of Hungary as *the other side*. It was clear to me now that there were fundamental differences between East and West. It wasn't just the imbalance of wealth, stark though it was. It was more elemental. What I was feeling—and struggling to articulate—was the difference between a society that was open and one that was closed. A society that had a place for individuality and ambition, for quality and enterprise, for trust and respect, for just about anything that could be imagined. And one that didn't.

I did my best to conceal my disappointments. I was polite. I was curious and friendly. I understood that asking people questions was an impressive thing to do, so I asked questions. I inquired about the janitor's health and asked the bus driver if he was looking forward to his day off. I listened patiently when people told me of their problems, even though I hadn't the slightest interest in them. I came across as deferential and contemplative—much older than my years. But that was just a trick. I believed that impressing people would keep me safe. I wanted to be safe.

Only Gyuri knew of my sadness. He had his own struggles, different from mine. But he had already suffered through a year alone and had some insight to offer.

"I don't like it here," I told him. It was that simple.

"Okay, so what do you want to do about it?"

"What can I do?" Each time I asked the question, I hoped there would be a different answer.

"Nothing. That's what you can do. Nothing. So you'd better adapt."

I hated that word, *adapt*.

"Andris, you're making things hard for yourself," Gyuri explained. "Find some friends. There are good people here. Go out and meet them."

This was not what I wanted to hear. My friends were not in Budapest, but in the little speaker in that Bakelite radio, which we had gotten back from Uncle after serving two weeks of punishment. When I turned on the radio, the miles melted away. Every morning I squared myself for the routine of the day, and every night I lost myself in the world of music. I hoped things would get better, but I learned the hard way that a problem ignored is not a problem solved.

I pretended that I was present and eager at school. I raised my hand more than anyone, hoping to get noticed. Zsuzsi was the nerd in our family—not me—but I desperately wanted approval, and being labeled a drip seemed a small price to pay. I often got carried away, even going so far as to tell my history teacher that I had read *Das Kapital.* Mr. Draskovics burst out laughing.

"Son, that is great," he said. "I am sixty years old and I have not read Karl Marx, but I guess you are a genius."

And yet, despite my stubbornness, I felt the hard edges of my unhappiness begin to soften. As time passed, I found myself getting used to Budapest. I even found myself liking it. Time and again I would stop in front of a great building and imagine what it must have looked like in the past—before the war, before the communists took over, before it was collectively owned. The Gresham Palace down on Roosevelt Square had once been the headquarters of an English-owned insurance company. It had been occupied by the Red Army during the war, and was subsequently sectioned off into communal apartments. But when I stood before it in those lonely days, I liked to picture the men of the illustrious Gresham life insurance company conducting business in this, their world headquarters. Imagining these men in their smart suits and umbrellas, I felt a little less isolated, as if Hungary were still connected to commerce and, with it, the outside world.

Some two decades after the war, all the bridges crossed the Danube once more. I would stop in the middle of the magnificent Chain Bridge whenever I could, just to enjoy the view. At that distance I could not see the marks left by the war; I could see only the charming face of a beautiful city. It might have been damaged and wounded, but it was still a dignified cosmopolitan center. Even in its infirmity, Budapest had a majesty all its own.

When the warm weather came, I'd spend time at the public swimming pool like we did in the old days, when Father would sit with his paper and I learned to read upside down. In summer the more courageous people would put tape recorders in their windows and play Chubby Checker or the Beatles. It was as if the young people behind those windows wanted to make a statement: We are part of *that* family. *We love this music*, this defiant little act said. *We love that lifestyle. Please someone help us, we are stuck here. Can you hear our radio? Can you hear us?*

There was more rock and roll than I imagined there would be when I first returned to Hungary, but much less than I wanted. I was determined that one day, I would leave all this behind, but I understood that I should try to make the best of it in the moment. Adapt.

Gyuri was different. He accepted Hungary as his final destination. At age sixteen, he was a lot taller than me. Handsome, too. This innocent-looking boy with curly hair and good manners was the center of attention. As soon as we arrived at school in the morning, we would part ways until classes ended for the day. I loved it when we took the trolley home. I felt safe again, swapping stories with my brother.

It was around this time that I made a new friend. Péter Békés lived right below us, wore Wrangler jeans, and played the guitar. We'd get together with a soccer ball in the dilapidated garden of Aunt Anni's apartment building, two guys kicking a ball back and forth and talking about girls and school and music. Mostly music.

Péter looked like Engelbert Humperdinck, one of

those English pop stars. Humperdinck wasn't my kind of singer—he was an old ladies' heartthrob—but he was on the radio all the time, and his photo was everywhere. Péter had the good sense to be embarrassed about the resemblance.

We'd been halfheartedly kicking around the soccer ball one day when Péter came up with an idea. "Hey," he said. "Let's go down to see the proletarians at the Danuvia Works on Saturday."

"You want us to go to the *kultur* where Gyuri has his dance lessons? That's lame." Practically every factory had a *kultur*, a social club set up by the authorities to support the educational ambitions of the Party and the trade unions.

"Yes," he said. "Exactly."

"You have fun, friend. Make sure to tell me all about it later, because I'm not going."

"András, you knucklehead. It's not just about proletarians and dancing. There's a band there, Liversing, and they play rock music after the dance lesson."

"Right. Boring music at the *kultur*? No thanks."

"It's not what you think, Andris. You know about the permits, right?"

"What are you talking about?"

"The music permits. My mother says they are a mechanism of control that allows or prevents bands from appearing in public."

"So what has this got to do with this Liverwurst of yours?" I thought I was hilarious, given that Péter spoke fluent German.

"Very funny."

"I do my best."

Péter continued. "You know there's this selection committee of the State Concert Bureau, and it hands out permits to perform in public."

"This is Hungary. There's a permit. The sky is blue. What else is new?"

"Listen, smart-ass. This isn't just paperwork. It's all about control. The bands have to know hundreds of songs, mostly the ones preferred by the selection committee. They have to pass the exams, prove their decency, and prove that they can read sheet music."

"How decent?" I wondered.

"Nothing provocative. Nice music and nice looks, I guess."

"I'm not sure the Yardbirds or the Pretty Things can read sheet music. I'm sure they don't need a government permit," I said.

"You're right. It's not about reading music. It's about the obstacles the authorities put in front of the bands. They decide who's a musician and who is not."

Hearing this, I felt wounded—naive. I thought that the whole point of music was to pick up your guitar and play what you wanted however you could.

"So what does this have to do with Liversing?" Now I was interested.

"Well, Mother told me that sometimes the authorities exile bands to play on the outskirts of town. 'You know, this is politics!'" Péter continued, not entirely sure himself what his mother had meant by this. "So Liversing, who call themselves a rhythm-and-blues band, well, they're kind of exiled."

"So you want me to see an exiled band? What are they going to play, the greatest hits of the Szeged Prison?"

"Ah, but you are so quick to judge. My friends say Liversing plays to a different style and much louder as soon as the dance teacher is gone. It's pretty wild, apparently. And you don't need a membership to get in. Come on, what's that saying— *You can't see from the outside the fire inside.* You know I'm right." Péter put his hand on my shoulder and gave me a shake. "Andris," he said. "You're coming with me."

CHAPTER THIRTEEN

The Danuvia Mechanical Engineering Works was an unattractive building in the Fourteenth District. It had been built years earlier, when the location was pretty far from the center of town, but as the city pushed its borders outward, the factory became part of the outskirts of Budapest.

According to Péter's sources, wild beat concerts were permitted at the Danuvia because the authorities felt it was a safe distance from downtown, where the real political dangers loomed.

We took trolley number 79 to the Eastern Railway Station, arriving late in the afternoon while the dance lessons were still going on. The man who stood watch at the door of the *kultur* seemed to be doing his best to dress up like the people you'd see in Western magazines. He was trying for Carnaby Street, poor guy, but he couldn't escape the confines of Angol Street—a now-ironic tribute to England and a holdover from pre-communist days. Comrade Doorman wore a colorful silk scarf tied skillfully around his neck. That he got right. But his tight trousers showed the surgical scars of what were once old suit pants, and they looked ridiculous. The big comb sticking out of his rear pocket was obnoxious, but nothing could compare to his long, pointy shoes, later known around Budapest as a "Jimi Hendrix." (These shoes had no relation to the real Jimi Hendrix, who would never have worn such ugly footwear, but someone somewhere thought that giving these things the name of the God of All Guitarists would make them cool, and the name stuck.)

I shouldn't have been so harsh in my evaluation of this man. He just wanted to look different, which in itself was admirable. I'm sure he didn't care about my judgment, though, as he leaned against the door with a Five Year Plan cigarette hanging from his lips.

I recognized that cigarette from the wrapping: gray, with a drawing of a red factory and a smoking chimney, and twenty coffin nails inside. That's what they called those cigarettes, coffin nails. I had heard that the Five Year Plan kind caused blindness, but it didn't seem to bother this man, whose sharp angles had been blurred by pálinka, the Hungarian brandy on sale at the club.

Inside the factory-building-turned-cultural-center was a dimly lit hall where the dance classes took place. As was the case the world over, girls sat on one side and boys on the other. The dance teacher stood in the middle. When a band struck up a Hungarian love song about how János left Marika or how Lujza left Pista, everyone got up to find a dance partner. I spotted Gyuri as he made his way over to a girl in a polyester blouse and modest skirt that grazed her knees. Gyuri himself was wearing the compulsory black suit with a white nylon shirt and black polyester tie. He hated it, but that's all you could get in the stores in those days, and that was the dress code.

"Is this what you dragged me here to see?" I asked Péter.

"Just wait," he responded. We were biding our time in the foyer, which smelled like a urinal. (The smell of toilets seemed to permeate every public place in Budapest in those days.)

Then they announced the last song of the dance lesson, "Young Lovers"—an instrumental made famous by the Shadows, a British band. A good transition to the next stage of the afternoon. The kids stopped dancing, and the teacher collected her stuff and left the room.

Quickly the room was rearranged for the beat concert. Chairs were pulled to the side and stacked up out of the way to give the audience as much space as possible. Jackets were removed and synthetic ties tucked away in pockets. The girls undid at least the top two buttons of their polyester-silk blouses. Gyuri had gone to the men's room, where he messed up his curly hair and combed it back with a little Brylcreem he carried in a tiny jar in his jacket. He and everyone else in the crowd looked different. Better. The doors were opened to the public and scores of young people streamed in. The room rushed to life.

I didn't think I would like the show. I guess in a way I didn't want to like it. But it was loud, as it had to be; scratchy, as it needed to be; and as powerful as everyone wanted it to be. It was rock and roll: revolutionary, young, world-changing rock and roll. I was blown away.

It was unlikely that Liversing had ever seen any of their favorite bands perform live in England or America, but they went out of their way to emulate what they thought a good rock band must be like. They were confident, noisy, theatrical, like they'd never seen the inside of barbed wire. I moved close to the stage to watch the amazing guitarist, a tiny man named Zsolt. He wasn't wearing a suit like his bandmates—just a dark-blue shirt with his sleeves rolled up—and he wasn't playing on one of those terrible Czechoslovak Jolana guitars, either. He had a sparkling blue Swedish Hagström Standard 80. I could only imagine what he'd had to do—what he'd had to pay—to get hold of that.

The stage setup was unusual for a beat concert. The red Party banner was displayed behind the band, and below it a sign bearing the slogan WORKERS OF THE WORLD, UNITE! The red, white, and green flag of Hungary hung on each side of the stage, and to top it all off a huge red star made of glass and lit from the inside hovered above the band. A fireman in full uniform stood guard, next to the Selmer and Vox amplifiers.

When Liversing hit the first powerful notes of the Kinks' "You Really Got Me," that inimitable *Da-dada-da-da, da-dada-da-da* followed by *Giiiiirl,* the crowd erupted. The band went on for two hours without pausing between numbers. They went at it hard, sweating like the energetic young musicians they were, doing everything to please their audience. They gave us what we wanted.

It was around the second or third song that I realized the band was singing mostly in gibberish.

"What is *darkis náj?*"

"That's 'darkest night,' you idiot."

"They have no idea what they are singing," I said. "The language of rock and roll is English, not balderdash."

97

"Then go to England, my friend. This is Hungary—you'd better get used to it."

The show was over by nine o'clock. The hall emptied quickly. The swing shift would be starting in just a few hours. The band cleared the stage while some of the boys looked on with envy. The members of Liversing were the demigods of the day, emissaries from a different world and a different life. Some of the boys volunteered to help, just to touch the instruments and the amplifiers. They talked to the musicians, shook their hands, and patted them on the back. Some asked for autographs before the instruments were schlepped to the gray East German–made Barkas taxi waiting outside.

The Danuvia Mechanical Engineering Works returned to its normal self, but the drab gray building, with its overall shabbiness and stink of urine, had faded into the background of this shining night. Gyuri, Péter, and I passed through the factory gate to see Comrade Doorman still at the door, his arm around a woman he had picked up during the concert. So the evening was a success for him, too. It had been a good crowd, energetic and loud. Best of all, no interference from the police. Comrade Doorman smiled as we walked by, a Five Year Plan hanging from his lips.

CHAPTER FOURTEEN

It had been a tough year, brightened only by Gyuri and Péter, and the letters my parents sent from Denmark. The ministry courier delivered the letters once a month. Open postcards, which came in the regular mail and bore the colorful stamps of Denmark, appeared more often. Once in a while we'd receive packages via the rare visitor from Copenhagen. Gyuri and I would devour those small gifts of magazines, chocolate, licorice—sometimes even a few bananas—as if they were air. We'd eat one piece of chocolate, one licorice drop at a time. Save the banana for a special moment. These once familiar items were now precious; they deserved a ritual.

My parents' letters were written on quality stationery. Seeing my mother's beautiful, almost calligraphic handwriting on the envelope made me feel proud somehow. She used a fountain pen; she never did get used to the Bic pen I bought on our first day in Denmark. The letters—always long and detailed, written with empathy and love—encouraged us to keep up the good work, to be nice to Aunt and Uncle. In every letter there was some confirmation that if we kept our grades up and did not need to repeat any classes, at the end of the term we would spend our last summer together in Copenhagen.

Dear Gyurika and Andriska!

Here in Copenhagen everything is the same, except for your absence. The weather is bad. Father is working hard and spends much time at the office. We will be traveling to Bornholm soon. Zsuzsi spends most of her time with her schoolmate Pia. They are funny and they started wearing strange clothes and are listening to music all day long. She is difficult sometimes, and Father spoils her. More than before, now that she is the only one around. Your cat Kitty is well, too, she had kittens recently in spite of the surgery last year.

Let us know if you need anything. You can write every month and deliver it to the Ministry and they will forward it to us. Be sure both of you to wear your Norwegian sweater I made for you. Father says Mr. Halász might be traveling to Budapest next month and we will send you some magazines your friend Finn keeps buying for you. It would be so good to have you around, you could help me in the garden like you used to.

My children, you know how much Father and I miss you. Your rooms are awaiting you when you come for the school break. I haven't removed anything.

Anyu

Be good, I am buying the Volkswagen soon, with the American extras. I was thinking it should be light blue. I am ordering the Blaupunkt radio with it. I have ordered the furniture. You will like it. Behave with Aunt and Uncle, do as they tell you. Be grateful you can stay with them.

Apu

I was ecstatic when school came to an end in June. I couldn't wait to go home—to Denmark. I wanted to jump right back into the middle of it all as if I had never left. I had had enough of Hungary, of the separation from my parents, of the separation from my guitar, of Uncle. Especially Uncle.

We flew direct from Budapest on Malév Hungarian Airlines, a mere two and a half hours. There was no refueling in East Berlin this time. No soldiers. Nevertheless, the approach to Copenhagen airport was as exciting as it had been during that first flight six years before. When I arrived back at our house at Gjørlingsvej I called my friends, eager to pick up where we had left off.

"András," Henrik Storr Hansen said, "I am so happy to see you! But what happened in Budapest? You sent me a couple of letters in the beginning, but then nothing."

"Ya, Simonyi," Bent Clausen said. "We thought you had been picked up by the secret police."

"Oh, sorry," I responded. "I got busy. You know how it is." The fact is, they didn't know how it was, and I had no desire to tell them. I wanted Budapest to move west. I didn't want to move Copenhagen east. "I'm just glad to be back."

"Why don't you stay?" Henrik asked. "You belong here."

Why indeed? While Gyuri and I were in Hungary, my parents had made up their minds to leave Copenhagen. They had bought all the beautiful Danish designer furniture, a complete designer kitchen, and the olive-green Gustavsberg bathroom from Sweden to be moved to Hungary. Cardboard boxes, wide reels of Scotch tape, and large balls of twine were all stored in the garage. Some boxes were already closed, marked with the Budapest address, marked with an umbrella icon to signal how they should be stored in transit.

If I had been old enough to know how to argue, to make the case for not returning to Budapest—why none of us should—I would have said that we belonged in Denmark. Father could be a terrific businessman, a real textile merchant. He would be the best in Copenhagen. Mother could have started a little shop where she would have a few seamstresses employed and make luxurious clothes for the rich women in the neighborhood. I had the little shop across the street from the baker in mind. This was what I had been thinking. But I was now fifteen years old, and I couldn't even talk my teacher out of giving me a bad grade.

There were moments when I sensed that Father wasn't sure of his decision. It was around this time that he first told me something he would repeat many times in the future: *These have been the best years of my life.*

"This is a plush life I have had now for six years. The best six years ever. Maybe this will be as good as it gets. I survived the war, I came back alive from the POW camp, and I had to rebuild my life from scratch. That was twenty years ago. Yes, we have been here for a long time. But staying here permanently…it's not the same as a temporary posting. Not at all. I am fifty now. I don't have the strength or the time to start all over again. I like this country, probably one of the best countries in the world. I wake up every morning thankful to have been given these years. You and Gyuri and Zsuzsi got a head start like no one else."

I listened, having no idea when my father's speech would end.

"You know, I feel really at home here," he continued. "But then things are changing in Budapest." I just shook my head. "Andris, you are old enough to understand that it's not easy to say goodbye to your country forever. I got a job offer. It's a good job. We have a nice apartment, and now it will be even nicer. I promise. You will see."

I promise. You will see.

But I did not see. All I could think about was how Denmark had taught me to appreciate freedom. What a loaded word that was. When the Party in Budapest spoke of freedom, it had no idea what it was talking about. "Freedom for the suppressed peoples of the world" was one of their political slogans. But what was this freedom? When my Danish friends ranted about the prime minister and called him an idiot without consequence, that was freedom. When thousands of us protested against nuclear weapons in front of the Danish Parliament without police interference, that was freedom. When I walked into the bookstore and asked for a copy of *Dr. Zhivago*, which was banned behind the Iron Curtain, that was freedom.

I wasn't ready to give it up.

"I don't want to go back! I don't like the school. I only have one friend there. My teachers here in Denmark want me back," I said, my head bowed. Then I lifted my eyes and looked first at Mother, then Father, and asked, "Can't we stay?"

Mother took over and cut the conversation short: "No we can't. We made all those sacrifices for you and Gyuri to get into one of the best high schools in Budapest. You have done a year. Gyuri now has done two. We are not going to waste that. Your father and I have made up our minds. I know it's tough to leave friends behind, but you'll find new ones. We are Hungarians and that's final."

There was no court of appeals. No higher authority. The verdict had been reached.

CHAPTER FIFTEEN

S ome years matter more than others. That was definitely true of 1967, the year that rock and roll changed in big bold leaps—and my last summer in Denmark. Everything was different now. Rock and roll was in turmoil. Even the concept of a song had changed. Some were still melodic and beautiful, but many of the new tracks were rough, even raw. The guitars didn't necessarily focus on producing a clean, distinct sound. Sometimes the notes came out dirty and distorted. Sometimes we didn't know what the sound was exactly, only that it was fresh and new. There were more improvisations and fewer pretty solos, and sometimes the rhythm would shift in the middle, making the whole track altogether more powerful. This was the year of Jimi Hendrix's "Purple Haze," Cream's "I Feel Free," and "See Emily Play" by Syd Barrett and Pink Floyd.

The lyrics, too, were different. Songwriters were moving away from sweet refrains about falling in love or hearts being broken. Now the lyrics were being taken over by real-world events. And they weren't always pleasant, like the Buffalo Springfield song "For What It's Worth" that spoke of battle lines and paranoia. This new music was about breaking with the past. The revolution that started with "She Loves You" had kicked into high gear, and the showdown with the establishment had become a full-fledged rebellion. Rock and roll was our weapon. We wouldn't be ignored.

As a sign of things to come, a new Beatles album, *Revolver*, had been released in the West over Christmas. A precursor to the truly revolutionary *Sgt. Pepper*, *Revolver* reached us in Budapest as soon as it was out in England. The music was mesmerizing. The first record I had to hear over and over again before the message behind the lyrics became clear, *Revolver* confirmed what I had long suspected: everyone might have listened to the same music, but we all heard something different. *Revolver* proved to me that rock and roll was an individual experience. That's why I didn't like the way it was dissected on Radio Free Europe and Radio Luxembourg by DJs who imposed their interpretations on us. I wanted to explore it myself.

These experimental new sounds were a departure from happy-go-lucky tunes like "She Loves You." Even those of us who noticed that the Beatles had evolved, that over the last four years their music had acquired a harder edge, were surprised by the raw sadness of "Eleanor Rigby." It was like nothing we had heard from the Beatles. "Taxman," too, was about a real-life conflict with authority, and "She Said She Said" featured a powerful guitar wailing through the whole song. Then there was the influence of Indian music.

Ravi Shankar and his sitar—an instrument we had never heard of before—were the inspiration behind *Revolver*. The guitar's South Asian cousin, the sitar was used in traditional Hindustani music and produced a much subtler sound. How surprising it was, then, to hear how well the instrument's natural dissonance fit in with rock's distortions.

We got to hear it for ourselves when Ravi Shankar appeared with his ensemble at the Academy of Music. Gyuri and I were thrilled to hear this musician who had come straight from India, a man who knew and was admired by John, Paul, George, and Ringo. Someone who was their friend, who had taught them how to play the sitar, the very instrument on *Revolver*. How crazy was that?

The concert was amazing. The audience seemed to appreciate this strange but beautiful music and gave Ravi a standing ovation. But Hungarians are polite concertgoers and they love to clap, so I'm not sure people liked it as much as they pretended to. Gyuri and I were captivated, though. We had a few of Ravi's records at home so it wasn't totally new to us. Even so, tonight we had come not just to listen to Indian music or to see the man who had inspired the Beatles' "Norwegian Wood" and "Love You To." We had come to meet him.

Ravi was a lot smaller than we had imagined. A diminutive man in his mid-forties, he wore the traditional long white dhoti paired with white trousers and sandals. He was friendly, patiently answering questions about where in India he was actually from, where he lived now, how long he was staying, and his understanding of Hungarian folk music. Small talk, really. When it was finally our turn, I asked him about the Beatles.

"How did you know I play with the Beatles?" he asked us, honestly surprised. "How is that possible?"

"Everybody knows the Beatles! Ravi, please, can you tell us about George Harrison?"

"George is a good student. He came to India to learn the sitar and to learn about Indian culture. But you know, what you heard tonight is really *my* music."

I handed him a picture of George Harrison and Ravi somewhere in India, sitting with their sitars. "Ravi, would you sign this for me, please?"

He asked me my name and wrote, TO ANDRÁS, RAVI.

As he handed me back the picture, I shook his hand and had a strange feeling that I was, in that moment, only one degree of separation from the single most important band in the world. I kept that picture for many years, safely tucked away in a metal box where Gyuri and I stored all our memorabilia: a collection of Beatles bubble-gum cards; one of Tich's cigarette butts, which I had picked up outside the Carousel; the autographed Ravi Shankar picture. It was as close as I would ever get to the Beatles.

That summer we could barely keep up with all the new bands coming out of Britain: The Spencer Davis Group broke up and Steve Winwood formed Traffic. Donovan went electric. The Kinks made a beautiful record called "Waterloo Sunset," catching the mood of the day with its melancholic sound. Then Cream came out with "I Feel Free," which blasted from the radio day in and day out.

My friends and I all wanted to dress like the men and women of Carnaby Street and San Francisco—and we did. We bought the most extreme and colorful outfits we could find, at times surprising even the good citizens of Copenhagen. I bought a black shirt with myriad tiny roses printed on it. Gyuri had one with pink, yellow, and blue stripes. We both got corduroy pants, tremendously cool in those days. Mine were burgundy. Gyuri's were green. We adorned our cords with wide leather belts and wore colorful shoes made of cloth. We also bought a roll of canvas in the colors of the Union Jack and got Mother to sew pants for us, perfectly tailored and incredibly loud. We turned heads everywhere we went.

There was so little pretension then. Everything felt honest and pure. There was room for everyone and everything. It was like the floodgates had opened and the old structures were being washed away to make way for the new. It was as if we were in the middle of a revolution—a nonviolent revolution. We knew that the older generation didn't really understand the music, the long hair, the clothes we wore, the way we spoke, the slang we used. But one thing was clear: we wanted something entirely new, even if we didn't exactly know what. We would find it through music.

Until that great summer of love in 1967, we didn't really follow what was happening in America and we barely knew the bands making waves on the far side of the Atlantic. Even my American friends preferred to listen to their English records. But one by one the Americans were gaining ground: Jefferson Airplane, the Velvet Underground, Janis Joplin, Scott McKenzie, the Mothers of Invention, and of course the Doors. Those, on top of the few we already knew of in Budapest—Sonny & Cher, Elvis, the Four Tops, the Beach Boys—made for a full-blown American invasion. We heard that San Francisco had turned on its head, that music had changed the way people lived there; that hippies were now running parts of America. This was the revolution, and it was unstoppable. It was like rock-and-roll music now stood on two feet instead of one.

And then the Jimi Hendrix Experience arrived: "Purple Haze," "Foxy Lady," "Third Stone from the Sun." Jimi was something else from the start. He was more than just a guitarist. He had other guitarists scratching their heads trying to figure out what he was doing and how he was doing it. His music and guitar playing were fresh and new. He played notes the way no one had ever played them before. The pulling and pushing, the bending of the strings, was aggressive and beautiful. He played unfamiliar chords and used the entire scale, switching from low to high and back. It was like he was playing multiple guitars at once. His showmanship—the stories we read about Jimi's shows, like when he set his Fender Stratocaster on fire onstage, fascinated us. We loved him.

But the big sensation that summer was undoubtedly the new Beatles album *Sgt. Pepper's Lonely Hearts Club Band.* Whether you were in Budapest, Copenhagen, London, or New York, you were waiting for the moment when you would hear it for the first time. The combination of electric guitars, electronics, and a classical orchestra with string instruments and brass was yet more proof that the Beatles were the kings of the rock-and-roll kingdom.

When I first heard the album, I couldn't get the magical "Lucy in the Sky with Diamonds" out of my head. After hearing the song just once, I was convinced the DJ was right. This was a song about LSD. How else could I imagine skies made out of marmalade? But all the songs were memorable, even the cheerful "With a Little Help from My Friends" or "When I'm Sixty-Four."

The Beatles had traveled an incredible musical journey, from *Hard Day's Night* through *Help!*, *Rubber Soul*, and *Revolver*. Now this. *Sgt. Pepper's Lonely Hearts Club Band* caused a sensation. This was a new sound. A new kind of storytelling. Once again, the Beatles didn't disappoint. I thought about this a lot in the following months. Was this record really that great, or was it that I wanted it to be great, that I wanted the moment of the Beatles to last? The Beatles had dominated my life for four years now and I wasn't ready to give it up. I wanted them to keep giving. We all did.

Copenhagen Radio, Radio Luxembourg, and the new Radio Veronica broadcasting from the English Channel would all play the record again and again. Each song was revolutionary in its own way, each a masterpiece. The Beatles had done it again. They'd made history.

After that summer, nothing was the same.

CHAPTER SIXTEEN

If you were lucky enough to own an electric guitar, you belonged to a privileged class. It might have been the electricity, which was a wonder in itself. More likely it was about the volume and power. We knew all the brands: Framus, Höfner, Burns, Gretsch, Rickenbacker, Gibson, Vox. But there was one that stood out from all the others: the Fender Stratocaster.

Jimi Hendrix would go down in history as the man who reinvented the electric guitar. But that wouldn't have been possible without his American Stratocaster. He wouldn't have looked the same. He wouldn't have sounded the same. He wouldn't have *been* the same.

The Stratocaster is a beautiful instrument. The frets are precise and the neck nicely finished. A double-cutaway guitar with an extended top horn, its machine head is shiny chrome, the volume knob like ebony, the whammy bar solidly anchored. It may still be the sexiest guitar ever made. When someone in Budapest finally had the great luck and honor to buy one, paying the price of a car for it, getting it through the maze of the customs office, and at long last bringing it onstage to show it off—he was like royalty.

Then there was the Czechoslovak Jolana. For years I'd been unfair to those who couldn't afford anything better than this lousy guitar. In my youthful entitlement, I'd laugh at them. Ridicule them simply because they didn't have the luck to own a Golden Framus like I did. Built in a former furniture factory, the Jolana was a terrible instrument, ugly and poorly made. *Jolana* was a curse word in our circles, and for good reason: The body would crack and the neck would twist. The pickups sounded bland and would fall to pieces. The volume knob would fall off. The tuning machines wouldn't hold the strings properly, and the East German strings—the only ones they had—would get out of tune and break constantly. The bridge and the nut wouldn't stay in place. The frets hurt your fingers. It was a miracle anyone could play that instrument at all.

And yet thousands of young Hungarians built entire bands around that instrument. It was the love of music and rock that made these young people embarrass themselves and walk onstage with a Jolana. Hundreds of guitarists learned their first Beatles or Rolling Stones song on a Jolana. They all sounded terrible. Nevertheless, thank God the Jolana existed at all—it paved the way for rock and roll.

CHAPTER SEVENTEEN

The family returned to Budapest for good that August. I came armed with *Sgt. Pepper*, the *Are You Experienced* album, *Buffalo Springfield Again, Younger than Yesterday* from the Byrds, *Something Else* from the Kinks, and hundreds of feet of tapes. Our appetite for rock and roll was insatiable. It scared me that after a wonderful and strange summer, I would be stuck behind the Iron Curtain again.

I was really lucky. Aunt Ágnes, Péter's mother, was a famous choreographer who knew a lot of creative people—dancers, writers, actors, actresses, and musicians—so their home was filled with a who's who of the Hungarian artistic word. Péter's family also had excellent artistic contacts in the West, primarily in West Germany and France. That was one of the things that helped forge our friendship—his familiarity with the West.

Péter and I were a team from the start. We knew that if we could get our equipment together, we could start a band. My little Dynacord amp was great for this purpose, but not powerful enough to serve multiple instruments and a microphone all at once, so we went hunting for a new one. The problem was, everybody else was looking for one, too.

"Demand is higher than supply," Péter said one day during rehearsal. "Our only hope is the black market. Even those crappy East German Regent amplifiers are difficult to come by."

Fortunately for us, Aunt Ágnes worked with many of the local beat musicians, so she was able to put us in touch with someone who might be able to help us. That's what led us to meet the members of Scampolo. We had heard about these musicians before, as the state-run youth club on Vigyázó Ferenc Street was actually referred to as the Scampolo Club, because the band played there regularly. At the heart of the band were an Elvis look-alike named Laci Komár—who had a great voice and great moves to match—and rock pioneer and guitarist István "Judy" Faragó. They hailed not from the fancy neighborhoods of Budapest, but from the deep countryside. Unlikely rockers, these guys were working-class heroes and living proof that nobody owned rock and roll—it belonged to everybody.

The Scampolo Club was a better venue than the Danuvia, which we had visited quite a few times. For one thing, the Scampolo was a real club, built before the war, when Budapest had been a worldly city, full of cabarets and nightclubs, populated by a healthy middle class. Of course, this was long ago; the once grand cabaret was now just an echo of the past. By the time Péter and I went there, it would likely have belonged to some state institution, in this case a real factory that provided cultural activities to its workers. Something utilitarian and drab. But there were still shows. *A lot* of shows.

Our first night at the Scampolo, Péter and I were surprised to see a huge crowd gathered outside. Until that moment, we didn't realize how lucky we were to have been given special passes. The people at The Scampolo Club were different from those who frequented the Danuvia. For one thing, the audience was full of *jampec*—teddy boys who showed off their Western clothes and accessories, a message that said: we are part of the *nyugat*—the West. I liked that.

The lights were already dimmed when we entered the club; the band was in the middle of a set. The keyboardist—Gábor "Gabi" Presser—was hammering away at his Italian-made red Capri Combo organ, a grin on his face. Judy, the guitarist, was impressive despite his size. Like Zsolt from Liversing, he was small, but he played well, with a degree of confidence that belied his height. Judy had a nice West German Höfner guitar, which looked like a Fender, lending him a high status as a guitarist. Komár, like the singer in Liversing, was singing gibberish, but it didn't matter. I liked the way he played his air guitar and moved in unison with Judy as he sang Presley. The band was perfect, his movements were perfect, just like the real Elvis. They surprised us with their set list: "Gimme Some Lovin'" by the Spencer Davis Group, "Black Magic Woman," the Fleetwood Mac version, and the like. The crowd was ecstatic—moving to the music and screaming.

After the concert, we shook hands with Judy and complimented him on his improvisations in the middle of their numbers.

"You know," he said, "a few years ago improvisation was prohibited."

"Really?"

"Yes, but we did it anyway. There were special inspectors who would come around to the clubs. If there was any deviation they would stop the music, report the musicians to the police, and take away their license. There was one night when we were right in the middle of improvising with a sax player when these men showed up and stopped the show. They said we'd get in trouble for playing American jazz music."

"What did you do?"

"We told them they were the ones who were in trouble."

"*That's* what you told them?"

"Yes. We told them that they had just stopped us in the middle of playing a Russian folk song and that our Soviet comrades would be upset if they found out."

"Did they let you go?"

"Sure, and then they were the ones who were scared. Lucky for us, they were clueless about the music we were playing, our version of Gershwin's 'Summertime.' Gershwin was certainly not Russian."

We walked backstage to meet with Gabi to see if he really had the amp we were looking for. Péter introduced us both.

"We came to see the amp."

"Have a look. It's ten watts. It's been adjusted for the new plugs. Of course you will need loudspeakers."

It was a big, battered tube amplifier made by Siemens before or during the war and probably used at train stations for public announcements. We tried it out—it wasn't great—then took off the back panel to see the inner workings. That's when I noticed the emblem of the Third Reich: an eagle with a swastika in its claws. Something Gábor likely hadn't noticed; otherwise he would never have touched the amplifier, being Jewish. It wasn't just that the amp was ugly and that it didn't sound right. No way could we buy an amp with a swastika. We left empty-handed.

Perhaps buying the amp wasn't really important after all. It was far more important that we got a chance to meet Gabi. I was honored when he invited me to visit him at his home, a two-room apartment on Dob Street in the old Jewish quarter, close to the local marketplace. I'm not sure what I expected, but his small apartment was orderly—too orderly, I thought, for such a great musician. Instruments and sheet music were stacked on top of one another in the room reserved for him by his elderly parents, with a huge Bösendorfer concert piano taking up most of the space. Gabi's parents were both Holocaust survivors and it was his love for them—and maybe loyalty to his fans—that caused him to remain in Hungary, unlike so many of his fellow musicians. He showed me the basement, an old air raid shelter with heavy metal doors, which still had gas masks scattered around. The heavy shelter doors were useful when Gabi rehearsed there, because no sound could escape through them. He kept his organ and amp there.

In this tumult of ideology everywhere, it was good to share ideas with someone who talked about things like studying music, the difference between opera and rock, and how he loved playing classical as much as he loved being onstage with a rock band. Gabi treated me like his little brother and shared thoughts with me that I wasn't used to—the thoughts of an adult. He discussed everything with me.

Gabi soon joined Omega, a famous Hungarian band who needed a keyboardist and a songwriter. I saw them play at the Budapest House of Culture in front of an orderly audience, nicely seated, and well dressed. This well-behaved crowd didn't match the exuberance of the music—songs from *Sgt. Pepper*, "Purple Haze," and of course some of Gabi's own music. Following in his footsteps, I too became a member of the Omega family.

Gabi's engagement with Omega resulted in massive success. He was soon aware of the immense power he had, being able to move large crowds with his music. But the more famous and popular he became, the more he realized he wasn't free to write or perform whatever he wanted to. "Comrade from the ministry told me that he could revoke my license anytime, so I needed to be careful. But then he went on to ask for two membership cards to the Omega Club for his nephews. That is how they are."

Like Scampolo, Omega had their own club. Other bands did as well. "This is the crazy world of Hungary," Gabi would say. "Where beat music is allowed, but not just any beat music. Where there are clubs that are not real clubs, where the authorities want you to think they are omnipresent, even though we all know they can't be everywhere."

It was a country, he said, where Comrade Horváth from the ministry surely would have banned rock music if he was told to do so by the Party. But they didn't *have* to, and so *they* didn't. After all, their own sons and daughters, nephews and nieces loved the music.

CHAPTER EIGHTEEN

I wasn't thrilled to return to Hungary, but living with my parents was everything. I was doing my best to play the part of the cool teenager, but in those first days back in Budapest nothing meant more to me than my mother and father's good-night kisses. As much as I missed Denmark and all its freedoms, I knew the value of all I had: two strong parents who loved me, who would provide all that I needed to explore the territory between child and adult.

Gyuri and I remained close. If anything, our time together in Budapest had brought us even closer. Alas, my relationship with my sister suffered during our time apart. As kids, Zsuzsi and I didn't have a lot in common. In fact, we seemed to have been in a continuous battle for our parents' attention. This only intensified during the strange year when Gyuri and I were in Budapest. In that period of separation, an invisible wall of indifference had formed between us. Regrettable, but that's just how it was. Father, meanwhile, became a senior executive in a textile foreign trading company. Mother went back to the State Insurance Company, where she had worked since the mid-1950s. We moved back into our beautiful three-bedroom apartment on the fourth floor of a Bauhaus-style building, built just before the war. It boasted a spacious layout with a large living room, dining room, and three bedrooms. The apartment was grand by Budapest standards, maybe any standard. Some people speculated that the Party had a hand in the acquisition, but that was ridiculous. It was my mother who had found the apartment on her rounds selling insurance policies two years before we left for Denmark.

The tenants at Fürst Sándor Street 33 were about to file for divorce, and that compelled them to sell the apartment for a ridiculously low price. My mother, the financial genius, got a loan from the People's Savings Bank, threw in our savings (she had always known how to make two forints out of one), and bought the place. One piece of real estate was allowed per family, and this was going to be ours and ours alone. Thank goodness we were spared the subtenants many of my friends were subjected to, the strangers who would move in with a family out of either financial necessity or Party edict. We were all so grateful that our family home was just that—*our* home.

Our apartment became Little Denmark in the middle of Budapest. Father, knowing the quality of goods available in Hungary, had planned every last detail. The impeccably designed living room furniture, the rosewood dining table with leather chairs, the beds, the nice lamps all had a stamp saying MADE IN DENMARK. Everything—the Bang & Olufsen radio, the Philips turntable, the Grundig tape recorder, the Blaupunkt TV set—projected quality. My parents had saved conscientiously for six years to make this cozy home for us all, to ensure that our return would be as comfortable as it could be.

Father and Mother created an island, a pocket of the West in the East. So long as I was at home, I could do whatever I wanted. To me, the border of the Iron Curtain began at our threshold. Within the confines of our home, I was allowed to read books that I could have been arrested for owning on the outside: Solzhenitsyn's *Cancer Ward*; Koestler's *Darkness at Noon*; Orwell's *1984*; Leon Uris's *Mila 18*. I consumed a lot of books in those days, Salinger's *Catcher in the Rye*, Buzzati's *The Tartar Steppe*, Moravia's *Two Women*, and a lot of Hungarian writers who were published before the war. But none of them made such an impression as those banned books.

At home I was allowed to listen to Radio Free Europe, Voice of America, and Radio Luxembourg as much as I wanted. I could ask any question of Father and he would answer honestly—no lies. I grilled him about the political situation across Europe. I asked his perspective on the Russians and the Arab-Israeli conflict. Perhaps most important, I asked him about women. I trusted my father. I trusted my family. But when I walked out that door, everything was different. I became alert and watchful, fearful and suspicious. By the time I climbed down the four floors and passed through the gates of the house, I was an entirely different person.

In the outside world I got used to watching my back. I was always alert, always worried that someone was listening in on my conversations. That man on the other side of the street was only pretending to read that newspaper. That fellow in the car parked outside our house was most likely watching who was entering and leaving the building. We were all slightly paranoid, but not without reason: This was a police state, after all. Even the social events organized by the Communist Youth League were supervised and reported on. Which was why my friends and I, like so many others, organized parties in our own homes.

The *házibuli*, as house parties were called in Hungarian, were private affairs. Mostly they were friends-only events designed to keep out the police informants who had a mandate to seek out enemies of the state. We had just passed the tenth anniversary of the 1956 revolution and the authorities were growing nervous—for good reason. The previous insurrection had started small. What began with a conversation here, a message there, had grown into a full-blown war for independence. Now, some ten years later, the Party understood that the majority of Hungarians had not given up hope that one day their country would be rid of the Russians and of communism itself. Of course they were wary of private gatherings.

Those of us who hosted house parties were vigilant, but that didn't mean the snitches didn't get in. They showed up out of the blue, introducing themselves as a friend of a friend of a friend. Who could send them away when they had established such credentials? Sometimes it was just naivete on our side, sometimes it was their cleverness. The authorities wanted to know what was going on behind closed doors, but there had been a softening of the hard rules and the Party was supposed to leave us alone in our homes, so they weren't sure how to deal with the phenomenon of the *házibuli*.

Sometimes the authorities reverted to their old ways. I

once attended a house party given by my friend Ferenc when the music was interrupted by the incessant ringing of the doorbell. It was the police—two in uniform and the other in plainclothes—who had come under the pretext of a noise complaint. Whether true or false, we had no way of knowing, but it did give them the right to intervene.

The uniformed officers looked blasé as they asked us to identify ourselves, one by one. Not the plainclothes officer, though. He was tough and wanted us to be afraid. The way he poked Ferenc in the chest, the way he questioned some of the older boys, he was determined to provoke. It was the plainclothes officer who called the shots, who walked boldly around the apartment examining books, picking food up from the table without asking.

"Just looking at all these fascinating books," he said perusing the shelves. But he wasn't interested in literature. He was looking for forbidden publications. And he found none. After the police had taken down everyone's name they looked into all the rooms, and even inside a large oak chest to see if someone might be hiding there. They took Ferenc in for questioning—an obvious warning. If the house party was the nucleus of a political opposition movement, it had to be shut down. Some *házibuli* would eventually turn into pockets of resistance. But for us, then—we just wanted to have fun.

Our house parties were mostly spontaneous events that needed little more than a tape recorder and a safe place to assemble without fear of neighbors or the police. "Roll up the rugs, push the armchair to the side," someone would shout through the music. That was the signal that it was time to dance, but only after we had consumed the usual party snack of heavily seasoned pork fat on a fresh slice of bread. And beer. And terrible cheap wine. Lots of it.

When Coca-Cola was introduced—we called it Cola—the American beverage became a staple at house parties. There were rumors that Coca-Cola contained a drug—the famed cocaine that we had heard about—and at first some of my friends were so sure that Coke contained the addictive stimulant that they swore they got high just from drinking it. Cola was a luxury item and a status symbol, a little piece of America previously available only beyond Vienna. Most Hungarians had never had a sip of the bubbly drink (and in this, again, I was one of the lucky few), so we were truly surprised when it hit the supermarkets in Budapest. According to the propaganda of just a few years before, this particular brand of soda pop was the ultimate symbol of the horrors of American capitalism. Produced by the mighty imperialist company called simply The Coca-Cola Company, the beverage was consumed by every American teenager and appeared in every American movie.

When Coke first arrived in Budapest, I rushed to the supermarket on Lenin Boulevard, where I spent all my savings on twelve stubby glass bottles of *the real thing*. I carried the Coke home with pride and stashed it under my bed, sharing it occasionally with Gyuri. I was certain it would soon be off the shelves again. But as I would shortly find out, Coca-Cola was now bottled here! Apparently one of the state-owned liquor companies had negotiated a deal to produce Coke, the first in the Eastern Bloc. Clearly we were moving to the West, one small step at a time. In the fight between the Party purists who looked to Moscow and those who saw our future more closely aligned with the West, the latter had scored—and scored big. There was no stronger indication that the winds of change were blowing through Hungary. Coca-Cola was here to stay.

Like many others in Budapest, we had a small wooden summerhouse, way outside the city. Sometimes my parents went for the weekend, leaving the apartment in our care. They gave us permission to invite friends over, which we interpreted broadly. We had tapes. We had music. We had house parties. Mostly it was our friends from school who came, but sometimes our neighbors Gábor and Juli Antall would stop by. I liked Juli and considered her a friend, but I was unsure of Gábor, whom we addressed formally as Mr. Antall. The Antalls were an odd couple. He was a large, serious man, a lot older than his wife, who was friendly and cheerful.

Mr. Antall had a high position in the government. It was widely known that he worked closely with the minister of culture, but I was in the dark about what he actually did. I suspected that he might have been the person who sent out the orders about the "intolerable, anti-socialist behavior of some youth groupings, which call themselves beat orchestras." He might even have had a hand in coming up with the dreaded S-T-B rule. *S* for "support." *T* for "tolerate." *B* for "ban." God forbid that you were a painter, writer, artist, or musician who landed in the B category. Your career and any chance at a public appearance were over. But these categories turned out to be arbitrary, with no clear definitions and no written regulations, which meant that sometimes the rules would abruptly change overnight. You and your guitar might be taken away for playing a particular song one day—but play the same song a day later and authorities might not say a word. As my musician friends would tell me: "You never knew what would happen after playing a new song for the first time."

S-T-B rules covered every genre. Rock music was in a gray zone from the start, and hovered somewhere between *tolerate* and *ban*. Rarely was it outright *supported*. Even before these categories were established, the authorities had issued stern warnings about the dangers of rock music, like this one addressed to the editors in chief of all written media, strictly under the supervision of the Party. Aunt Ágnes showed it to us—she had received it from a friend:

> Hardly a day goes by that a paper does not mention—with or without photographs—this latest American craze, this hula-hoop. Unintentionally, and perhaps guided by goodwill, they are making propaganda for this fad. That is exactly what they did with this other insanity, rock and roll. And still this latter is now all over us. The best way for us to combat this craziness and the likes: silence to death, don't talk about it.

It didn't work.

Not that the minister cared so much about the music himself. Unless the issues were really political, he left our depravities to small-time bureaucrats like Mr. Antall. Our neighbor's presence at our house parties showed that he didn't share his minister's views on rock-and-roll music. I suspected it was Juli's influence. She knew how close I was to those "youth orchestras." She couldn't avoid hearing me practice my guitar and play my records. Neither of them could. Lucky for me, they didn't seem to mind.

As far as I knew, Mr. Antall interpreted his orders loosely and never got anyone into trouble. To the contrary. "You know how much I like what your friends are doing as musicians?" Mr. Antall told me one evening. "Their closeness to the roots of Hungarian folk music is really impressive, but they should refrain from this doublespeak in their lyrics, talking about longing for London and things like that. That is not helpful. How can we hold back real radical thoughts or antisocialist behavior if we allow popular bands like them to behave this way?"

I didn't agree, but there was no point in arguing, especially when the explanations he gave were often in stark contrast with the expressions on his face. He looked like he wanted to say what my father jokingly told me about official policy: "On that issue, my view does not coincide with my position."

CHAPTER NINETEEN

Like every other kid in Budapest, I wanted as many of the great rock-and-roll records as I could get my hands on. Singles were great, but LP's—now, *they* were a big deal. The Doors, Traffic, the Band, the Grateful Dead, the Rolling Stones, and anyone else we had heard over Radio Luxembourg. Either Father would get us the record from abroad or we would buy it ourselves on the black market.

The black market was well organized. I'd place my order with this guy I called Scotty, a well-dressed high school dropout who smoked expensive American cigarettes and knew who to contact. I never knew Scotty's real name, but he could be relied upon to contact Hungarians who traveled outside the country or foreigners who were planning to visit Budapest. Scotty placed the orders and set the prices. He made a small fortune.

Despite our many privileges, money was always a problem. Gyuri and I pooled our resources to scrape together enough to pay for whatever record was on the top of our wish list. As a last resort we'd sell something, like a pair of old loudspeakers we once shifted for about eight hundred forints—maybe forty dollars at the time. We used that money to buy the Doors' *Waiting for the Sun* record, which set us back five hundred forints. Another time we sold a few magazines—a hundred forints apiece, two hundred for the nude magazines!—and bought the *Hair* album for six hundred. Records were pricey, considering that a tram ride was 1.00 forint and a loaf of bread, 3.60.

We didn't begrudge the high prices. Each album was worth it—every note, every groove, every admiring look it would bring. It wasn't just about the music. A record was a status symbol, plain and simple. The newer, the more colorful, the more exclusive, the better. When I got a new album, I would walk around town with it tucked under my arm for everyone to see. I thought I was being cool and casual, the way I always made sure the cover faced away from me. I didn't realize how obvious I was.

It was great to get a new Beatles album, but the impact wouldn't last long because the high demand meant that the black marketeers and smugglers would focus on that record. But if I managed to get the newest Jimi Hendrix album—*Electric Ladyland,* for example—now, that was something. When I first heard "Jumpin' Jack Flash" on Radio Luxembourg, I knew that I had to get the EP. I knew it in the way a fifteen-year-old boy knows anything: with driving passion and absolute certainty. Wouldn't it be nice, I thought, if I could walk into a store and put my money down on the counter and buy it just like that? Surely that's what kids in America did. And not just America, but England and France, Denmark and Japan. Just about everywhere in the world except for Hungary and the other great nations trapped behind the Iron Curtain.

I decided to give it a try.

I walked into the state record store on Lenin Boulevard, next to the Western Train Station. The store was modern and austere. The floor was covered in black and yellow tiles, with some kind of design in the middle of the room. I couldn't figure out if it was artistry or a mistake.

"What are you looking for?" came the clerk's unfriendly hello.

"Would you happen to have 'Jumpin' Jack Flash' by the Rolling Stones?" I asked. "You know, their new record? You might have heard it on *Sunday Cocktail* on the radio."

The clerk was a bespectacled young man in his late twenties, tall and thin with slightly long, greasy hair.

"No, sorry, I don't. It's a great record, though."

I didn't really expect him to have it, but I was kind of surprised that he knew what I was talking about.

"That's too bad," I said. "All the kids are listening to the Rolling Stones. It's a shame you don't stock their records."

"Yes, yes, it's a shame, but what can I do? You think I don't want to sell stuff like the Rolling Stones or the Kinks or John Mayall?"

"Well, why don't you?" I knew I was pushing.

"I sell what they get me to sell. It's that simple." We went back and forth on the subject for a few minutes. The conversation was all very mechanical, but then he surprised me. "Why can't we buy a decent record player? Why can't we buy a nice pair of leather shoes? Why is my dad driving a Trabant and not a Mercedes?"

Our conversation was futile and we both knew it. The state store was full to bursting with records—classical and homegrown pop, Vivaldi's *Four Seasons*, Beethoven's Fifth—but no Rolling Stones. Officially, the blame was placed on economics and those bastard musicians and record companies who asked too much for the copyright. The state planners weren't going to waste hard currency—meaning dollars, pounds, or deutsche marks—just to satisfy a few long-haired bums. Why should the state spend even one forint on those culturally alien records? The fact that there was a huge demand for this degenerate music made no difference. Not even when fools like me made some complaint at the stores.

Fifteen years earlier, say in 1952, the year I was born, a customer would probably have gotten a pretty heavy prison sentence for speaking as I had. The charge would have been that I was a foreign agent, an agent provocateur for the West. But times had changed and the system was softening. This clerk was used to angry customers and it didn't seem to bother him. In fact, after our exchange I was so comfortable with him that I asked if he wanted to hear a joke, slightly politically loaded, just to bring home the absurdity of my quest.

"It'd better be really good, my friend," the clerk said. "I got customers waiting."

"Okay. Parrot walks into a state grocery store where the shelves are stacked with cabbage, paprika, and onions. He asks for a banana.

" 'We don't sell bananas,' the employee says.

"The next day Parrot goes back to the store and asks the same question again. The employee is clearly upset.

" 'Parrot, I told you we don't sell bananas. If you come back asking the same question again'—the employee points to the cross on the wall with a Jesus—'I will nail you on the wall, just like him.'

"The next day Parrot does it again.

"The employee loses his temper. 'I told you not to ask for bananas.' He nails Parrot to the wall, wings stretched, next to the crucifix.

"Parrot is surprised and turns his head toward the cross, and asks Jesus: 'Did you ask for bananas, too?'"

The clerk laughed long and loud. In fact, he laughed so hard he had to take off his glasses to wipe the tears from his eyes. "That's a really good one!" In return for my great joke, the clerk gave me a tip. I should go to this private store he knew on Rákóczi Avenue that sold records from the Rolling Stones and other bands. I had heard about this store before, but never wandered far enough to visit it.

Our family had always had a record player. The old one Father bought in 1959 had a white plastic arm with a brown felt plate, all built into a nice cherrywood cabinet. I had no idea what make it was, but it was frequently the center of family evenings. I liked the way Father made a ritual about listening to his records. I remember the black, white, and blue cover of George Gershwin's *Porgy and Bess* with the Decca label. Father was very fond of Gershwin—he also had *Rhapsody in Blue*, though *Porgy and Bess* was his favorite. A present from England, the album contained a note explaining that this particular record could be played five hundred times. Father wanted to put it to the test, and so we played *Porgy and Bess* over and over again. The whole family knew the songs by heart.

Later, when we acquired a tape recorder, Father taped hundreds of records, a blend of all kinds of music: classical to jazz, folk music to church music. He didn't really understand the beat music Gyuri and I listened to, but he never said anything against it, either. In fact, Father gave us his empty reels to record whatever we liked. We weren't alone in having a tape recorder—by now almost every boy did. So we shared. Somebody, somewhere would make a decent copy of a record, and then others would come around and copy from that tape, again and again, until it was worn thin. I even joined a tape recording club at the House of Culture in Buda, the same place where Omega had once played. The members were treated to pop records otherwise not available, curiously provided by the state. But it was the state that made the selections, a not-too-ingenious way of control. And there was another catch. Everyone who went to the recording club was subjected to an ideological lecture.

One such talk was given by a singer-songwriter in his late thirties with hair like Roy Orbison's, but who was considerably less talented. Pompous and presumptuous, he was well aware that because he had been dispatched by the district council of the Communist Youth League, he was the one who stood between the club's records and our tape recorders. We *had* to listen to him no matter what.

I recall one of his lectures in particular because it was about Bob Dylan. Hungarians loved Dylan; his protest songs inspired many. But this Roy Orbison knockoff made us angry with his talk of Dylan's hypocrisy. Bob Dylan was a fake, he said, because he traveled by private plane while singing about the misery of poor people. He was a big liar, just another product of the American capitalist machinery. I hated this man for humiliating my hero in public, but I didn't bother to confront him because, like everyone else in that class, I wanted to move on to the taping session. In the end, I decided that the poor selection of records wasn't worth the price of listening to someone smear the good name of one of my favorite musicians. I quit after a few weeks.

Things were changing in Hungary. For years travel outside the country was all but impossible, but by the mid-1960s authorities had begun to allow *some* travel to the other side. This happened slowly. Very slowly. Selectively, too. Hungarians who returned from the West brought home scarce goods, including records, either for their own use or to sell on the black market. But smuggling wasn't for the faint of heart.

The few who were allowed to travel would feel frightened as they approached the border with Austria, which was the gateway to the West. Everyone had something to worry about. Those leaving the country would fear discovery of the few American dollars or West German marks hidden somewhere in the seams of their underpants, or between the layers of their suitcase. Smuggling hard currency was a big crime, and the punishment was severe. Of course the authorities knew everyone carried contraband currency. Nobody would believe that you were traveling on the twenty dollars you could buy legally from the state-owned bank. So Hungarians took ingenious steps to fool the authorities. My friend Bálint would scotch-tape his illegal dollars on the sliding door of the compartment in the train, so that when the customs officer entered his compartment the money would disappear inside the door case. It was almost foolproof.

You faced a different kind of scrutiny on the way back. Although the state permitted you to bring one or two records into the country, if you "smuggled" in more than that, they might get you. Records were not contraband, but behaving like a greedy capitalist was. More than a couple of records would be considered "quantities for trading," and again, the penalties were severe. For one thing, you'd be blacklisted—banned from traveling outside the country for years, even decades. It wouldn't matter how many times you applied for an "exit permit," you'd be rejected again and again for improper behavior. It wasn't just record albums, either. Anyone attempting to import "improper goods," which is what coveted sex magazines or blacklisted books were called, was met with a similar punishment. Besides being banned from travel, anyone with a good job (such as a manager or professor) would be demoted and humiliated for good measure.

Most Hungarians understood the way things worked and prepared by carrying additional goods for the sole purpose of buying off corrupt officers. An extra record or porn magazine, a bag of Italian coffee, a few bars of Rexona or Lux soap would do it. If there was a demand, there was a supply. In the end, market forces won.

But that particular day all I wanted was "Jumpin' Jack Flash." I ended up at the store on Rákóczi Avenue, the one the shop clerk had alluded to, which had the technology to copy music from a disk to what the man called a floppy—a thin piece of plastic with the music imprinted on just one side. How he created these floppies was a mystery to me.

"Fascinating. How do you do this?" I asked.

"Intellectual property," he replied. "A trade secret."

The owner of the store, one of the few private small shopkeepers, was a serious-looking man fully aware of his privileged situation. He had original records in cellophane wraps, almost the newest ones, and his products were way overpriced, even by black-market standards.

But after a little negotiation about the price and some storytelling, he allowed me to look at the floppy process, which fascinated me. The smell of the plastic as it was molded into a record you could actually play made the whole thing magical. The quality of the floppy was awful, and it wasn't cheap. What's more, because it could only be played once or twice, it had to be taped immediately or its contents would be lost forever. Still, it was a solution to my problem.

CHAPTER TWENTY

I t was tough to be a Hungarian teenager in the 1960s, especially one who wore his hair long, who displayed a peace sign on his T-shirt, and who wore his jeans long enough to mop the pavement—the American way. All of these things were considered culturally suspect by the authorities and treated as acts of aggression by the police. Nobody wanted to cross paths with the Rendőrség—the Budapest police—but we'd see them on street corners, beating their batons rhythmically in the palms of their hands. *I've got my eye on you*, they seemed to say. *I'm watching.*

We had all heard about the riot police and their tendency to beat up young people who had the audacity to gather together in groups larger than ten. But I'd never had a run-in with the Rendőrség, except for the time I was picked up by the police after having visited the Chinese embassy with a couple of friends. China was communist; Hungary was communist. It didn't occur to me that the Hungarian authorities considered Chairman

Mao a dangerous enemy in same category as President Johnson.

But that was the extent of my contact with the police, until one day when I was doing nothing more than looking out the window on trolley bus 76. I had been traveling on that bus regularly since I was a little boy; in fact, I grew up with the sound of it as it drove under our balcony. I knew all the different cars on the line. The one I was on that day was a tired, older Soviet-made model that smelled of the mix of engine oil and sawdust they used to sweep the floor. It was a familiar smell, though not a pleasant one, and I resisted getting used to it.

Life had been bearable in the private little universe I had invented for myself, with a little help from my friends and family. I should have known that it wouldn't last. The day I had my brush with the law, I got on the 76 by the zoo, which was the closest stop to Heroes' Square, where I had been hanging out that afternoon with Péter. We had been to band practice, where we struggled with guitar chords. The songs were still in my head. I was humming my parts as we came up to the traffic lights.

There were only a few passengers on the trolley bus that day. One was an older woman who had seen better times, wrapped in clothes that, once elegant, were now worn thin. She wore a woolen coat, a silk scarf, and a pair of well-polished black shoes. And a hat—a very nice hat, in fact, which was quite unusual in those days. Something about the way it sat on her head suggested that this woman knew *exactly* how a hat should be worn. I liked the way she carried herself with pride, as if to say that the system couldn't break her.

A man and a woman in windbreakers were also riding

the trolley that evening, probably on their way home from work. This young couple sat slumped in their seats, perhaps because they had made a stopover in one of the *kocsma*, the ever-stinking pubs, where they could get drunk on bad alcohol for nothing. Then there was the group of Young Pioneers, proud in their red scarves. They were chattering away, perhaps on their way home from an outing at the Amusement Park next to the Zoo.

Five stops from the Zoo, a police officer got on. He looked like most policemen, somewhat angry and proud in his gray uniform, his pistol in his shoulder strap, baton in hand, the red star on his cap. This *hekus*, as most of us called the police, started staring at me the minute he got on the trolley. In fact, he didn't take his eyes off me. He was menacing and intense, and as much as he wanted everyone to know that he represented authority, this *hekus* clearly wanted to intimidate me. And he did.

For my part, I just sat quietly and stared at the trolley floor. I intended to make no mistakes. I knew that the best way to avoid a dog bite was to avoid eye contact with the dog, and I figured this was much the same situation. Don't provoke. Just pretend you don't exist. Keep a low profile like you're nothing—just air. Of course, that was impossible. As small and skinny as I was, I was still underscoring my presence by wearing a tie-dyed T-shirt and jeans. The Levi's were my trademark and a status symbol. Unfortunately, the pair I was wearing were badly torn on one leg, and my bare knee was visible. Torn jeans weren't the style in the 1960s, not like they are today. I had just worn through mine and didn't have another pair. I didn't think that was reason enough to stop wearing them.

Unfortunately, as I feared, the policeman was desperate

to teach me a lesson. He didn't take his eyes off me, not for a second. He must have noticed how uncomfortable I was. That in itself made me an easy target. And of course he was well aware that nobody on the trolley would stand up for me.

After a torturous ride home, I could see my stop up ahead. I gathered my things and pushed the red button above the door, signaling to the driver that I wanted to get off. That's when the *hekus* made his move.

"Show me your ID," he said in a stark, authoritative voice.

Asking for your ID for no apparent reason was the first step in a surprise attack, the weapon of choice for the bully police officer. It was a clear statement that, in his view, something was wrong— *with you.* You were suspicious. You called attention to yourself in such a way as to require police action. I handed the officer my ID and he paged through the little burgundy booklet. It had all the information he needed: name, age, address, mother's name, occupation, employment status. Mine said I was a student.

He read the address and realized that I was going to get off at the next stop, so he knew he had only a little time to perform his duty.

"What are you wearing?" the officer asked.

"A farmer," I responded. That's what we called blue jeans in Hungary. "They are torn," I added, a preventive strike.

"Yes, but why is it torn? Do you have to wear it like that? Didn't your father or mother teach you how to dress properly?" he asked.

"I fell." I was surprised at how easily the lie came. "I

was playing soccer with my friends and I fell." I couldn't admit that I had been wearing my jeans like this for weeks and would continue to wear them until my cousin Georges in Belgium sent me another pair.

"Well, dress up properly next time," he said, hissing like a snake.

The conversation didn't last for more than a few seconds, but it seemed like his towering figure was standing in front of me forever. I stood frozen, wishing that the clumsy trolley would move faster, arrive earlier, open its doors sooner. Finally, as the trolley stopped I turned around to quickly get off. But the *hekus* was faster than I was, and before I could move he kicked me with his military boots—hard. I flew off the stairs of the trolley and landed hard on the pavement. My body and ego were both bruised. I felt such injustice at what had just happened, but I couldn't do or say a thing. It was the first time anything like this had happened to me. I had hoped that someone would come to my rescue, perhaps offer a word in my defense. But only the half-drunk couple looked up, and they nodded in agreement with the police officer. The cop looked satisfied at their approval. The old lady stared out the window with a sadness in her eyes, but she probably had problems of her own. The Young Pioneers were curious and frightened, but the teacher told them to turn their heads. They obeyed.

I stood tall and made a point of breathing slowly to counteract the growing fury I felt. I knew better than to react in anger. It wasn't that he had hurt me—not physically at least. It was the humiliation that had enraged me, the helplessness I felt. Who the hell did he think he was to treat me like this just because I was wearing a pair of jeans he didn't like? I wanted to challenge him, to tell him that I would report the incident to his superiors, who would surely send him off to some remote town by the Soviet border. But who was I kidding? This wasn't some record store clerk. This was the Rendőrség and I was just a high school student with long hair and torn jeans. I cut my losses and ran home.

I was still shaking as I opened the gate to our building. Once inside, I sat down on the steps next to the old elevator, trembling and hoping Mrs. Rozsbor, the old concierge, would stay in her apartment. I didn't want her to see me like this. I didn't want anyone to see me. After about five minutes I had regained my composure and quietly walked up the four flights of stairs to our home.

Gyuri was at his desk when I told him what had happened. He said that I shouldn't let it bother me, that this had happened to many of *his* friends and that they still wore their jeans. He told me that I was a hero and that kids in America went through much the same thing. "You'd never believe it, but American boys and girls get beaten up for their looks. Sometimes really badly. I guess we Hungarians are just like they are. Your torn jeans or theirs, not much difference."

CHAPTER TWENTY-ONE

I loved going to the movies. When I watched an American film, a rare opportunity, I'd imagine being Tony Curtis or Elvis driving one of those big cars—a Pontiac GTO convertible or a Ford Mustang. Western movies were only selectively shown in Budapest theaters. We'd get the occasional reel featuring Cliff Richard and the Shadows, but I didn't really care for them, even if Hank B. Marvin's guitar playing was quite something. I wanted to see James Bond and the films of Alfred Hitchcock. I wanted to see *A Hard Day's Night* and *Help!* From time to time a few Western movies would be shown at the club operated by the Interior Ministry, but admittance was restricted to a select few. If you knew someone who worked at the ministry—even a friend of a friend—you might occasionally be allowed in. Otherwise you were out of luck.

Every week on Wednesday, Péter and I would go through the film programs on the last page of the *Népszabadság*, the Party newspaper. We were always on the lookout for films that promised something special.

Movies that might have a nude scene or two, that had a good fight, or that starred Gina Lollobrigida, Claudia Cardinale, or Ingrid Bergman were must-sees. A film that had a pop band playing got extra marks. That we would see no matter what.

Despite the Party having a hand in selecting the movies, there were some pleasant surprises, such as *Go Go Mania*, which featured my favorite bands: Eric Burdon and the Animals, Billy Kramer and the Dakotas, Chris Farlowe, the Spencer Davis Group, Peter and Gordon, the Honey-combs. They were all in that movie, lip-synching to their hits, except the Beatles, who performed live. When Péter and I discovered that *Go Go Mania* was playing in a small theater on the outskirts of Budapest, we took a long tram and bus ride to get there. The Endre Ady Theater, named after the famed Hungarian poet, was in a beautiful state of disrepair. Built to service a small enclave of houses for state employees in the 1920s, this lovely little theater was itself an art deco gem, with a nicely designed ticket office and sturdy wooden chairs that represented the period.

The venue was almost empty when we got there, with just a few seats occupied by other young people who, like Péter and me, wanted nothing more than to see their heroes on the big screen. The movie opened with a scene from a Beatles concert. There they were, larger than life, playing "She Loves You" in front of a concert hall of screaming girls.

"Look at all those girls going crazy," Péter said to me. "How great would that be?"

Then came the Animals with "The House of the Rising Sun" and that amazing guitar intro everyone wanted to play. After that the film showed the Spencer Davis Group and the Nashville Teens, the first British rock band to have ever played in Budapest. Péter and I returned for a second show, after ducking out to a neighboring pub for some *virsli*—Hungarian hot dogs.

We didn't really understand why some movies were shown and others were not, only that those considered alien to "socialist cultural values" did not get picked up by the state film distribution company, MOKÉP, which had a monopoly over which movies made it into the country. We didn't understand the logic of censorship; we only knew that it was an invisible and powerful thing that denied us opportunities to experience what teenagers around the world were enjoying. Then there was the "safety valve" that the Party opened from time to time to allow us to blow off some steam, a way to let us sample Western culture without endangering the system. That's how we got to see some real movies, not the lame selections like the pirate movie *Captain Blood* or *Cartouche*, a French adventure film. The movies that were released through the valve showed contemporary life in the West in all its depravity. And it was just as Hungarians had expected.

Perhaps no film displayed Western decadence like Michelangelo Antonioni's *Blow-Up*. The Party screened this wonderful movie in a small art-house theater in the center of Budapest. The choice of venue was a deliberate decision by MOKÉP, designed to contain the numbers. Only a few thousand, at most, would get to see the film during its run.

The theater was across the street from another "landmark," a butcher's shop where, every year a few days before the celebration of the Great October Socialist Revolution, a beautiful, life-size bust of Comrade Lenin was displayed. Not so surprising in communist Hungary, except that this particular statue was artistically carved out of pig fat. People would come from miles to see this prizewinning sculpture of Comrade Lenin. Only a few dared laugh.

It was a cold and rainy November day when Péter, Gyuri, and I went to see *Blow-Up*. But we didn't care about the bad weather. Nothing would keep us from seeing Vanessa Redgrave and, more important, the Yardbirds. The film was almost new by Hungarian standards, having been released in the West about a year and a half earlier. Demand for the movie was high and the line at the ticket counter was long, but we weren't going to miss our chance. Italian director Michelangelo Antonioni was known for being critical of America, for showing how American culture dominated Western society. That's likely why his film passed the censors. But it wasn't the reason we wanted to go.

This was London on the big screen, a larger-than-life look at young people just like me—if I had been lucky enough to reside in England. *Blow-Up* centered on David, a wealthy young photographer who lived a lavish life in groovy London and took random pictures until, one day, he realized he had photographed a crime. This part of the movie appealed to me, too, as photography was something of a tradition in our family. Father was exceptionally talented with his Exakta camera. His aunt Ata was a world-renowned photographer, known for her photos of the 1956 revolution, the fashion photos she took for big Parisian fashion houses, and the dreamy pictures she took of her children. Ata was close friends with Robert Capa, arguably the most famous of all press

photographers. And since Mother had worked at the Kodak film factory before the war, the process of enlarging
photographs was familiar to me.

I loved assisting Father as he covered the bathroom window and turned it into a darkroom, switched on a red light,
and got down to the business of enlarging his negatives.
I'd watch as he poured chemicals into square dishes, then
submerged the photo paper. Seeing the pictures appear
on the paper was magic. How could I not see this movie?

The main character's life appealed to me. His London
home, his job taking pictures of a semi-nude Jane Birkin
with his Hasselblad seemed like a dream. Not to mention
that he got to sleep with Vanessa Redgrave and drive a
white Rolls-Royce convertible. That was the life. David
was something of an eccentric, spending his money on
beautiful useless things like an old wooden airplane
propeller. Just for the joy of it. He didn't have to worry
about censors or uniforms. He didn't have to concern
himself with anyone listening in on his conversations and
reporting him to the authorities. He worked. He partied.
He made a lot of money.

And yet, as much as David's life was something of a
fantasy for me, the story in itself wouldn't really have
made a huge impact were it not for the nightclub scene
in the middle of the movie. In an attempt to tease out
the details of the murder, David drove his Rolls-Royce
to a club in Soho. He walked through an alley where
the distorted sound of an electric guitar could be heard.
Then he followed the music into a nondescript little hole
in the wall where . . . the Yardbirds were playing! Jeff Beck
was on one side of the makeshift stage and Jimmy Page
was on the other, playing "Train Kept a-Rollin'."

My jaw dropped. Péter's jaw dropped. The sight of one of our favorite bands on the big screen was breathtaking. When Jeff Beck heard a cracking sound emanating from his amp that wouldn't go away, he smashed the amp in frustration, destroying his poor guitar in the process. And when he tore off the neck of his guitar and threw it into the audience, the polite English crowd erupted. They loved him. This was the energy of rock and roll, and it was pure and beautifully destructive. I don't think the censors really understood the incredible impact that scene might have on us, how it might influence rock musicians in Budapest. The raw power of rock had always eluded them.

It was David the photographer who emerged victorious in the fight for the neck of Jeff Beck's guitar. But once he was outside the intense atmosphere of the club, something seemed to deflate in him and the artifact suddenly lost its appeal. He threw it away. That I didn't understand. Antonioni wanted to say something about the alienation of society, I guess. I knew all about that, but I still would rather have had Jeff Beck's guitar.

Péter and I felt a certain sadness as we walked out of the Film Museum that evening. We wanted to be in swinging London, in Soho, in that club. We didn't want to be on a dark street in Budapest where the only attraction was a statue made of lard. I don't think we were alone in our melancholy, because when the movie ended and the credits rolled, the audience was quiet. This film was something special and we all needed to process it, which might have been why there was none of the usual after-show chatter. *Blow-Up* reminded us all about the life we should be living.

CHAPTER TWENTY-TWO

You must tip your hat. Like this," my father said. "That's what a hat is for. So you can tip it."

We were wearing our gray felt Stetsons with the enormous brims and the thick silk ribbons. It was one of those rare occasions when we were walking together down Pozsonyi Street, father and son. How could I not be proud?

"You look like my favorite jazz musician!" Father said.

"Who is your favorite jazz musician?"

"Nat King Cole. He is the best. I can listen to him for hours."

"Oh, the guy who sings that song you like?"

"Yes," said my father, laughing. "The guy who sings that song I like. He always looked sharp. And he wore a hat like yours."

I had told my parents about the incident with the policeman. My mother was fretful and said that I should just stop this jean-wearing nonsense. My father took a less conventional approach.

"You know, clothes really do make the man," he said.

I had heard this before. "Yes, but I'm a teenager."

"So what is a teenager if not a man in training?" Father had an answer for everything. "Why don't you try dressing differently. See how people react."

I wouldn't have been interested in giving up my blue jeans, but there was an American film at the time, with Faye Dunaway and Warren Beatty, two stars I knew from magazines. It was about the gangster couple Bonnie Parker and Clyde Barrow. I wasn't really familiar with the characters they were playing. A sexy couple with a love of guns was all I knew. I gathered that they were gangsters in rural America, which meant they lived somewhere more remote than New York or Chicago.

I hadn't seen the movie—it was off-limits to Hungarians—but I'd heard the Georgie Fame song on the radio many, many times. It was okay, a little hokey maybe, but I loved the sound of machine-gun fire in the background. I knew a little about Chicago gangsters from a book I'd read about Al Capone. And I'd been to Csikágo a few times, that other Chicago, the one in Budapest's Seventh District, which was an equally dangerous but perhaps less exciting place. There were no big black cars with men in nice suits hanging in Csikágo, just nasty little crooks who would beat you up and rob you if you weren't careful. Of course there were no such things as gangsters in this country, and no underworld. Officially, that is.

I showed photos of Bonnie and Clyde to my father, pointing out the suits Warren Beatty wore. Always double-breasted. Always with a vest and a white shirt, a wide tie with a big knot. He said that it was elegant, and that it was time for me to own an elegant suit. That's how

I came to have a double-breasted suit made of English wool, with my own white shirt and a fashionable silk tie. My first suit.

Father had some fabric stored in an old vulcanized-fiber suitcase on top of the wardrobe in the hallway of our home. Fortunately, gone were the days when the secret police would raid your house, looking into its farthest corners to find items you might have been, in their words, "hoarding." If they couldn't find what they were looking for, these leather-clad policemen might plant evidence that they'd then confiscate, and you'd be taken away as a capitalist pig. It was ingenious, really. A very effective method of getting rid of those considered to be the enemies of the people, including your own personal enemies. That was the 1950s, though. Thank goodness for the '60s. Father's stash of fabric was safe and so was he.

We hauled the suitcase from the top of the wardrobe and spread all the fabrics out on the floor in the living room. They were blue, brown, black, and gray, plain and striped. Most had numbers and writing woven into the lining material: "Finest wool and silk. Made in England. Dormeuil." or "Richards 100% Wool. Made in Hungary."

"These are from the Richards factory," Father told me. "From before the war, when Hungary was one of the great makers of textiles in the world. And this one is made by Dormeuil from England. I got it from Mr. Stolz from London. It would be worthy of the Duke of Edinburgh. He could have his suits made from this," he declared proudly.

The gray fabric with the herringbone pattern was very much like the suit Clyde wore in the movie. I chose that.

"Ah, Andris. This is elegant. Diplomats wear suits made of fabric like this," Father said. "An exceptionally good selection, indeed."

Father took me across the Ferdinánd Bridge to meet with his tailor. The door opened slowly to a frail man in his sixties. He was small like Father, and he had a thin French mustache. Mr. Lévay held a piece of shiny white chalk in his hand, and he had a small velvet pillow attached to his forearm, with dozens of pins sticking out. His glasses hung around his neck on a string, as did a measuring tape—white on one side and green on the other.

Ah, Mr. Simonyi," Mr. Lévay said. "Welcome. It is good to see you as always. Do come in." Theirs was an old-fashioned relationship, based on familiarity and respect. They addressed each other as mister or sir, ignoring the new style of address in which men and women alike were referred to as comrade. Mr. Lévay wasn't a communist and he wasn't a member of the Party. My father was a Party member, as were almost all government officials. But Father thought highly of Mr. Lévay for his craftsmanship, and for his integrity.

"I brought you a new customer," Father said. "He has a picture he would like to show you. We also brought this herringbone." Father rolled out the fabric.

"I think I will enjoy working with it, Mr. Simonyi. It is rare that I come across something like this one." Mr. Lévay put on his glasses, taking the cloth between his fingers.

It was a ritual conversation between two men with mutual respect and a deep knowledge of their respective professions. Father had been in the textile business for thirty years, Mr. Lévay likely longer. He had owned a big textile business before the war, with forty employees. Like all other businesses employing more than five people, it was nationalized after the communist takeover in 1948. Two men showed up one day, one a thug in a long leather coat, and took the shop into the possession of the people. All Lévay was allowed to take was his hat.

Now Mr. Lévay's home was his workshop, his workshop was his home: a tiny hallway, an equally tiny dining room, an even tinier studio. The old oak furniture pieces were way too big for the small space, but they were dear to him. Mrs. Lévay would have been desperate to hold on to the furniture, as she would have been to keep the Herend china displayed in a glass cabinet, another fragile reminder of the family's lost wealth.

"Before we get to work, my wife would like to say hello," Mr. Lévay said. And with that a cheerful woman showed up in the doorway. She seemed truly pleased to see my father.

"Good day, Mr. Simonyi, so nice to see you. And your son. Such a fine boy. Please give my best to Mrs. Simonyi."

I was impatient, growing cross that these niceties were holding up the important work ahead of us. I showed Mr. Lévay the picture. "I would like that one," I said. "The American gangster. Do you think you can do it?"

"Can I do it?" Mr. Lévay came alive at the question. "This is the style we had in the '30s. You should have seen the beautiful suits we used to make those days. I like this double breast and the vest that goes with it. The vest will have a silk back, of course. We can do it, young man," he said, turning to my father for approval. "I just don't understand this worship of gangsters in America," he added. "All this shoot-'em-up glory. They should be better citizens."

Father and his old friend shared a nod, maybe even a wink. They understood that a little criticism of America never hurt. Just to be on the safe side.

Mr. Lévay put everything he knew into the making of the garment. He was meticulous about the details like the lining in the jacket, which he made from the silk in his own reserves. He angled the peaks on the lapels just right—one of the most striking features of Clyde's suit. I asked him to make flaps for the trousers. I wanted to be able to wear them with suspenders or without, so we discussed that, too. We brought made-to-order buttons from Mr. Sutoczky, a specialty button maker who lived on our street. They were made of cow horn, nicely polished. Six big ones for the breast, one for the inside, and four smaller ones for each sleeve.

In all, I had five fittings with Mr. Lévay. I didn't think we'd ever be done, until one day he said, "Well—how do you like it, young man? All you need is a Stetson and you will look like an American gangster."

Years later when I recalled this time with my father, I realized that it was his way of passing on what he valued most: a respect for other people; the acknowledgment of quality and individuality, of people over politics or position. I think my father wanted to show me how an honest profession can help fill a life, even in hard times. He might not have cared that much for my jeans, even if he surely felt my pain, but this was about so much more. This was about showing me that dignity and decency are more important than ideology.

CHAPTER TWENTY-THREE

H air was always an issue. Long hair, to be precise. Teenage boys grew their hair to express their individuality, to rail against conformity and the power of the status quo. My friends and I wore our hair long to distinguish ourselves from the crowd. We considered it protest in its purest form. And yet, as much as we viewed long hair as a tool of silent resistance—as a means of dissent against a system that wasn't created for us and that we didn't believe in—it also served to demonstrate our love of rock and roll. Because along with the electric guitar and the raw vocals, the outlandish costumes and the crackling energy, it was long hair that set rock and roll apart from all other music.

The authorities knew that they were virtually powerless against rock's growing popularity. They also understood that it was a movement as much as anything else. Loud and extreme, rock extolled the virtues of independent thought, personal freedom, and respect—the power of the individual. It was no wonder that the authorities considered it a threat to the collectivist ideology of communism. Neither was it any wonder that males with long hair—that most visible sign of rock and roll—were easy prey for the police. Even Gabi Presser, who was by then a popular figure, had been held for questioning after a show at Lake Balaton, where he had been touring.

But it wasn't just the police. Gangs from the workers' district would travel to the center of Budapest armed with batons and metal bars with the sole purpose of picking a fight with anyone with long hair. I was with my friend István Králik when we became the target of one such bashing. Králik and I were in City Park when three thugs sneaked up on us and started shouting "Nasty faggots!" and "We'll teach you a lesson about fashion!" and "Assholes, we'll give you a haircut!" They didn't expect Králik to pull out his own weapon.

"You want to fight? Let's fight," Králik shouted, and with that he pulled out a rubber cable with steel balls attached to the end. It was a powerful bludgeon—he could have killed someone with it. When the hoodlums didn't back down, Králik swung his weapon over his head, as if to strike. That did it. The gang ran off in the opposite direction and I counted my blessings that I had such a heroic friend.

The issue of hair was dealt with matter-of-factly at school. If your hair was considered too long—and it could be that it had grown just slightly below your ears—you'd be called out by a teacher, likely in groups of three or four. "Here, take this," Mr. Müller would mumble while holding out a handful of coins. "You don't have to pay me back, Simonyi, but don't come back without that haircut. And you, Friedman, you too! And you and you!" he would say, pointing at his victims. Then he would tell us that we should all be ashamed of ourselves, there would be no future for long-haired louts like us, and what were our parents thinking letting us go out of the house like this.

We felt it was important to break the rules. The boys rebelled with their hair and the girls rebelled with their clothes. High school students in Hungary were compelled to wear a jacketlike blue robe over their clothes, the way the teachers did. The girls were told to be "decent" and to wear skirts that covered their knees. These were young vibrant girls coming into their own, and they wanted to show off their legs, their tights, and their personalities. It was, they felt, a risk worth taking. Some of the boys would comb their hair to make it look shorter at school, but the girls did the opposite, coming to class with their skirts rolled up above their knees, sometimes sticking a pin or a ribbon on their robe to make it their own. The more rebellious ones would also apply lipstick. A way of demonstrating their individuality *and* teasing the boys.

The teachers' response was typical. One day they wouldn't seem to care, while the next they would take on the role of Party enforcer, giving the students a stern lecture, pulling on their earlobes, or sending a note home to their parents. I had such a good relationship with my own mother and father that I didn't worry when the teacher sent me home with a letter in my own blue notebook. I was pretty nonchalant about the whole thing when I passed it to Father to sign.

"What is this, Andris—a note from your teacher about your hair?"

"Oh, yeah. A few of us got them," I replied.

"I don't care who got them. A note from school is unacceptable. Go get a haircut and don't let me see another message like this again."

I was shocked by my father's response. It upset me more than the bad haircut I was forced to endure. We talked about it the next day.

"I am sorry, Andris. Frankly, I don't care about your hair, or your guitar playing, or those crazy clothes you like to wear," he said. "I respect you for going your own way. But you need to scale back sometimes. I can't always be there to protect you. It's not always about being right or wrong. Sometimes it is just reasonable to give in."

Father was right, of course. And as I would realize years later, the clashes that were prompted by hair and short skirts didn't necessarily have to do with breaking the rules—not the dress code, anyway. Sometimes a teacher called out a student because he was looking for some small way to assert his position, a way to make his voice heard. A number of our teachers had been raised in the ultra-conservative era before the war, when Hungary was a rigidly Catholic country dictated by class. Authority was feared and respected then. Men were considered superior to women and, as a rule, age in itself decided who was right and who was wrong. With these clear points of reference gone, our teachers lived within the blurred lines of communist ideology, where they tried to reassert their own authority by picking small fights instead of engaging in large battles.

It was around this time—the mid-1960s—that Hungarians started using the phrase *Goulash Communism.* The people who did this were proud to distinguish Hungary from the rest of the Soviet bloc by naming their political system after the hearty cowboy soup made popular by the cattle herdsmen, otherwise known as *gulyás*. A simple dish, goulash was a mix of anything the herdsmen could carry: beef, onion, green paprika, potatoes, tomatoes, carrots, and of course ground red paprika—lots of it. Herdsmen, just like my mother, would add a little of this, a little of that—usually an ingredient you'd be better off not asking about—that would make the whole experience tasty, but hard to digest. *Goulash Communism* seemed a fitting name for the current state of affairs.

CHAPTER TWENTY-FOUR

All rock bands start the same way. You get your first guitar, even though you have no idea how to play. You
sweat to learn those first few chords. You find other kids
who are equally terrible and try to emulate your musical
heroes. You share the sparse equipment available. Then
you find a drummer. Suddenly you find yourself in a band
and spend all your time rehearsing. You can hardly wait to
be on a stage, any stage, and perform. You want to please
the girls and show off to the boys. You want to have fun.

Péter and I were eager musicians but not very good.
Like many children, I had studied the piano from a young
age. And, like many children, I hated it. Nevertheless, I
had hoped that some of the rudimentary skills I learned
at the keyboard—all those hours of scales—would translate to the guitar. It didn't happen. They were such
different instruments, each with its own musical vocabulary. Never mind great keyboardists like Jerry Lee Lewis,
Little Richard, and Steve Winwood—to me, the piano
was a waltz. The guitar was rock and roll.

My piano lessons hadn't made me a pianist, so I'm not sure why I thought that taking guitar lessons would make me a guitar player. Nevertheless, Péter and I talked our parents into getting us an instructor. Mr. Teacher Sir (that's what we called him) was a jazz guitarist my parents had found at the Operetta Theater. He taught us important things like upstrokes and downstrokes, the significance of pausing, and executing a pull-off. But when it became clear that he wasn't going to be the one to teach us how to play "Since I Met You Baby" like Spencer Davis, Péter and I challenged him.

"No, that's not the way it goes," Péter said.

"It sounds different," I chipped in.

We should have realized that the effect of one lone guitar couldn't replicate the sound of a professional group, professionally recorded, but we were little pricks and thought we knew everything.

"Trust me," he said. "These are the chords."

"Sorry, Mr. Teacher Sir. I really don't think so," I said. "You sound nothing like the record."

That was to be our last lesson.

We were on our own from that point, straining for the right chords, learning the fretboard. It was hard going, but oh so sweet. Sometimes Péter and I would fight over missed notes or a messed-up rhythm. He was disciplined and a better player than I was; that much was obvious. I struggled to keep up. But I was stubborn and I wanted this more than I had ever wanted anything, so I kept going.

Nothing was as important to me as music. Not schoolwork, that's for sure. Péter and I got together to practice three, maybe four times a week. In between sessions we'd be home alone, each in our rooms, sitting with our tape recorders or record players. We breathed in the music—every song and every note—and as the spools of tape played out, I allowed myself to imagine a different version of my life. I was strong and free. I could go where I wanted and do what I pleased. In this dream I lived in Budapest, but a Budapest more open than the one I inhabited, where liberty was the rule and skill and ambition were given freedom to grow. When I listened to music, I could believe in my dream. I don't think I was alone in this. How could I have been?

Péter and I made sure to check out our competition. We saw some good bands and some mediocre bands. We saw some really awful bands. If you can imagine an Eastern European version of the worst of *American Idol* with musicians playing out of tune and mispronouncing the lyrics, you'd be close. But no matter how good or bad, there was also something radiating from the stage. These guys knew they were doing something extraordinary.

We picked up our guitars anytime we could, carefully transcribing songs from the tape recorder, note by note. We'd do this for hours. We weren't great. We taped ourselves so that we could hear our efforts played back to us. We were always disappointed. Gyuri did nothing to spare our feelings.

"What is that supposed to be?" my big brother would ask.

"This is 'Satisfaction,'" I would reply. "It's by a band called the Stones. The ... *Rolling* ... *Stones*? You might have heard of them ..."

"The *Rolling Stones* would be rolling over in agony if they heard what you did to their song."

I played those three immortal notes again, showing

off my fuzz-box. Gyuri, always the cutup, pretended to double over in pain.

"You try it if you think it's so easy," I told him. Then I did some acting of my own and pretended to unbuckle my guitar and hand it to him. "Come back in three days," I said. "We'll be ready."

"Keep trying, little brother. I'll come back in a year and we'll see."

Here's the thing about persistence: eventually it pays off. One day our playing sounded a little less like the wail of a small, feral animal. You could make out a melody, hear the difference between chorus and verse. There was a rhythm to what we were playing, a tuneful logic. It didn't seem an outrage to call our efforts "music." We were ready to form our band.

Péter and I had talked endlessly about forming a trio: guitar, bass, drums. We started by swapping his six-string East German guitar for a bass—not an easy thing to do. His dream of a Fender was just that, a dream, so he settled for a white Kovács brand.

We needed an amplifier, too, which we had been on the lookout for ever since the "Nazi amp" incident. If I was a Brit, I would have gone to a music store on Denmark Street in London. But this was Budapest, where a Selmer or Vox was very hard to come by, a real scarcity. Obtaining one might take years, if you were lucky. Another option was finding a secondhand amp in a consignment store. We needed one fast, so we headed to St. Rokus Hospital, where Péter's father was head gynecologist. At that time hospitals made much of their own equipment and had workshops staffed with skilled people who repaired ECGs,

X-ray machines, and the like. When there was a shortage of spare parts (and there was always a shortage of spare parts), the workshop fabricated them as best they could. We had heard of a man, Mr. Zamek, who supplemented his day job fixing medical devices by designing and building amps, which he then sold on the black market.

Mr. Zamek's workshop was in the hospital basement. It was a messy room lit by cold neon tubes, and to me it looked like the lair of a mad scientist. An old iron vise had been fixed to the workbench, and a dozen steel files were strewn next to it. Hammers and screwdrivers were everywhere, and there was a smell of resin from a soldering iron. Mr. Zamek was busy fixing an integrated circuit for one of the medical instruments. Stacked next to him on the workbench was medical equipment waiting to be repaired. I recognized an oscilloscope and a couple of tangled blood pressure cuffs. I couldn't identify most of the devices, but with a quick scan of the room I spied an amplifier. Péter saw it, too.

"Ah, so you like this, eh?" Mr. Zamek placed the amp on the workbench. "I just finished it."

We actually did. A small amp in an aluminum case with a leather handle, it had three homemade plastic knobs—one each for volume, treble, and bass.

"Cool," Péter said.

"Cool," I repeated.

"German tubes. Japanese resistors. Hungarian genius." Mr. Zamek pointed his thumb at his chest, laughing at his own joke. He plugged it in and connected it to a speaker under his workbench.

"Can I try it out?" Péter asked. He'd brought his guitar along just in case.

"Of course."

Péter played a few notes and looked satisfied. It wasn't bad. "How much are you asking for it?" he asked.

"Two thousand five hundred," Mr. Zamek replied.

That was a lot of money, probably more than Mr. Zamek's monthly salary.

"Can't you go cheaper?" we asked.

"Can't do. Can't do. There is someone already interested. You take it now. It will be gone tomorrow."

Péter pulled me aside to discuss the transaction. We were eager to upgrade our playing, and we both knew that getting a bass amp was our logical next step. I wasn't sure about spending so much money—even though it was Péter who was putting up the funds—but we needed an amp and this was pretty much our only option. We bought the amp in the end. We were glad to do so.

CHAPTER TWENTY-FIVE

Péter and I weren't quite legends—not to anyone but ourselves. Still, enough kids knew about our band that getting a drummer wasn't going to be much of a problem. But we didn't want just any drummer, and we certainly didn't want one of the many boys who played drums with the Young Pioneers. That regimented ra-ta-ta-tat wasn't *real* drumming. Not to us.

We held auditions—a pretty lofty word, given the circumstances. We were looking for someone who knew what it was to be part of a group, someone who wasn't a show-off. We were looking for chemistry, although it would have been pretentious to use that language at that time. The question was simple, really: Did we like him or not?

There was Balázs from my school. He was terrible, couldn't find the drum in front of him. Then there was Zsolt from Péter's school. He was worse. He didn't even own a drum. Laci from our street was good, but he was way too old and wanted to be paid. In the end we didn't find our drummer. Aunt Ágnes did. She was friends with István Baló's mother and thought we should get together. We met at a rock concert somewhere in the Sixth District.

"Eh, hi?" Péter said. "Um, are you Baló?"

"Yes, and you are Simonyi?" he responded.

"No, I am Békés, that's Simonyi," Péter said, pointing to me.

"Let's go to the buffet and have a drink," I suggested. We got ourselves some beer—Kinizsi beer, the cheapest there was. It wasn't great, but there were times—and this was one of them—when it was Kinizsi or no beer at all.

"How do you like the band?" I asked. It seemed like a good icebreaker. I had no idea who they were. By now there were so many bands that I couldn't keep track.

"They're okay. But the drummer is a little sticky," he said.

"*Sticky?* What do you mean by *sticky*?" I had never heard that expression before, but it made him sound like a pro.

"He's not a great timekeeper," he answered. "He always comes in a little late. The bass is much more precise." István had hair like Art Garfunkel. He was taller than me, about Péter's height, five foot nine, but he looked really young. Much younger than his fourteen years.

"So, about this band of yours," he asked. We were taken aback. Whose job interview was this?

"We're going to be a trio," Péter said. "Like Cream and the Jimi Hendrix Experience. A blues band."

"I think I want to play in your band," he said.

"Well, let's get together and give it a try," I said. We didn't want to promise anything before hearing him play, but I had a good feeling about this guy.

Péter and I were excited. We knew that we needed a drummer to make us look and sound like a real band.

When István came for the first rehearsal at Péter's home, he brought the snare, the bass drum, a cymbal, and the top hat. We made room for the drums on the carpet, setting up my amp on one side and Péter's amp on the other.

"This will be loud, really loud!" Péter said with a lopsided grin.

We asked István if he knew any of the songs we played, and we rattled off a list of our favorites by Cream, Traffic, and Fleetwood Mac.

"Play them for me and I'll do my best. But let's jam first."

Péter and I had no idea what jamming was, and we said so.

"Well, you take some basic chords, agree on the rhythm, and play whatever you feel is right," he explained. The first few notes sounded strange, as we had never played with a drummer before. Still, we were surprised at how good it all sounded and, more important, how much better Péter and I played now that we had a third member of our group. I had to pay attention not just to Péter, but to István—although his real partner was Péter, the bass player. We *jammed* together for a while, enjoying the novelty of it as much as the sound. And just like that, we had our drummer. We were a band.

István's family had a large house in the fancy Buda section of town, which came with a big garage. Very few people those days had big houses and fewer still had a garage of any size. Lucky for us, István's parents were famous journalists who were never at home, so they moved the family car out of the garage and let us set up our equipment there two or three times a week. We practiced long hours until we were thrown out of the house or until the neighbors complained.

At one point we had a discussion about obtaining an official permit. We were so good together, we thought we might play some gigs.

"Do you know how hard it is to get an official permit?" István asked.

"I have no idea, but Iván Rusznyák, the guitarist from Gyuri's class, got one," I said.

"My teacher told me that unless I want to become a professional musician, I should stay away from the authorities. Maybe in a few years," he continued.

"Come on," Péter chimed in. "We could play some real concerts. We could earn real money if we had a permit."

We went on like this for a while, Péter and I pushing for the permit, Baló pushing back. It was two against one at this point, but when Aunt Ágnes told us that she thought it was a stupid idea, we gave up on it. Not before getting a big *I told you so* from István.

Péter was philosophical about the whole thing. "It doesn't matter," he said. "We'll play whenever and wherever we can. Surely we'll be able to find a place that wants a rock band. Somewhere we could play for small change, or for beer. Or for free. Because there will always be the girls."

Now we had to come up with a name. One day as I was sitting in the dimly lit air raid shelter in the basement of Gábor's Dob Street house, listening to him play his Hammond organ, I spotted some buckets of red, black, and blue paint. I asked Gabi if it was okay to use the paint while I listened to him play. I'd always loved fooling around with paint and felt that if I hadn't wanted to be a musician, I would have been an artist. Gabi had no objections, so I started brushing abstract forms on the whitewashed wall, then randomly adding whatever words came to my mind, such as *heavy, blues, Levente* (from Illés, another Hungarian band, which I didn't particularly like), and *Märklin*—a reference to my model train set. Then I stood back and looked at the wall. "Bingo!" I said. "That's the name of the band. The Heavy Levi Märklin Blues Band!"

"That's a terrible name" Gabi said. "You can't have a name that mocks other musicians. And this Märklin thing is weird. And it's way too long. Find something shorter."

"Yes, but I want it weird. I want people to notice and re-member. The stranger it is, the easier it is to remember," I said, as if I knew what I was talking about.

"You need to come up with something different. Some-thing you *all* agree on." It wasn't an opinion. It was a verdict.

I wanted the name of our band to reflect the power of our music, to convey the immense energy that rock and roll generated. So as I was contemplating another name, the word *generator* seemed to be a good starting point. Péter had previously said something about being called the Generator. A four-syllable word that tripped off the tongue was surely a good place to begin. But there had to be a reference to the blues, of course, and purple and blue are the color of sadness. That's how I came up with the name the Purple Generator.

I called Péter later that day. "The Purple Generator!" I said. *Lila Generátor* in Hungarian. "What do you think?"

"That sounds awesome. I am not saying you are a genius, but close. In fact, you just stole my idea—I was about to suggest the very same thing. But you can get all the credit for it when it's printed on our first album."

The Purple Generator started playing to ungrateful audiences. They didn't appreciate our music. They wanted to hear the Hungarian hits, such as "Az Utcán" (On the Street) by Illés or "Mi Fáj?" (What's Hurting You?) by Metro. But we couldn't and wouldn't play these songs—we were into Western music.

I remember a gig at the Petőfi Gymnasium, Péter's alma mater. It wasn't the perfect venue—there was no real stage—but we had an audience, so who cared? We were playing our repertoire, which was everything except Hungarian hits. Some people were clearly disappointed and didn't mind telling us. "Don't you know other songs? Like Illés and Omega and Metro?"asked a boy named Pali.

"We don't play that kind of stuff."

"Well, that's a real pity, because we prefer that kind of music." This was Juci, Pali's girlfriend.

"So you don't like our music?"

"No, that's not what we mean, but we can't dance to your songs. We don't know them."

"Okay, the concert's off, we're going home," I said into the mike. "Pali and Juci don't like our music. We're packing up."

"No! No! No! Please stay!" the little crowd of about twelve shouted. Our loyal fans, how cool. I loved this rock and roll.

CHAPTER TWENTY-SIX

G etting a band together is hard. Keeping it together is harder. The real challenge was to get the sound right. And so we rehearsed. A lot. There were moments we loved and moments we didn't. Sometimes we cheered and sometimes we cursed like sailors. Even so, we wrapped up every session with the knowledge that we were better than we were the last time we practiced. And the next time we got together we'd be even better.

After about a year of rehearsals Gabi offered us the opportunity of a lifetime. "You guys are good," he said. "Why don't you come down to the Omega Club one Sunday afternoon. You can be our warm-up band." So many young rock bands wanted Gábor to listen to their music just to confirm their existence. But it was my band, the Purple Generator, that he had asked to be his warm-up act. Talk about a big deal! I mean hundreds, maybe a thousand kids flocked to see Gabi every Sunday. And now we were going to open for his band in front of a live audience at the prestigious Omega Club! This was the big time.

We practiced diligently, and when we thought we were ready for the concert we invited a few of our classmates to hear us in the garage.

"You guys are great!"

"I never thought you all would be so good."

"Yeah, Brian Epstein is on his way to Budapest to sign you up."

It was the validation we needed. But we had a problem. We were spending so much time rehearsing that the Balós and their neighbors were getting tired of the noise. So Péter spoke to the super of his building on Dózsa György Street, who agreed to let us use an empty room next to the coal storage in the cellar. It didn't cost us anything and there was no written contract. All the super asked was that we keep the place clean. Péter got hold of an enormous bass cabinet to service his brand-new West German Echolette bass head, which he had finally gotten from his mother and which now produced an incredible sound. István brought down his entire drum kit—five drums, top hat, and the two cymbals—and with my little Dynacord and the AKG mike, we created a full sound.

We continued to practice hard every day, as any band would. By the time we got to the date of the concert, we were really good—even by Gyuri's standards.

"You could maybe try 'Satisfaction' again," he said with a sly smile.

The day of the gig we showed up early for the sound check. A real sound check with a technician to test our instruments and our microphones. We spent at least forty-five minutes saying "check-check" into the Shure mikes, adjusting the level, the treble, and the bass. It was pretty awesome.

We were so much younger than the members of Omega, but that didn't seem to matter. We were even granted the honor of changing into our stage garb in the very same dressing room. They all welcomed us. Gabi of course. János Kóbor, aka Mecky, the front man with long blond hair. Laci Benkö, also on keyboard. György Molnár, aka Elephant, the lead guitarist. Then Tamás Mihály and József Laux, aka Blöro. I changed into a gauze shirt and jeans, and a white Afghan coat—trendy in those days in London—with stringy fur hanging on the bottom and around the wrist. A white fur coat wasn't exactly what people were wearing in Hungary those days, but it was a present from Denmark and I wore it with pride. Elephant offered his help.

"Come on, let's tune your guitar. I have an A tuning fork in my pocket." He plugged the jack chord into my guitar and the other end of it into the impressive Marshall stack, like the one Eric Clapton played on in Cream. When Elephant handed me the tuning fork, I hit the mike stand with it, held it to my ear, and compared the tone of the tuning fork with the A string of my guitar. It was way out of tune, and I was glad Elephant had helped me out.

"Okay, that should do it. Make sure your guitar is always in tune," he said. "Nothing matters more."

Tamás Mihály, the bassist, saw the sickly little white bass Péter was going to play.

"Use my Fender," he said.

Péter couldn't believe his ears. "You're really going to let me play your bass?"

"I don't think you'll break it," he said, smiling, as he handed it over.

István was allowed behind the Ludwig set of József Laux—maybe the nicest set of drums in the country, maybe in all of Eastern Europe. He was so obscured by the drum set that the audience could barely see him.

And then it was time to perform. The colorful floodlights blinded us and we could see almost nothing of the audience, but that turned out to be a good thing because we were so nervous. Our first number, "Homecoming Blues," was a song we had heard on a Taste album. István was totally out of rhythm and lost track of the song. Péter was out of tune and started in the wrong key. I forgot the words and hit some bad notes. But none of that mattered. We were on a real stage. We were loud and we were having fun in front of hundreds of boys and girls watching with envy.

We got better after that first song. A lot better. Our confidence grew with the encouragement of the crowd, and when we hit the first few notes of "Crossroads," I could feel the energy in the room elevate. They loved us! Omega stood in the doorway to the green room adjacent to the stage, watching. Gabi gave a thumbs-up, the ultimate confirmation. The boys were yelling and the girls were cheering. I guess no one had expected us to play so well. We played one number after another without stopping. When we got to the last song on our set list, "Need Your Love So Bad," the audience rose to its feet.

In the middle of the concert, I suddenly felt something very strange. I forgot all about the people around me. I wasn't nervous or worried any longer, I just got lost in the music and floated above the crowd. Nothing like that had ever happened to me before. It was supernatural. I was high, but it wasn't from anything I had smoked and it sure wasn't from pálinka. It was just the magic of the music, the electric guitar, something you could call Strato Magic. That was the moment I realized why it was worth fighting the oppressive bureaucrats—the moment I understood why musicians would suffer for those precious moments onstage. This was the ultimate freedom.

Suddenly, Gabi appeared on the side of the stage and shouted: "We're not ready to go onstage yet. Just keep playing." Unbelievable.

So we played one of our own compositions, a song inspired by Jimmy Page. The audience loved it. We improvised after that, jamming in front of a live audience. That went on for at least twenty minutes. We stopped only when Gabi signaled to us that Omega was ready to take the stage. "Give a big round of applause to the Purple Generator," Gabi shouted into his microphone from behind his new Hammond organ. "Aren't they great?"

There is nothing, really nothing, that compares to standing onstage strumming your electric guitar, singing and playing from your heart to an appreciative audience. I didn't think my love of rock and roll could grow any stronger, but it did in that moment. I remain forever grateful to both Péter and István for having been such great band members. And forever grateful to Gabi and all the members of Omega for allowing us to take their stage.

We sat for hours and hours—Péter, Baló, and myself—trying to wind down, but we couldn't. We walked all the way home, talking, dissecting the performance, sharing moments.

"Did you see that pretty girl asking me to hold her?" I asked Péter. "She said that she wanted to be my girlfriend."

I felt like a rock star.

CHAPTER TWENTY-SEVEN

I was a huge Steve Winwood fan. I had known the Spencer Davis Group since "Keep on Running" hit the British and European charts. I'd missed the group when it appeared in Budapest the year before, in 1967, but Winwood wasn't with them any longer so I didn't really mind. Without him, the Spencer Davis Group was just another band. When Steve formed his new band Traffic (my friends and I referred to him as Steve), I placed their NEVER ENDING TRAFFIC logo on the wall of my room, the wall of the summerhouse, my schoolbag, my guitar case, my books—every flat surface.

Steve was my role model as a musician. Refined, cool, and English—there was nothing pretentious about him. In all of the pictures, he stood out as a self-assured but understated person, as if to say, *I know who I am: I'm an English rock star. But that doesn't mean it has to be written all over me.* "Dear Mr. Fantasy" was my favorite song, and I'd play it on repeat for hours. I'd lay down on my bedroom floor, my head between the loudspeakers, close my eyes, and escape into a dream. Steve was the epitome of the cool rocker and I considered him a friend ever since my first "encounter" with the Spencer Davis Group. I prayed that Traffic would come to Budapest.

My prayers were answered.

It was early June and the sky was gray when I spied the poster on Rákóczi Avenue:

Concert by the English group Traffic
at the Sports Stadium, July 7, 1968
Supporting act: Jimmy Cliff and the Grease Band

I couldn't believe my eyes. Of all the bands... Traffic! Had I wanted this so badly that I imagined the poster? Was this a mirage? I walked down the street and turned a corner. Another poster. I walked a little farther and there was a third! It *was* true. Traffic *was* coming to Budapest. I had to tell Gyuri. I stepped into a phone booth to share the news.

"This isn't normal. Real rock stars don't come to Budapest," I said. "No band of this stature has ever been here. This must be a mistake."

"Just go and pick up tickets," he responded.

I didn't need to be told twice.

It became a summer of waiting. Each morning I woke up and counted down the days before I would see Traffic onstage. It would make all the difference in my life—not just as a teenager, but as a musician. *My* favorite band, *my* musical idol, playing in *my* city. It was one thing to have Traffic's records, but quite another to see them live. To be under the same sky, to see them up close, maybe even meet them in person. Only someone long deprived of such opportunities could truly cherish the moment. This was going to be a watershed event for rock and roll in Hungary, for tens of thousands of young Hungarians.

With three tickets in hand—one for me, one for Gyuri, one for Péter—I knew that as much as seeing Steve play would be a dream come true, I had to meet him. In person. Face-to-face. I had to shake hands, maybe talk to him and ask for an autograph. This was my opportunity. I would never get another.

My first task was to find out where the band would be staying. I called all the best hotels, speaking to the receptionists in English.

"Hello, I am visiting from England and was hoping to meet up with some friends. Can you check your bookings, please, and let me know if you're expecting any visitors from England around July 7. Mr. Winwood? Mr. Capaldi? Mr. Wood, maybe?" I've never had a heavy Hungarian accent, more like a he-could-be-from-anywhere accent, so my voice didn't give me away.

My assignment may have proved my dedication to Traffic, but it was a fairly stupid idea. I should have known that the hotels wouldn't provide me with any information. These front-desk clerks all worked for the secret police and weren't so easily fooled. Western visitors were routinely spied on—even ordinary Westerners. But this was a famous English rock band, so the authorities would observe them more strictly than most. They could corrupt the youth of Hungary! They could incite a revolution! Things could get out of hand, as they did after the concert by the Spencer Davis Group, when kids turned over trash cans and smashed store windows.

It was Father who held the key. He contacted one of his friends in trade, who told him that rooms had been reserved by the State Organizing Bureau (ORI) "for some English musicians" at the Hotel Szabadság. An appropriate choice considering *szabadság* is the Hungarian word for "freedom." So I went to Rákóczi Avenue to investigate the hotel and do a little reconnaissance. I checked out the entrance, went inside the foyer, peeped into the restaurant, had a word with a busboy.

The last few weeks before the concert were spent in agony, but then came July 7. I got up at six to get ready, which was ridiculous as the concert wasn't until much later in the day. But I couldn't wait. I checked our tickets more than once to make sure I got the date and time right—also silly because the date and time were etched into my mind.

Gyuri, Péter, and I got to the Sports Stadium early. Although our designated sector was in a good part of the stadium, there was no assigned seating. We wanted to make sure we got the best seats we could. As we were walking to the main gate, I noticed hundreds of policemen in the neighborhood, including some in plainclothes who were all too easily identified. We walked into the stadium between rows of police and members of the "Young Guard," the paramilitary arm of the Communist Youth League, who stood by with armbands that read ORGANIZER.

The Sports Stadium was somewhat smaller than its brother, the People's Stadium, right next to it. But it was still huge. The fact that Traffic would be performing here was symbolic. This was musical history in the making, a sign that the world cared about Hungary. More precisely, that Winwood, Capaldi, Wood, and Mason cared about Hungary.

We got very good seats in the "fighting arena" just a few yards from the stage. We were in the center of the stadium, where the hockey games normally took place. Between us and the band there were "only" metal bars and the police. We wanted to be close to the stage, close to the music, and close to the musicians who would be playing in front of the big stacks of Marshalls. Jimmy Cliff, the opening act, one of the apostles of reggae music, was very good of course, but he wasn't the one we had come to see. As he was playing—and he played wonderfully—dark clouds rose over the stadium. I'm sure I wasn't the only one worried that rain would wash away the concert and our dream with it. But then, as if by some divine act, just as Traffic was coming onstage the sun came out from behind the clouds. The long-awaited moment had arrived and even nature was on our side.

The musicians—Jim Capaldi, Chris Wood, Dave Mason, and then the "man" himself—looked very cool as they walked onstage. Winwood, wearing an Indian gauze shirt, waved to the audience and sat down behind his white organ. "Hello, Budapest," he said into the microphone. Jim Capaldi walked to his drums, Chris Wood hung a saxophone around his neck, and Dave Mason picked up a guitar and hit a few chords. The stadium was quiet with just a few shouts of "Traffic" and "Winwood" breaking through the crowd. I was on standby, ready to take pictures with my camera. I was angry that I hadn't brought my Philips cassette recorder, the way some others had. But then Traffic started playing and I forgot about everything. There was nothing else, just the music.

"Coloured Rain" was first.

Winwood mesmerized the audience with his organ playing, a jazzy sound made even more striking by the distortion. When the crowd figured out that he was actually playing the bass lines with his feet like a classical organist would, they went wild. He was especially fantastic when he played "Blind Man" and "Feelin' Good," neither of which I had heard before. Simply fantastic.

The police were very visibly present. They weren't there to enjoy the music, of course, rather to spot "irregular behavior." It was up to them to make sure that no one shouted anti-system slogans. The police scanned the crowd constantly, ready to "lift out"—that was the official term—anyone who deviated from acceptable standards of behavior. All was going well when Steve shocked the audience by saying, "The next song we would like to dedicate to the police. It's called 'Who Knows What Tomorrow May Bring.'"

"What was that?" I asked Gyuri and Péter. "Will the police intervene? Stop the concert? Take them away in handcuffs?"

"Incredible," Gyuri said, visibly worried. We froze. Hundreds, maybe thousands of kids all froze.

"Maybe they didn't understand. Maybe the interpreter was smart enough not to translate. Or maybe they can't reach their superiors and they don't know what to do," Péter added.

"Or maybe they are Traffic fans. Who knows?" I said, as it became clear that the concert wasn't being stopped and the music would continue. Clearly the police didn't understand the joke—if it was even meant as one. There was no change in anyone's behavior, although a smattering of laughter and cheers could be heard from the crowd, from the people who did understand the message. *Good for you, Steve*, I thought.

The last song was "Mr. Fantasy," my all-time favorite. There's something mystical about that number, and the guitar part is difficult. Steve played his light-green Fender Stratocaster, which was probably made especially for him. It seemed to me that the people at the Fender factory would probably beg a genius like Steve to accept the gift as their small token of their respect and appreciation. That was what I was thinking when I saw a strange-looking fellow bring the instrument to him onstage.

It was a magical moment. Chris Wood switched from saxophone to the organ, Dave Mason played bass, and Capaldi was on the drums. Listening to "Mr. Fantasy," we were all filled with happiness. I longed for time to stand still, for the moment to last forever.

CHAPTER TWENTY-EIGHT

G yuri, Péter, and I felt nervous as we walked away from the stadium that night, mainly due to the large presence of security forces. Police vans, which we mockingly called fairy-tale cars, were parked along the streets. Lots of them. The mounted police were on high alert, their horses as nervous as we were. Gyuri felt uncomfortable and decided to go home through the back streets. I wouldn't be swayed from my mission, so I doubled my steps and walked toward "Hotel Freedom."

But a few blocks from the stadium, out on Thököly Street—the main street in the district—some of the boys from the concert started kicking trash cans, shouting political slogans, and smashing windows. They vanished into the side streets when the police came into view; nevertheless, some were picked up and whisked away. The police weren't afraid to use force, to swing their batons and use their handcuffs. I was scared. I certainly didn't want to be locked up, but meeting Steve Winwood seemed worth the risk.

I was relieved to get to the Hotel Szabadság. It wasn't quite the Waldorf Astoria, which I had seen in photographs, but it wasn't bad, either. An old hotel, bombed out during the war, most of it had been rebuilt in the modernist style a few years earlier, with the exception of the main entrance, which was kept from the old days. I remember the color dominating the building, a greenish blue. The huge revolving door at the main entrance was the original one, which had seen movie stars, royals, generals, German Nazis, and then communists pass through. And now British rock stars.

Foreigners couldn't just stay anywhere in Budapest; they had to stay at designated hotels, to be kept track of. The designated hotels put in real effort, as even the communist government wanted to project quality and wealth when it came to foreigners, East or West. The Hungarian authorities wanted to show that we were better than other East Europeans. Of course they did. Even communists were competitive. And the Party wanted to be appreciated by the West—by the Brits, the Austrians, the French and West Germans. That mattered almost as much as Moscow's acknowledgment.

The Hotel Szabadság was their opportunity to impress. The interior was nicely redone in the style of the 1960s. The designers had some limitations—this was Hungary, after all—but it was obvious that as much as they had studied modern hotels in Paris, Rome, London, and New York, they wanted to show off our great Hungarian architectural heritage, too. The result wasn't bad. Certainly nothing to be ashamed of. The walls were covered with walnut panels. The marble floor—except for the shabby job the tile setter had done on the grouting—gave it grandeur. The chandeliers were modern, too, tubelike lamps hanging on wires, maybe twenty or thirty of them. Modern shell-like armchairs, red or black, were arranged around coffee tables in the lobby. A staircase led to the second-floor restaurant, winding around the foyer like a snake.

But there was something about this hotel that made it especially suitable for receiving visitors from the West: eavesdropping devices installed in most of the rooms. Bugs were fitted to the phones, under the bed, even in the bathrooms. Everyone had heard the story of a guest who had one day complained to his wife about the faulty toilet, only to find it miraculously fixed the next morning. The Party didn't stop there. The Hotel Szabadság was frequented by well-dressed prostitutes, women who were rumored to be paid agents of the secret service or who otherwise had been blackmailed into the act. They faded into the background, these women, as did well-dressed men who watched over the guests.

If I could just get inside the hotel, I'd stand a much better chance of meeting Steve and the rest of the band. It wouldn't be easy, though. Security was now heavy, with plainclothes officers standing at the entrance, next to the doorman. Who else would wear a suit and tie in the scorching sun?

I needed some of that famous Hungarian ingenuity to get inside the hotel, but it eluded me. I thought of trying the I'm-a-visitor-from-England line, but I abandoned it when I realized I would be asked for my passport. In the end I tried the direct approach.

"Hey, wait, you can't go in there," the doorman said when I tried to enter the hotel. The plainclothesmen looked on, ready to interfere.

"I just want to wait inside for the band. You know, the ones who played at the stadium."

"Yes, they are staying here, but you can't come in anyway. You are not from the State Organizing Bureau. Or are you?"

"No, I am not."

"Beat it," he said. "Stand over there with all the others. They are waiting for your friends, too."

So I joined the little crowd of hard-core fans, some of them holding the *Mr. Fantasy* album to be signed, others a picture of the band. Suddenly a small bus appeared at a distance, a police vehicle in front of it.

"Here they come!" a voice shouted.

The police car arrived, followed by a white-and-blue East German Robur bus with ORSZÁGOS RENDEZŐ IRODA ORI painted on the side. My heart was beating fast. First a couple of men and a woman, probably the roadies and the translator, stepped off. A mix of Hungarians and Englishmen, clearly distinguishable by the way they were dressed up. The crowd cheered as Mason, Capaldi, Wood, and finally Winwood exited the bus in style, the way real stars do. They waved to the little group that had assembled to meet them, stopping for a moment to shake hands and sign autographs. They were followed by bodyguards.

You look at pictures of musicians in the fan magazines. You listen to their records and see them onstage. But when they're so close you can touch them, observe their faces, look them in the eye... That's something else entirely. They look familiar, but different somehow, too. Everything is the same and everything has changed. There I was in the city I grew up in, on a street I'd walked a hundred times—and there was Mr. Fantasy himself.

I knew I had to pull it together. This was it. My one and only chance. I faked calm and pushed myself to the front of the crowd where Winwood was signing autographs.

"Hello," I said. "Welcome to Budapest." It wasn't the most inspired opening line, but it would have to do.

Steve looked up from signing an LP and smiled at me. He seemed kind, if somewhat reserved.

"Hello, who are you?" he said. "What's your name?" I liked his thick English accent.

"My name is András. I was at the concert." He was only four years older than me, but I felt like such a kid.

"Did you like it?" he asked while continuing to sign.

Did Steve Winwood just ask me if I liked his concert?

"I did," I said. "I really did."

"Thanks. You guys were a really responsive audience. I could tell that a lot of you knew the songs we played. That always feels good," he continued.

Words were coming out of my mouth—English words—but they seemed to float above me, disconnected. I felt separated from everything that was going on around me. Yet there I was.

"I know all your songs. I have all your records. You know this was the best concert I have ever been to. I will remember it forever. Thank you for coming to Hungary. And thank you for the comment on the police. You could do that, we can't."

He smiled.

I had wanted to say hello to Steve Winwood and now I had told him what I wanted to tell him. Yet there was more. I had a question.

"Steve," I said, with what I thought might be my very last breath. "Can I ask you who your musical hero is?"

"Ray Charles," he responded without missing a beat. He had stopped signing autographs and was talking only to me. "Have you heard of Ray Charles?"

"The blind American singer?" I asked. "Of course. He sings your song 'Georgia on My Mind.'"

"No, it's *his* song," Steve said, referring to the fact that, while it might have been written by Hoagy Carmichael, it was Ray Charles who made the song famous. I didn't want to tell Steve that I liked his version better.

"Ray Charles," I repeated. It was all I could manage.

"But you know you need to be careful about meeting your hero. Most of the time...well, he may not be the person you think he is."

I reflected for a moment, and then to my astonishment I said quietly—so quietly that I was sure he wouldn't hear—I said, "Too late, Steve, too late.

"I play in a band, you know. My band plays one of your songs," I continued.

"You're a fellow musician then, are you? Do you want to come inside, meet the other members of the band? Hey, Albert, let me introduce..." And he turned to me to ask me to repeat my name.

"András."

"Yes, meet András."

"Count Albert is my name, but just call me Albert," he said, extending his hand. I was shaking hands with the man who had given Steve Winwood the green Stratocaster to play "Mr. Fantasy." Count Albert looked messy and worn. He had a narrow, aristocratic face that was framed by long, straight hair. His eyes were ringed with faint purple circles.

I was now among the lucky few who split from the crowd and walked past the guards as they respectfully greeted Winwood and the rest of the band. He must have known that without him, the guards would never have let the little Hungarian in.

The doorman recognized me and grabbed my arm.

"He's with us!" Albert said in a strong, clear voice. "He is coming with us."

The doorman was clearly disappointed.

Inside the lobby Steve was surrounded by people asking for his autograph. I was standing next to him as he responded to each request. Then, as he was about to leave for his room, he turned to me and said, "Nice meeting you, András. I'm a bit tired, you know, it's been a long day. But I very much enjoyed talking to you. Maybe we'll meet again one day. Be good and work hard." And with that we shook hands.

I wasn't sure what I was to do next. All I knew was that I wanted to hold on to the moment as long as possible, and that the doorman was lying in wait for me. Albert must have understood this, too.

"Hey man," he said. "Do you have anywhere to be? Maybe you'd like to come out with some of the guys. We could go downtown and get something to eat, maybe listen to some music."

"Um, sure. I could do that," I stammered. "I mean, yes—of course."

"Great. Hang out here for a few until we get ready. We won't be long. Think of a nice restaurant with some good local music. Gypsy music."

I sat down in one of the shell-like chairs. Albert's idea

of "a few" was different from mine. I was beginning to worry that the management would throw me out. The doorman kept looking at me with suspicion, wringing his hands in a way that was vaguely threatening. Just when I had almost given up, Albert, Chris Wood, and Jim Capaldi spilled out of the elevator.

"Hey man," Albert said. "Andreas, here are the guys. Guys, here's Andreas." He missed my name by just one letter. This was a pinch-me moment.

"So, have you thought of a fun place to go?"

I cautiously suggested the Apostolok—the "Apostles" restaurant.

"This Apostles restaurant. That's a fitting place for a count?" Albert asked.

"The fittingest," I replied.

The Apostolok was a decently good place downtown by the Elisabeth Bridge on the Pest side of the city, by the Danube. The restaurant had survived both the war and the communist takeover, in spite of the connotations of the name. The food was excellent, and the service was good. Nothing to be ashamed of.

"This was built at the time of the monarchy, when Hungary was prosperous," I told them. "I hope you won't be disappointed."

"Don't worry. If the food is good and the music is good, that's all we need," Jim Capaldi pitched in.

"Yes, that's all we need," the ever-quiet Chris Wood nodded.

Budapest, with its million inhabitants, was still more like a village for those who lived in the center of town, who frequented clubs, who listened to Radio Free Europe and Radio Luxembourg. That's why, walking into the

Apostolok, I knew that all eyes were on us. Everyone knew who these Englishmen were, although they were likely wondering who I was. A waiter led us to our table, and we squeezed ourselves into the boxlike booth. A short time later we were joined by other Hungarians who said they were artists: painters, filmmakers, and musicians.

"Hello, my name is András," a tall, thin guy, with long hair, said in English.

"Can someone help translate?" he continued in Hungarian.

"I can," I said.

"Good. Tell them that I am a filmmaker, and that I was there in the stadium, and if they don't mind I'd like to sit at the table. I am a great fan."

I didn't mind translating, and my namesake was nice; he wasn't pushy at all.

"Go ahead, sit down," Albert insisted, and we made room for the other András.

Then there was a musician, a well-known bass player I had heard Gabi talk about, even though I didn't recall ever seeing him onstage. He, too, settled in at our table. We had a real conversation about music then, about instruments, about the problems rock musicians had in this country. The Hungarians couldn't stop asking questions, and the English responded with a great deal of patience.

And I still couldn't believe that I was sitting at a Budapest restaurant with Jim Capaldi and Chris Wood, and my new friend "Count" Albert. Wood and Capaldi came across as quiet and reserved.

"So András," Chris Wood asked. "Where is this secret police of yours?"

"They're everywhere."

"Everywhere?"

"See those guys sitting across the room? I'm almost certain they're from the secret police. But don't worry, they wouldn't dare interfere with people like you!"

"So why are they here, then?" Capaldi asked.

"Because of us. Because they want to know what *we* are up to," the other András said, picking up the thread of the conversation. "They're afraid of me and our friends here, more than they are afraid of you."

Capaldi waved toward the secret police, who reluctantly smiled back. Not everyone smiled, though. Some older Hungarians sent disapproving glances our way. "We get those looks all the time in England, too. It's just that older people, they don't understand us," Albert quipped. Then he grilled me about things to do in Hungary, the country's history, the paintings on the wall. He asked about life in Hungary.

"It must be difficult to be a musician here?"

"It's not easy," I told him. "But we make an effort. Instruments are hard to get. Records, too. But some of our bands are really good. I have a band, too."

Count Albert thought *the Purple Generator* was a great name for a band. I wished Péter was there to hear him say that. And just when I thought the evening couldn't get any better, it did.

"Look," Albert said. "We have a lot of Hungarian forints to spend and there isn't much we can do except burn them. They won't allow us to take them out of the country." Albert reached into his pocket and pulled out a stack of hundred-forint bills, the highest denomination. Lots of them.

"We'll stay as long as the money lasts. Want to help us spend it? We could use a tour guide."

Nice! As we were discussing where to go—I had suggested Lake Balaton—a Roma band came to our table to play. They wanted to impress the English guests and they did, playing their instruments masterfully. Capaldi, who had some Roma blood in his veins, was impressed by the man behind the cimbalom. A native Hungarian instrument that looks like an open piano with two sticks that hit the strings, the cimbalom is a difficult instrument to play. Capaldi got up from his seat, walked over to the band, and tried it out. Then a young Roma violinist played a short virtuoso piece, and when he finished, Capaldi hugged him.

Way past midnight Capaldi, Wood, and Count Albert with all the Hungarians in tow went back to the hotel and I went home, happy to know that I would be joining them for a trip to Balaton the next day. I gave Albert my phone number. My mind was racing as I walked home, through Csikágo, the rough neighborhood of the Seventh District, then on to Andrássy Boulevard, where I caught a tram on Lenin Boulevard. Bakers at Glazner, the bakery on the corner of our street, were already loading a truck with fresh morning bread, and I picked up a loaf.

CHAPTER TWENTY-NINE

T he phone rang early the next morning.

"Are we going?" asked Albert.

"You bet we are!" I replied.

I left a note for my parents on the kitchen table saying, "I am off to Balaton with Traffic, don't worry!"—as if I were just going to the store to pick up some milk. I was back at the Hotel Szabadság by nine.

Albert was sipping his coffee at the restaurant when I arrived. The rest appeared a few minutes later, looking worn and tired like Albert, but happy enough. The other András joined us. We took a taxi to the Southern Train Station, where Albert insisted on paying for all of us. But he wanted to be among Hungarians, he said, so we didn't need to travel first-class. There was nothing pompous about these guys.

Albert was enjoying himself on the train, drinking an immense amount of alcohol he had bought at the station kiosk, including a bottle of Unicum, a bitter schnapps and a Hungarian specialty. He didn't get drunk, but he sure was friendly, talking to the Hungarian passengers.

"Anyone speak English?" he asked.

A tubby boy with a Beatles haircut said he did.

"My name's Albert. What's yours?"

"Máté," the boy responded. "Are you from London?"

"We live in the country, not far from London. How come you speak English?"

"I listen to Radio Luxembourg. You know Radio Luxembourg? Good music!"

"Yes, I know Radio Luxembourg. I listen to it as well. Want a cigarette?" Albert pulled out a red box with a gold rim.

"Dunhill. *Hoppáááá*," the boy said. "This is very good cigarette. Thank you." Almost all the boys and one of the girls took one. Máté lit the Dunhill while the others put their cigarettes into their shirt pockets, a valuable possession to be treasured.

"Fuck, what a great guy this English!" one of the boys raved, in Hungarian. "Who is he?"

I was proud to tell them that Albert was with Traffic, and that *I* was with him.

"Oh, boy, so he is famous!" Máté stated rather than asking. "I know Traffic. 'Hole in My Shoe.'"

Albert grinned at the mention of the song and shook hands with Máté.

"Nice kids," he said.

In a few hours we boarded a big boat in the harbor of Tihany on Lake Balaton. Balaton is our sea, the place to be when school's out. Every summer boats like this were on the lake providing entertainment for young people. They were operated by the travel organization of the Communist Youth League, Express, which ensured the guidelines for "decency." They failed, because young people came to enjoy themselves and sometimes their behavior wasn't "decent" at all. Summers are hot in Hungary, and sometimes it got pretty steamy.

As it turned out Liversing was playing on our boat, with our friend from last night on bass. The band was on top of their game. Their sound was good, so much better than when I had heard them at the Danuvia on Angol Street. They wanted to impress the English. Albert was smiling, rolling his funny cigarettes and puffing away. He looked satisfied, his face appearing even thinner between his long, dark hair hanging on the two sides.

With a bottle of wine in hand, Albert sat next to me and talked of his travels and what it was like to be a roadie. He was a lucky man, he said, because he had the best job in the world.

"Don't you ever want to go onstage and play with them?" I asked.

"I don't have to be onstage to feel like I'm a member of the band. And my guitar playing is nowhere near theirs."

"I saw you hand the green Stratocaster to Steve?"

"You noticed that?"

"Yes, that was a beautiful guitar. Then Steve played 'Mr. Fantasy.'"

"But you know what? Without me, the band would hardly be able to play," Albert told me with a laugh.

"Tell me about the Cottage, Albert. What's it like?" We were sitting cross-legged by the railing on the boat, with the music blasting, but far enough from the loudspeakers to have a decent conversation.

"It's a big white house, which isn't like a cottage at all. It's a mansion. There's a stage outside in the garden," he explained. "We can play as late and as loud as we want. You know, there's magic there."

I was thinking that I, too, would love to have a big house like that and imagined myself sitting there with my friends, with all the instruments around. Nobody slept that night. We just stayed up talking about all kinds of things. Around six o'clock the next morning, Albert, Wood, Capaldi, and I were back at the station in Balatonföldvár, waiting for the train back to Budapest. This is where we would say goodbye.

Jim and Chris shook hands with me, but the count hugged me and said: "We are friends now. I'll send you some records. Be a good boy, and study hard. Practice your guitar." And as a sign of our friendship, he gave me the address of the Cottage.

I felt a terrible emptiness as their train disappeared from sight. Something I'd felt only once before, when my grandfather had died. Like falling into a black hole. For two days I'd been part of Traffic, one of the greatest bands ever; part of their world. Now they were all gone and once again we are separated by an insurmountable wall, an impenetrable curtain, that damn Iron Curtain.

For weeks afterward, I was excited about the arrival of the postman, and thinking that the records, the ones Albert had promised, would arrive. They never did, but I was almost certain that he had sent them. Someone, I thought, maybe the postman, had kept them for himself.

In October that year a nasty article appeared in the Hungarian press about Albert, real name Albert Heath.

The Hungarian piece was an inflammatory story, supposedly in response to something originally written about in the *New Musical Express*. According to *Youth Magazine,* Count Albert had to justify his "prolonged stay" in Hungary to his bosses, Traffic. The Count apparently argued that the Hungarian authorities held him in the country for five days. *Youth Magazine* "exposed" this as a lie and said that Albert "had been seen among other places at the Apostolok restaurant and on the cocktail boat on the Balaton, attempting to try out all the alcoholic beverages available." I was right, they were being followed. We all were.

CHAPTER THIRTY

I was riding high after the Traffic concert. It might have been the proximity to rock greatness—or maybe it was just the experience of hanging out with a bunch of cool guys, knowing I could hold my own—but I felt more at home with myself than I had in a really long time. I was starting to relax, to let down my guard. And as I did, I felt as if I was coming to know who I really was, regardless of where I lived or what language I spoke. I felt good. I felt strong.

I should have known it wouldn't last.

It was Péter who broke the news. It was early, maybe 7:00 a.m., when I heard an urgent knocking at our door. I opened the little security window to see who it was. My friend looked worried and pale.

"Open the fucking door," he said. And then, "Haven't you heard?"

"Heard what?"

"Czechoslovakia was invaded at midnight," he said. "Bill Ramsey called from Munich to ask if we're all right."

"Invaded? By whom?" I asked.

"The Warsaw Pact," he said, breathless. "They marched into Czechoslovakia and are confronting the people in Prague." And then, "Andris...Bill said there were Hungarians among the occupiers."

I was dumbstruck.

Péter continued. "Alexander Dubček, the Czechoslovak leader—you know, the strange-looking guy with the big spectacles, the one who looks worried in every picture? He was forced to resign. Bill said that many of his artist friends are fleeing Prague. Some have already been rounded up. It's the end of the Prague Spring. He wasn't able to say more because the phone went dead."

I thought my eyes were open to the harsh realities of the world. I thought I had a broad view of politics and culture. Hadn't I lived in both East and West? Didn't I listen to banned radio stations and read forbidden newspapers? I knew that my teachers were giving us contradictory and confusing messages about what was happening politically—and how we were expected to respond to it—which was why I relied on my parents, who had the courage to explain things honestly to me.

I thought I knew what to expect. But I never expected war.

Over the past several months Gyuri and I had been comparing the news on Radio Free Europe or Voice of America with the official media—Radio Kossuth and *Népszabadság*, the Party daily. Father taught us to read between the lines.

"See this article?"

I wondered why he was asking. "It's about the great

meeting the leaders of the Hungarian party had with the Communist Party of the Soviet Union."

"No, that's not really it. There's a hidden meaning you have to learn," he said. "Sometimes it's what's missing from the text that's most important. What's *not there* is the thing worth knowing. When the authorities say that the leaders of Hungary and the Soviet Union had a fraternal exchange of views, but don't mention what really happened, trust me, Andris—there was a real shouting match. You know who almost always wins that shouting match, don't you? It's not us. It's not the Poles. It's not the Czechs. Like it or not, it's the Soviets. That's the way it always is. And that's why we need the Czechoslovaks. Maybe if we stick together we'll be strong enough."

Father also told us to be on the lookout for vague descriptions and smooth talk, for people who say "trust me."

"Trust only a few and certainly not those who suggest they know the unquestionable truth. There is no unquestionable truth. Nobody knows all the answers. It's right to question things you don't understand."

I knew a lot about the things that had gone on in Czechoslovakia over the past months, again from Father.

"The Czechoslovaks are trying to go their own way, like we, too, are trying something different. Remember I told you about the experimental economic reforms?" Yes, he had told me about the reforms. "But they'd better be careful. If Dubček makes the mistake of challenging the domination of the Soviet Union, they'll get tough. Let's just say that Moscow thinks *one size fits all* is a good model."

He loved to use metaphors from his beloved profession.

"How stupid would it be to make clothes in one size and expect everyone to feel comfortable wearing them, big or small, fat or skinny."

His face was serious. He didn't mean this as a joke.

"These elements of reform Dubček has introduced—they're similar to our own but even more relaxed, and that could be a problem. They've 'loosened up the system,' as the Party jargon would suggest. There's more debate—real and healthy debate. Artists and journalists can finally breathe."

That made Father happy. And when he was happy, I was happy. But as with everything behind the Iron Curtain, it was happiness restrained by caution.

"This could all be too much for Brezhnev. If Czechoslovakia tries to leave the Warsaw Pact, others will no doubt try to follow. The Soviets will never let that happen. They won't think twice about using force."

Father was right. He just didn't expect to be right so soon.

The day before the invasion we had celebrated St. Stephen's Day with street parades, formal commemorations, and an air parade over the Danube complete with fireworks at night—a big sensation! It was *panem et circenses*—bread and circuses, as the saying goes: keep the people well fed and entertained. Hungary's national day was also called the Day of the New Bread, because it coincided with the new harvest, the first time bread would be baked from the newly harvested wheat. For years I thought the Day of the New Bread was a communist invention. Only later did I understand that it originated from pagan traditions and was revived by the communists to counter the religious celebrations of St. Stephen, the first Hungarian king.

Everything seemed right and peaceful that August 20. The year 1968 had been one of hope when I had let myself believe that Hungary could soon be a country where reading a book by George Orwell or watching *Dr. Zhivago* would not be a crime. And now this.

Father explained the seriousness of the events unfolding around us. "Look, boys, the truth is that it's war."

"You mean *real* war, with tanks and everything."

"Yes, with tanks and everything."

Péter, Gyuri, and I stood stunned. We listened carefully as Father described the situation.

"This is pretty much what happened when the tanks rolled into Hungary twelve years ago, when they crushed the revolution they nowadays call counterrevolution. You can't remember, you were too young."

But I did remember. I was four when the Russians invaded Hungary. I had heard the gunshots and watched from our window as men, women, and children crowded onto trucks with their few belongings. It seemed to me to be a nice idea to travel on top of a truck, and I vaguely remembered my parents arguing about whether to board one bound for Austria, or stay. The way my parents spoke, their tone of uncertainty, scared me as much as the armed man in civilian clothes, gun slung across his shoulder, excited me. I didn't really understand what was going on, nor did I understand the significance of the red, white, and green band on his left arm, but even at the age of four I knew that things were serious, that this wasn't just another excursion organized by the trade unions.

Days after the Russians rolled into Budapest with their

heavy weapons, I heard a ferocious rumbling in our street. Tanks. Gyuri and I rushed to the balcony, two small boys who stood mesmerized by the magnificent green tanks with the red stars. These were Soviet tanks, but what did I know? This was exciting.

"Gyuri, look at the man on the tank," I shouted. "He has a gun!"

"Look, there's another one behind him. And another," Gyuri said.

"You come inside!" Mother screamed. She knew the soldiers were fierce, that they had orders to *shoot to kill.* What she didn't know was that they were armed with Kalashnikovs, a new breed of rifle never used in combat before those early days of November 1956. It was a grim honor for Budapest. And now, twelve years later, I was imagining those same Kalashnikovs trained on families in Prague who were crying in despair or boarding trucks bound for Vienna.

My father picked up the map from the bookshelf and described the military situation in as much detail as he could, filling in the gaps in the scarce information. He made clear that the Czechoslovaks didn't stand a chance, even if there was resistance from within the population. He urged us to understand the motives behind the occupation, which in his mind were fairly simple.

"The Soviets won't allow their empire to collapse. If the Czechoslovaks succeed in breaking away, nothing would prevent us from chipping away, either. The Poles would follow. The Russki are scared of that, just like they were scared of the domino effect of Hungary becoming independent in 1956," he explained. "This is the first real crisis you will have to face as grown-ups. I want you to understand the possible consequences."

I was thrilled to be thought of as a grown-up.

"What are you going to do now? What should we do?"

"You do nothing. Stay home until I tell you it's okay to leave the house. I'm going to try and find Otto." Uncle Otto was father's friend and a former colonel in the army. "I can trust him to find out what's really going on. The official radio won't tell us the truth. Reading the newspapers tomorrow is pointless. The foreign stations will be jammed."

My father opened the big closet in the hallway, looking for the raincoat he didn't really need on such a sunny day. His mind was probably elsewhere. He continued talking as he pulled on his coat.

"It's awful that Hungary is one of the invaders." He looked sad and angry as he said this. "We of all nations should know what it means to be invaded by the Soviets and what will follow. The least we should have done is stay out of it."

"Why?" This was Péter's question. It was also mine.

"Because of dignity, because of honor. Because that would have been the right thing to do."

State radio explained the importance of this most recent military action, how it was necessary for the survival of the Socialist Camp and the preservation of the achievements of the Working Class of the Socialist World. They spoke of solidarity, a word I had heard endlessly repeated on radio, too often to take seriously. The news was dry, matter-of-fact.

Radio Kossuth

The Hungarian News Bureau was authorized from an authoritative place to announce the following:

To fulfill the request by the Party and State leadership of the neighboring Czechoslovakia the Government of the Hungarian People's Republic in cooperation with other allied countries is lending support, including military support to the brotherly Czechoslovak people in order to prevent the dangers of a counterrevolutionary turn caused by the internal antisocialist and external imperialist forces.

There was a twist in the news later that day:

The Hungarian leadership followed with extreme interest and special attention the positive developments in Czechoslovakia since the beginning of the year in their efforts to correct the previously sectarian mistakes. However, it turned out that the developments later did not serve the interests of the Czechoslovak people.

Read between the lines!

This statement must have resulted from a big fight within the Hungarian Politburo, as the decision to participate in the invasion would not have been made lightly. Clearly there were some in high positions who regretted the failure of Dubček's experiment. Like most of my friends, I had a deep sympathy for the Czechoslovaks. We shared a common fate behind the Iron Curtain, each in our own barracks in the Eastern camp. No two captive nations were closer. Czechoslovakia was a hostage. Her failure was our failure.

Father was angry and sad when he came back. He didn't tell us what Uncle Otto had told him; he just sat for long silent minutes lighting one cigarette after another. He was, no doubt, contemplating his future. In the months before the invasion, Father had been invited to take part in a committee that was preparing some market-friendly reforms to be introduced on the first of January, the coming year. Dubček had just come to power and was attempting similar reforms, and we were all watching carefully. As the radio announcer had said at the time, "Hungarian leadership followed with extreme interest and special attention the positive developments in Czechoslovakia since the beginning of the year."

The market reforms that Father was involved in were intended to open Hungary up to the rest of the world. They advocated less central planning, more private initiative, and a relaxed relationship with the West. Hungarotex, the textile company where father was second in command, was working with Western businesses like Levi Strauss and Company in San Francisco. Attuned as he was to both social and economic issues, Father tried to find a middle ground that would combine the best of both worlds.

His boss at the company, Uncle György, was a family friend and one of the "reformers," as Father would refer to himself and his colleagues. The two men exchanged information about the world situation at their weekly game of canasta, and during weekends together at our summerhouse. The card playing wasn't important, and neither was the fresh country air. These gatherings were about an honest and vigorous exchange of ideas, the chance to talk about what they had read in the *Neue Zürcher Zeitung* or the *International Herald Tribune.*

Father had been hopeful when he saw Hungary and Czechoslovakia moving in the same direction. Now, with Dubček gone, he was worried. What would happen to our own country? "The conservatives—the ones who still mourn the death of Stalin...they'll surely use this as a pretext to fight back," he said. "With the full backing of their friends in Moscow."

That afternoon we sat in the kitchen behind closed windows—Father, Péter, Gyuri, and me—and tried in vain to tune in to the Western radio stations. Radio Free Europe and the VOA were being jammed, with the broadcast coming in only when music was being played. Finally, on some unfamiliar wavelength, we managed to catch the Hungarian broadcast of the BBC. That's when we heard the details of the invasion. The commentator spoke of half a million foreign troops marching into Czechoslovakia. We sat there for hours, all very quiet, the radio turned down low so that the neighbors wouldn't hear, although we suspected they were listening to the same broadcast. Mother joined the conversation. She was worried, of course, but she tried to ease our fears by insisting that she was needed in the kitchen. Even in the worst of moments, she thought of feeding our family.

My father's future was on the line that day. Would the small capitalist-style reforms he had supported come to a screeching halt? Would he be able to keep his job, a position from which he had been able to influence an opening to the West? Father had no doubt been labeled a capitalist by hard-line communists for the way in which he advocated elements of a market economy and the limited freedoms that came with it. This could mean big trouble for him.

Father received a few worried calls from friends who spoke in a kind of coded language. One friend advised, "Don't go shopping on Lenin Boulevard today," a clear warning to stay away. Another said that her husband had been drafted on twenty-four hours' notice. Our neighbors on the floor came by to ask if we were okay, and perhaps to ask Father for some advice. Our neighbor on the fifth floor, a high-ranking editor of the Party newspaper, but sympathetic to the Prague Spring, also came down to share his concerns.

"This is bad, really bad," Father told us. "But you know, in life you have to make compromises from time to time. That doesn't mean you should ever give up. You should *never* give up. I am fifty-one years old and may not live to see real change, but you might." He was bent over at the kitchen table as he said this, cracking walnuts to distract himself from the worry of the day. Father's frail figure—physically weakened from the hardships he'd suffered in the war, from the lasting effect of the typhoid fever—hid a man of determination and strong will and character.

"I can tell you. In a few years either this country will be free, or it will be doomed forever. The Czechoslovaks were right to try and change things, even more ambitious than we are, but they couldn't deal with the overwhelming force and internal opposition."

"But what went wrong?" I asked.

"Maybe some of the brave steps questioning the monopoly of the communists came too soon. I really don't know. Perhaps they should have made some compromises. Moved slower. I don't really know," he repeated. He was clearly in doubt about the reasons.

"Still, they were right. And the Russians were suspicious from the start. They decided to interfere a long time ago," he continued as he cracked another nut and slowly peeled off the shell. "At least the nuts are good this year." Father loved the large walnuts, which were in season at this time of the year.

"But it will be very difficult for them now, because there will be reprisals; people will land in prison. The lucky ones will be exiled. Their best writers, musicians, artists will be banned, imprisoned, or expelled. We know how it goes."

"What will happen here?" Péter asked.

"We are now alone."

CHAPTER THIRTY-ONE

A s 1969 approached I became aware of political propaganda in a way I never had been before, and with it,
the increasing vitriol of the Party. America was the one
constant. It was the bad guy, responsible for all the ills of
the world. My friends and I were immune to the skewed
presentation of the United States, but not everyone
could see through the Party's lies, because not everyone
listened to Radio Free Europe or had a father to help
him wade through all the propaganda.

The Prague invasion had been a tremendous shock,
made all the more upsetting when we heard that Dubček
had been assigned to work on a garbage truck. The news
about his whereabouts spread like wildfire, and wherever
he showed up to collect trash, hundreds of Czechoslovak
citizens showed up to greet him. His day on the job
turned into a day of demonstration—and both lasted
just one day.

There was great confusion among my teachers as
to how to treat this, and other news coming out of

Czechoslovakia. Before the Prague invasion, teachers had been told to prepare lessons explaining the slow reforms to their students. Previously they had been instructed to tell us why elements of market economy and cooperation with the West, as well as with the East, were compatible with communist dogma. Not an easy thing to do at the best of times. Now my poor teachers had been directed to do an about-face, to condemn the very things they had so recently promoted. I could see the divide among them. Some used doublespeak when talking about Czechoslovakia. They were supportive of the official line in class, but in private would express sadness over the invasion. Then there were those who took a hard line and applauded the invasion and, with it, the increased condemnation of America.

The Party spent a lot of time running down the United States. That didn't make sense to me. If America was such a bad place, why expend so much effort to explain just how awful it was? I guess it was because America was a mythical place to most Hungarians. Especially young Hungarians to whom it was a beacon of hope, a symbol of all that was worthwhile. I wasn't alone in wanting to visit the great American cities. All of my friends wanted to see New York, Chicago, Detroit, San Francisco, and Los Angeles. The USA was enigmatic and powerful, a place of optimism and wealth. The East was dull, full of sorrow and poverty. I thought a lot about America, but I never gave much thought to our immediate neighbor, the Soviet Union. It might only have been 150 miles away, a five-hour train ride, but it was a closed and secretive world, a place of cold power and darkness. I always felt like I could be an American. I never believed I could be a Russian.

It's not that I hated the Russians. In fact, Father had taken great pains to make sure that we didn't hate them. He would tell us how, during the war, he had picked up Russian as a POW in the city of Gorki somewhere on the Russian steppe. My father could easily have perished in the camp—many did—except, there too, he was considered useful because of his language skills.

He was lucky. Yes, a man who had been interred in a POW camp and fought in a fierce battle where so many had died could still be considered lucky. He had fought in the Battle of the Don, an ugly episode in an ugly war. Tens of thousands of Hungarians died fighting the Soviets, including Hungarian Jews like my father, who were herded before the troops to sweep for land mines—because pigs were considered more useful than Jews. But as he was wandering on the Eastern Front in the terrible cold, a Russian officer saved his life. When a soldier tried to pull my father's boots off at gunpoint, a passing officer saw what was happening, drew his gun, and *shot his own soldier.* Then, the Russian officer let my father go.

He would never forget that episode. And even when Father realized that the Soviet Russian communist experiment would end in disaster, he still made sure that his children understood that there were exemplary people from every country. I guess that's why he took us to see the pilot and cosmonaut Yuri Gagarin.

I was ten years old when this global hero came to Denmark. Father knew of my intense interest in space, how I had followed Gagarin's 1961 orbit and made sure that Gyuri, Zsuzsi, and I got to greet this rock star of the skies when he arrived at Kastrup Airport. I remember the enthusiastic crowd and Gagarin's broad smile, how he patted us on the head, put his hand on my shoulder. We shook hands and stood next to the man for a few minutes, as hundreds tried to get a glimpse of him. Years later, I was privileged to tell this story to astronaut John Glenn—a small East-meets-West moment for me.

Despite my love for all things Western—especially music—I didn't get too excited about the connection between rock lyrics and politics until the Russians invaded Czechoslovakia. That's when I became politically aware, and not just about what was happening in Europe.

It had been almost two years since I had lived with my aunt and uncle in the big house on Dózsa György Street. I rarely saw them anymore, even though they lived a floor above my buddy Péter's home, where I hung out most days. I saw my cousins from time to time, but I did my best to stay clear of Uncle, whom I had never forgiven for taking our radio.

My cousin András was making a name for himself as a professor's assistant in the Faculty of Mathematics at Eötvös Loránt University. I looked up to him as a sort of genius. A sharp, critical thinker with a tremendous aptitude for numbers, the exacting mathematician didn't subscribe to some of the more intractable ideals of the Communist Party. And although we never really discussed it, I don't think he supported the Russian intervention in Czechoslovakia, either.

At one of our rare family get-togethers—because despite my problems with Uncle, Father and Mother would occasionally invite them over—András pulled a comb from his pocket and showed it to me. It was shaped like the body of a fighter airplane, without its wings.

"This is a comb made by the Vietnamese comrades," he explained. "You know what material this is? It's the precious metal of an American fighter plane that had been shot down. The American bastards were spraying Agent Orange on the Vietnamese people! They're killing them for imperialistic reasons. They are murderers." András rarely got excited, but he had an intense passion in his voice as he talked about the Americans. "Look," he said, pulling out a picture of a downed F-4 aircraft. "This could be the plane the comb is made out of."

Some of the American songs I was listening to in those days were about the draft and the war in Vietnam, like the *Hair* album. At first I had no idea what *Hair* was about, other than that it was a collection of great songs, some of them funny, some of them—according to *New Musical Express*—sexually obvious and explicit. I didn't mind that. The lyrics had words I had never heard before, like *sodomy, fellatio, cunnilingus.* I had to look them up in the blue *Oxford Dictionary* on Father's bookshelf.

I didn't have detailed access to the storyline of *Hair*, so not all of it made sense to me. I loved the psychedelic album cover and the iconic photo on the sleeve—the green and red mirror images of a Jimi Hendrix Afro—but the LP's liner notes didn't do much to help me understand what it was all about. The word *Vietnam* wasn't mentioned, so there was no real context for what was happening. It took me a while to understand that it was all a protest against the war. It really sank in when I received a letter from my American friend Billy Hanson.

He started out as usual, with some niceties about his mother and father. Then his words turned gloomy.

My friend, this awful war is tearing us apart.
Brother received the draft, called up to serve in
the Army. He chose to leave for Canada, because
he does not want to be part of this war, this
killing. He's not the only one. His conscience
will not allow him to take part in this. I feel so
sorry for those who are sent over there. We pray
every day that it will end soon.

Thinking about Billy's brother desperately trying to
evade military service made me wonder if maybe something *was* wrong with America. For me, America was
Mr. and Mrs. Hanson. It was my friend Billy and my
teacher Ted. (Even if he did tear up my comic book.)
America was Jimi Hendrix and Janis Joplin. President
Kennedy, who had been so tragically assassinated. But according to state television, America was bad and President
Lyndon Johnson was evil.

Could it be true? I had to find out for myself.

There was a lecture at school about the Vietnam War. The
speaker was comrade secretary of the Communist Youth
League, a certain László Such-and-Such. A high-ranking
leader in the CYL, Comrade László was in his forties, with
his remaining hair turning gray. He seemed a little too old
for the youth movement, but he must have had the right
credentials. How else would he have become the secretary of such an important organization? Despite Comrade
László's eloquent use of the Hungarian language—and
his impressive use of bureaucratic talk—he wasn't very
convincing when he spoke about America. Just angry. He
was practically foaming at the mouth when he talked about
Lyndon B. Johnson, whom he compared to the devil.

"The just liberation struggle of the Vietnamese people is connected to our own struggle against imperialism. The unity of the fraternal socialist camp is strong, and the Americans will be defeated, thanks to the support of the Soviet Union."

Really? The unity to overrun small and defenseless countries like Czechoslovakia? With this last comment Comrade László lost what little credibility he had remaining.

When we were allowed to ask questions, someone from the back row quietly asked, "And what about China. Aren't they helping?"

"Who said that?"

Évi stood up. She was one of the brightest students in class.

"I know that Hungary supports the Vietcong, but I was wondering if we are joining forces with China on this?"

This spontaneous question had obviously not been cleared before the event. "If any of you have in mind asking about the Warsaw Pact and Czechoslovakia," the teacher coached us before the lecture, "I am warning you: don't! If you do, I will personally ask the headmaster to kick you out of school. Is that understood?"

The comrade secretary did nothing to clear up my confusion about America. When he spoke of the Americans, it seemed to me that perhaps the comrade didn't really know what he was talking about. He probably wouldn't have agreed with the message of the Country Joe and the Fish song "I-Feel-Like-I'm-Fixin'-to-Die Rag," but it seemed like he was trying to tie them together in some way and I didn't like that. Country Joe hated the war because it was an unjust conflict that was causing untold casualties. Comrade secretary hated the war because he hated America. Maybe they weren't that close after all.

I had been listening to Country Joe and the Fish lately, and had picked up on something melancholy in the songs of this psychedelic band from San Francisco, despite the folksy overlay of their music. I understood that "I-Feel-Like-I'm-Fixin'-to-Die Rag" was about the Vietnam War, but I was at such a distance from it all, and so bombarded with communist propaganda, that I found it hard to put it fully into context. It seemed to me that Country Joe was trying to say things that were close to what that silly comrade and my cousin were saying—things critical of an American government that was inflicting suffering on the Vietnamese. But Country Joe was much more credible to me than the comrade secretary. I put my trust in American rock musicians. They were, I thought, honest and decent people.

The songs of Country Joe and the Fish were rarely played on Radio Free Europe, and only once did I hear them on Hungarian state radio. It was in a program about Americans protesting the war in which the commentator emphasized the band's "progressive political" views. I didn't know what to make of it, but it seemed to me that if my friends like Country Joe were allowed to be so outspoken, then maybe the situation in America wasn't as bad as we'd been told. What would his punishment be here if he sang about the ugly invasion of a peaceful country? And I didn't mean Vietnam.

No doubt the overzealous Propaganda Department of the Communist Youth League had a daunting task. They had to condemn the United States, but they also knew they were on a "mission impossible" to placate young Hungarians who were enamored with American culture.

Sometimes *Ifjusági Magazin*, the monthly magazine of the Communist Youth League, and other publications "borrowed" articles from Western publications in order to look hip and to gain readers. They copied photos from Western magazines such as the *New Musical Express*, *Billboard*, and *Bravo*, but the paper and the printing itself were of such terrible quality that sometimes you couldn't even make out which one was Ringo and which one was John—or if it was really the Beatles at all!

The articles criticizing America were uninteresting and abundant. And they came from all over, even from Western newspapers like the *Morning Star* in the UK, which was actually a mouthpiece of Soviet propaganda. The fact that you could buy the *Morning Star* at any newsstand in Budapest rendered it totally irrelevant in my eyes. Propaganda was enough in one language, and the Party's "We Are with You Vietnam" campaign had gotten so out of hand that it was wearing us all down, even those who sympathized with the Vietcong. I guess it just backfired, like any propaganda.

A friend of mine, yet another Péter, had relatives in America. This Péter and I would get together in his family's small apartment close to the Western Train Station and look at the postcards his relatives had sent from different parts of the United States. Some were from Miami, others from Yosemite Park, and still others from San Francisco. I knew about San Francisco because it had one of the longest bridges in the world, with trams that climbed the steep hills. I also knew about it because I had heard of the Summer of Love a year earlier, and because San Francisco was where Scott McKenzie had set his very famous song.

This Péter regularly received packages from his American relatives: coffee, chocolate, jeans, and some things he considered useless, like a baseball. His aunt, who had fled the country in 1957, after the failed revolution, ended up in San Francisco. The uncle was an engineer who had started his own business. Now the family owned a big car, and a big house with a swimming pool. At least that's what the letters said, and I had no reason to doubt them. My own uncle Bandi owned a big American Plymouth in Antwerp.

Péter bragged about his American relatives and showed me a letter they had recently written from San Francisco. "The Americans just call it Frisco," he said.

> It's a nice place, very bohemian and we are running into a Hungarian couple all the time. Young people are out in the streets that are full of colorful little shops. It's a beautiful community and everyone is happy.
>
> There is a tiny little store selling pancakes on Main Street in Haight Ashbury. The woman is standing behind the counter from early morning until late at night, rolling the pancakes, like our grandmother used to. The place smells like our kitchen in the old days. Of course she is Hungarian!
>
> Mici is her name. She owns the store with her husband Karcsi. People stand in line to eat their

pancakes which she makes from a Hungarian recipe. The young people love them and eat them smeared with raspberry or apricot marmalade or an even spread of a mix of sugar and cocoa powder.

She also told us there is a nice girl, who wears sunglasses and colorful necklaces and jewels who comes to the store a lot, mostly at night. She wears a big Make Love Not War badge and is very nice. Her name is Janis and she sings in a band. She likes the pancake so much that she gave Mici some posters. I am sending the poster to you. It's signed. I don't know if you have ever heard about her? Maybe not!

Had we heard of her? Janis Joplin was one of our favorites!

The poster had strange, crooked letters in striking bright colors: BIG BROTHER AND THE HOLDING CO. PRESENTS JANIS JOPLIN! It was difficult to read the text, but the whole thing was so expressive that it told us all we needed to know—something amazing was happening in San Francisco. That gorgeous poster conveyed the prevailing mood in that city: crowded but peaceful, so colorful and friendly that I could almost hear the music. And no doubt the whole thing was drug-induced. But it was the handwritten message with its pretty signature that really brought home the magic of San Francisco.

I love you from the bottom of my... and she drew a heart in place of the word. *Janis.*

Péter had no idea what this poster would represent when he offered it to me. I carefully rolled it up, put a rubber band around it, and took my treasure home to hang in my room. I put the *Cheap Thrills* album on the Grundig tape recorder and just sat there, looking at it. I was now in San Francisco, too.

What was really happening there? I wondered. Cousin András on the one hand, Comrade László on the other, Country Joe and all that great music, and then this poster. I was confused. But then after a while things started to clear in my head and I came to the conclusion that the America I had come to love through Billy, through Ted, through the great rock and rollers—that America was alive and well. But maybe everything was not okay. Maybe America was a lot more complicated than I thought. Maybe there were many faces of America, and the one I knew was only one of them, even if it maybe was the most important one: the attractive, likable country of smart, creative, and brave young people.

The next time I visited my cousin in his home, I brought up the comb. I did so reluctantly because I didn't know how he would react, but I thought it was important because I did not want a disagreement to fester between us. I remember standing there looking him in the eyes and telling him that I had been thinking about the comb.

"So what are your thoughts? You still believe Americans are good?"

"Yes, but let me explain."

"Go on, I'm listening." But he wasn't really.

"I feel sorry for your Vietnamese friends. I really do. And I think war is terrible. I really do. But I don't think all Americans are like that. And I still don't think all Americans are bad."

This opened him up. "Why not? They are killing the Vietnamese," he said.

"The Americans I know are not killing Vietnamese. And I listen to these bands and singers, and none of them are killing anyone," I continued.

No, I really didn't think Americans were bad.

CHAPTER THIRTY-TWO

It was my last summer before graduating from high school. I had plans for Balaton—months of hanging out with my friends, long days spent swimming and sitting in the sun. But first I had to do time at the Golden Apple Agricultural Camp. In principle participation at camp was voluntary. In reality it was mandatory. Our time at the camp was considered part of the school curriculum, an opportunity for us to gain work experience and become better citizens. But really, it was organized labor disguised as education. I didn't mind the work, but they should have been honest about it.

I woke my first morning of camp to the sound of Thunderclap Newman. They were a fresh new British band with a lead singer-guitarist about my age, Jimmy McCulloch. I wanted to be like Jimmy. I wanted his guitar, a white Fender Telecaster. The keyboardist was a former postmaster, a big man with a big beard. I tried to picture a Hungarian postmaster from the Red Horn Socialist Brigade of the general post office quitting his job and joining a rock band. It was hard to imagine.

I was thrilled to hear "Something in the Air" blasting from the loudspeakers, even though I couldn't image how the authorities could be so ignorant as to not know what it was about. A song about guns and ammo and instigators? But there it was that first day, as it would be every day after that, blasting from the loudspeakers at the camp. We heard it when we woke up, when we walked to breakfast, when we finished work for the day, and before we went to bed.

In that hot summer of 1969, this revolutionary song about no specific revolution was an anthem to freedom. Just a year earlier there had been riots in Western Europe and America, all of which ended in violence. The papers carried photographs of police in military gear clashing with students on the streets of Paris, viciously striking protestors with their batons, hosing them down as they fought back with cobblestones. State television showed pictures of the riots in America in the aftermath of the assassination of Martin Luther King, of workers across Europe standing in front of factory gates holding signs with anti-government slogans. These were anti-capitalist protests, the government declared. A fight by the people against a repressive and exploitative system.

Maybe they were, maybe they weren't. But the authorities feared ambiguity—which, again, they considered infectious. They were no doubt pleased to see the mess that students caused in capitalist America and Western Europe, but they didn't want such protests here. They knew they had to tamp us down before we got "ideas" ourselves. So even though my friends and I were hoping for at least a small revolution, something we could be proud of, we knew the authorities had us under their control. A control that extended to the Golden Apple Agricultural Camp.

When I look back on my youth, it seems that way too much of it was spent in the company of supervisors. Perhaps it was. The supervisors at this camp were a mixed bunch. Some would allow us to have fun, as long as we got our work done. They graciously pretended not to see us holding hands or drinking a bottle of wine. Just carrying on like teenagers, really. Then there were the others, strict supervisors, some downright cruel, who made it their business to see that we kept to the rules: no messing around between boys and girls; no cross visits between the boys' and girls' dormitories; nobody outside quarters after curfew. They expected us to pick five crates of fruit each day, and to have fun in the manner mandated by the Communist Youth League.

I had become a member of the Communist Youth League by this time. It was a natural progression, like becoming a Drummer Boy, the first stage of organized indoctrination (which took place at age eight), or donning the Soviet red scarf and uniform to become a Pioneer at age ten. When I was fourteen someone from the district office of the Communist Youth League had shown up at Stephen I school and given us a silly political speech about being patriots and raising the Party banner. He explained the importance of being good young communists; then began the registration process, which included providing him with two small head shots, one of which would be glued into my little red membership book, the other affixed to a registration card that would be used to keep track of my activities.

Only idiots took their membership seriously. It was a

formality, a rite of passage, quite different from full Party membership. And even that wasn't as it seemed. In principle Party members exerted influence on political policy and had a say in the decision-making process. In the real world those privileges were reserved for the comrades at the top. Still, being a member of the Party was a requirement for most promotions, so people joined for that, if for no other reason. There weren't many true believers, despite what the authorities said.

The Communist Youth League had many carefully crafted slogans okayed by the Party higher-ups:

It is our revolutionary duty and historic responsibility to construct a highly developed socialist society.

Young people, studying is the way forward toward social progress.

May the everlasting friendship between the Soviet and the Hungarian people flourish.

Long live and prosper the unity of the international working classes in their struggle against imperialism.

I, like most of my friends, paid no attention to any of this. My thoughts were elsewhere, on girls and music. Since the Golden Apple Agricultural Camp had both, I was happy to do my duty. Our camp was in the south of the country, not far from the village of Gara and the Yugoslav border. From the tops of the trees where I worked picking fruit, I could see the separation between our two countries. There were rumors that the Yugoslav government wouldn't return defectors, but that wasn't entirely true. Occasionally, the Yugoslavs would turn back a Hungarian, an East German, a Czech, or a Pole. I had heard of two young men who had been shot and a third in their company who had been delivered to the Hungarian authorities.

As was so often the case, the fate of the individual was determined by the political climate. While the relationship between Hungary and Yugoslavia wasn't as bad as it had been in the 1950s, we weren't allies, either—not since Yugoslav leader Josip Tito broke ranks with his Soviet "family" and rejected the "offer" to become a member of the Warsaw Pact. Our southern neighbor wasn't exactly the West, nor was it the East. It wasn't a friend, but neither was it considered a foe. It was another no-man's-land, somewhat less dangerous to those who wanted to flee. If you desperately wanted to defect—and many people did—you could do worse than cross the border to Yugoslavia.

To legally travel to the West you needed an exit visa, a stamp in your passport called a window. Even though the system was somewhat relaxed now, more so than it had been at any time during the thirteen years since the bloody revolution, you still needed this "window" to travel outside the Iron Curtain. Hungarians could travel freely to other Eastern European countries, but travel to the West was still very difficult.

The coveted window could be withheld without any reason. Something you or a family member had done in the past. Revenge for a long-ago slight. A comment about Party leadership, perhaps, or some rough joke about Comrade Brezhnev, like this one:

Comrade Brezhnev is on a visit to an African country. He gives a big open-air speech:

"I bring you Communism!"

The people erupt, chanting, "Um-ba Brezhnev, um-ba Brezhnev, um-ba Brezhnev."

He continues: "All the power will be in the hands of the workers!"

"Um-ba Brezhnev, um-ba Brezhnev!" the people shout once more. This goes on for a while. Each time the values of communism are stressed, the crowd goes wild with "Um-ba Brezhnev!"

In the evening Brezhnev and the king of this African country go bathing. Changing into his swimsuit, the king looks at Brezhnev with what the Soviet leader assumes is admiration, maybe even envy.

The king says: "Such a big man, but such a small um-ba!"

That alone, told at the wrong place at the wrong time, would be enough for a REJECTED stamp on a visa application.

Tens of thousands of Hungarians wanted to see the world—and then return. Disappointed or not with the life they had here, these folks considered Hungary their home. They were the people who had a for-better-or-worse attitude toward the country, the ones willing to wait for the better days they believed were ahead. This was where they were born. This was where they would stay.

But many had had enough of the harassments and wanted to leave for good. Perhaps they could see nothing but a bleak future. Perhaps they had been separated from family who were already on the other side. Once these people obtained their travel documents, they never looked back. Of course they lied about the purpose of their visit. And they made meticulous plans, down to the last detail: the exact day, hour, and minute of departure from the rest of the tourist group to which they were assigned, carefully avoiding the plainclothes police embedded in the group, who watched their every move. They knew the route they would take, the amount of money they would need, the clothes they would wear. They had that all-essential phone number and address of an acquaintance who would help them on the other side. If they knew no one, they would rehearse what they would say to the first policeman they'd meet.

"Wir sind Ungarische Flüchtlingen. Bitte helfen sie uns."

We are Hungarian refugees. Please help us.

It would be enough.

CHAPTER THIRTY-THREE

F rom my perch in the orchard I could see field soldiers driving Soviet-made four-wheel-drive GAZ vehicles, maybe a mile away. They patrolled in teams of two, buddies watching over each other in case one of them got the urge to flee.

The soldiers carried Kalashnikovs, the submachine gun of the Soviet Red Army and other Warsaw Pact armies. The weapon, known as an AK-47, was also widely used by the liberation armies of Africa, Asia, and Latin America, guerrilla forces fighting for independence against imperialist suppressors, primarily the United States of America. A murderous weapon used to keep down the people of Eastern Europe, the Kalashnikov terrorized Hungarians, and for good reason. Valued for its simplicity and accuracy, this weapon could effectively target an enemy at up to forty-five hundred feet, although it was most effective at nine hundred. It functioned as both a single-shot and a repeating rifle, and even under the worst weather conditions was easy to maintain.

A self-taught Russian peasant-turned-tank-mechanic was the brains behind the Kalashnikov. Mikhail Timofeyevich Kalashnikov became a weapons designer after being shot in the shoulder during World War II, drawing the first sketches of the AK-47 as he lay recovering in a field hospital. Kalashnikov was considered a hero in the Soviet Union, and was the recipient of the Order of Lenin, the highest decoration awarded to a Soviet citizen.

The orchards were a beautiful but unpleasant workplace. We spent long hours in the burning sun picking apples or peaches, whichever was ripe that day. Every two hours we'd get a break, a chance to talk to some of the other kids in the small teams we had been assigned to. I was lucky to be in a team with György, a friend from home. György was in Péter's class and part of the circle of friends that included Péter, István Králik, Gyuri, and me. A good guy and a great athlete, György had been a water polo player on the best team—the Vasas—which had originally represented the Iron and Steel Workers Union. That the Iron and Steel Workers Union actually had a water polo team tells you a lot about Hungary. Sports teams were organized by profession or social background: The police team was the Ujpesti Dózsa; the military team was the Honvéd. The Hungarian Gymnastics Club—the MTK—was founded by Jews who were not welcome in the Christian clubs, or in the Franzstadt, which was a club in one of the workers' districts. With the MTK, Jews created their own club.

Picking fruit was fun at first. You're at the top of the tree, enjoying the competition with your friends and teammates. You pick one, you eat one. Then the hours go by and you realize how hard it is. One day turns into two, turns into three, and your body aches. The heat is excruciating. And it's boring. We longed for our short breaks, and most of all for the ride back to camp at the end of the day, where we were greeted once again by Thunderclap Newman.

Within an hour of returning to the camp, we'd all be showered and ready to go—to dinner and the nightly singsong at the bonfire. But I didn't want to be part of this mandatory fun. Neither did György. We wanted to visit the girls' dorm.

György was tall, strong, and handsome. All the girls wanted to go out with him, but he was in love with Mari, an upbeat girl with striking red hair who wanted to become a physical therapist. György dreamed of becoming a doctor, even though he'd likely never make it to the medical faculty in Budapest because he lacked the right family background.

"We don't have any connections. My parents aren't even members of the Party," he told me.

"C'mon, György, don't give up. You have good grades, right? That's got to count for something." It wasn't just that I was trying to make my friend feel better. I knew he'd make a good doctor, if only he could find a way in.

"Good grades might matter for someone else," he said. "But not for me. Not for someone whose parents are considered enemies of the people." This was a whole new level of despair. He continued, "I have the wrong pedigree, András. My family used to be rich. Not only am I a descendant of wealthy capitalists, several members of my family have defected. I'm done for."

He was done for, all right.

"I'm sorry," was all I could manage to say.

"You know, in Western Germany, you can be granted citizenship as soon as you arrive. We have German ancestry. They would even accept the Hungarian documents for my school degrees as proof of my qualities. This is important if you want to continue to study there and not start all over."

For a minute I was wondering why he was telling me all this, but I didn't think it important enough to ask. György's knowledge of documents and citizenship was irrelevant, as far as I could see. Why not just enjoy the music and the drinking in the girls' dorm? I played my guitar—softly, though. I didn't want to be caught breaking rules.

"You play that song by the Kinks, 'Dandy'? That's a good one!" one of the girls asked. I strummed the guitar and sang, others humming along.

"That song's great, but this wine is terrible," György complained, screwing up his face. It was the infamous Kövidinka, a real cheap drink. "Nothing better?"

"Nothing better. It's in line with our budget. You didn't complain when we were at your summerhouse a month ago and you got drunk on it."

"I didn't."

"Yes, you did. But that's irrelevant, because this is the only thing you'll get tonight," I said.

"Or water," Mari said, smiling, giving me support.

"Okay, okay." He took another sip from the bottle and pulled Mari close.

György was especially romantic with Mari that whole evening. There was a certain uneasiness about the situation. György was upbeat, but Mari seemed desperate.

They were holding hands like they didn't want to let go. I, too, felt that something was not right, but I couldn't figure out what it was. We passed the bottles around until all the wine was gone.

Around ten, before the singing by the bonfire in the courtyard ended, we climbed out the window and returned to the boys' dorm.

"I hope your dream of becoming a doctor will come true," I whispered to György when the lights went out.

"Who knows," he said. "Maybe God will help me out." He had never given away his religious side before, but it was there that night, something spiritual. A belief in something larger than his current situation.

Next morning scandal broke out in the camp. György and I, along with Mari and another girl, were summoned to the camp commander's office, an austere little room that smelled of floor wax. The four of us lined up in front of Mrs. Szenes while the specters of Marx, Engels, and Lenin glared down at us from the wall behind her.

Mrs. Szenes was furious. She looked shorter, smaller, and even more sinister than she usually did. Her eyes almost closed as she talked, and her Lenin cap was pulled down on her forehead. That spelled real trouble.

"You were in the girls' dorm last night." Her voice was low and menacing.

We stood there quietly, neither confirming nor denying. We were shocked that someone had given us away.

"Drinking wine." It wasn't a question.

We still said nothing.

"Drinking?" she now asked. "How did you get those bottles into the camp? And you climbed into the girls' dorm. Through the window."

"We were just over to talk and—" This was György.

"You were told not to, right?"

"Yes," we said in unison.

"Whose idea was it? Who initiated it?" She stepped toward the much taller György. It would have been funny if it weren't so sad. "You won't get away with this, Mr. Fehérvári. There will be serious consequences. I will see that this is noted at school. I will inform the schoolmaster of your behavior. But for now, there is work to be done. Dismissed."

György, Mari, and I sat together during the lunch break in the orchard. We talked very little while eating the stew and fresh bread, the meal for the day.

"What do you think she will do?"

"Szenes will punish us for sure," György replied in a surprisingly self-confident way. "But I don't care. Screw her!"

"And your parents, what will they say?"

"I am telling you, screw her!" he repeated. "I don't want to talk about it."

We returned to camp in the late afternoon, exhausted as usual. We lined up for the head count, also as usual. But something was wrong. We were counted once, and then we were counted again. The numbers weren't right. We were a man short.

György never did show up.

They questioned me, of course. And they questioned Mari, too. Both of us could say honestly that we didn't know anything about what had happened.

"But you were talking to him this morning!" they said.

"Yes," I confirmed. "But he didn't say anything to me."

"Nothing suspicious?"

I knew nothing, thank God. So there was no danger of saying anything wrong, no danger of betrayal.

The speakers were silent the next morning.

Some weeks later I received a letter from an unknown address. It looked like an ordinary piece of mail posted somewhere in Hungary. Some well-wisher had obviously smuggled it into the country, put a Hungarian stamp on it, and dropped it in the mailbox.

György was in a refugee camp in northern Italy, close to the Yugoslav border. He had walked ten miles from camp that day, to the border where his mother, father, and younger brother, Zolika, were all waiting. They had bribed a local peasant to help them avoid the soldiers. And who knows, perhaps the border guards themselves had been bribed. He apologized for the mess he had left behind. He hoped that I wasn't implicated in what he did.

He was happy at how things had turned out. Life at the refugee camp was a little rough, he wrote, but in a few weeks his family would be on their way to West Germany, to their final destination. When he got a permit to leave the camp for a few hours, he was able to go to a local instrument store and looked at all the fine guitars. "I saw a Fender Telecaster, like the one you've always wanted and I was thinking of you," he wrote. He also said in the letter that he missed the hours he spent with me. And that he missed Mari.

"Once I am out of here, I will go see your favorite bands on your behalf." He concluded by adding that he was hoping we would see each other soon.

It would be fifteen years before I'd see him again.

CHAPTER THIRTY-FOUR

American hippies were a big thing. Colorful, inscrutable, and free, they were all about peace and love. Other than that, I wasn't too sure. I thought I saw the expression of hippie culture in some of the acts such as the Mothers of Invention, Moby Grape, Janis Joplin, and Jefferson Airplane. Since they were all in San Francisco, I reasoned, it was a pretty safe bet that they were hippies.

The Animals had recorded a song called "San Franciscan Nights" that encouraged us to fly Translove Airways to that great city. The song spoke of angels and cops, of Harley-Davidsons. I didn't really know what to make of it all, but I listened to that song nonstop, especially on those hot summer nights when I lay awake in my bed thinking about San Francisco. Hippies were a summer thing, I thought. I had seen many pictures of them, but not one in which they were dressed in winter clothing, walking in the snow, braving bad weather.

I wanted to be a hippie, although I probably didn't go about it the right way. I'm sure lots of hippies wore neon shirts splashed with psychedelic flowers, but how many had their shirts sewn for them by a seamstress? My parents laughed at the new style, but most Hungarians weren't so good-natured about it. The Communist Youth, and I suspected the police, were instructed to fight this latest American craze. Hippie culture was contrary to socialist morals and behavior, a product of capitalism. If not stopped, it would spread through the youth of Hungary like the epidemic it was.

Of course that was a lie. Hippies were competition, and the authorities did not like competition. But I knew hippies weren't the lazy, thieving, drug-addled pariahs they were made out to be. They were young people questioning their parents and bucking the established order. Idealistic men and women searching for meaning. As it should be.

Meanwhile, Hungary was continuing a slow, steady opening to the West—particularly in business. This loosening of the reins was an economic necessity. It was also a small victory for people like my father who lived for the trade with his counterparts in England, France, and indeed the United States. Father was traveling to the West more frequently now, and sometime in 1969, for the first time in his life, he went to America. Such a visit would have been unthinkable just a few years earlier, but here he was packing his bags for meetings in the USA. Not just any meetings: Father would be sitting down with executives from Levi Strauss and Company.

"They got in touch with us," he told me. "They want to have their jeans sewn in Hungary because we have great seamstresses. And we are cheap."

"And the denim? What about the denim? That's the whole thing, the denim!"

Father laughed. "They will send the material, we will cut it, sew it, and send back the finished jeans."

"Does this mean that Levi Strauss and Company denim jeans will be available in stores in Budapest?"

"Maybe we can make that part of the deal. We'll see. But you know this will be intended for exports. They will end up in Western Europe and maybe even America."

"Tell them that your son is wearing their jeans," I urged. In this small way I would be included in the meeting with the Levi Strauss executives.

Father talked more about his trip and listed the cities that he would be visiting. Of course he would be visiting San Francisco—that's where the Levi's company was based.

"Can you maybe bring me something about the hippies?" I asked.

"What do you mean?"

"Just something about them. They are based in San Francisco," I said, as if they, too, had their headquarters there.

"We'll see," he said. That sounded like a promise to me.

Every day for two weeks Gyuri and I would sit with the *Great Atlas of the World* trying to figure out where Father was that day.

"So this is day nine. I think he's in New York today," Gyuri said.

"Certainly on the East Coast."

"Washington, maybe?"

"Yes, maybe, that's where they have the White House. And look, this is the obelisk."

Proudly wearing my American gangster Clyde Barrow–inspired outfit with sister Zsuzsi and brother Gyuri in 1967. *(Photo: Denes Simonyi)*

British band Traffic at the Budapest Sports Stadium, July 7, 1968. They were playing "Dear Mr. Fantasy," the last song of the concert. *(Photo: András Simonyi)*

When I wasn't playing guitar, I was drawing. This artwork commemorates the 1968 Traffic concert in my diary. *(Courtesy of the author)*

Gyuri with his friend Tamás Váradi, showing off their American-made Lee jeans. *(Photo: András Simonyi)*

Fans line up for an Omega concert. Budapest's Youth Park was an important music venue throughout the sixties. *(Photo: Péter Groza, Fortepan)*

Friends from the Karl Marx University at a "house party." Note the Coke bottles under the table, a sign of opening to the West. *(Author's family archives)*

A happy Gábor "Gabi" Presser at the time he founded Locomotiv GT, arguably the most influential rock band in Eastern Europe. *(Photo: András Simonyi)*

Private András. In spite of all my efforts to avoid the military, I was drafted into the People's Army for a year's service. *(Courtesy of the author)*

As a guest guitarist in the Rottenbiller Street Studio of the State Recording Company, September 1971, taping the first Locomotiv GT album. *(Photo: Tamás Barta)*

Sometime in 1973, after Lotte, my Danish girlfriend, taught me how to smoke "properly." *(Photo: Gyuri Simonyi)*

Participation in the work of AIESEC became a permanent feature. Here mingling with the delegation from Finland. *(Author's family archives)*

Father catching up on paperwork from the Textile Factory, May 1949. He had returned from a Soviet prisoner of war camp just two years before. *(Author's family archives)*

Mother, at age twenty-four, in front of her family's home in Vác, Hungary. She's wearing brand-new leather gloves she made herself. *(Author's family archives)*

A rare color photo on the Danube in Budapest around 1956. Gyuri is flanked by Zsuzsi and me. Mother is in the back trying to keep us in line. *(Photo: Dénes Simonyi)*

We always had a record player with an impressive record collection, including western records. This one was rigged up to an old Phillips radio, a prewar relic considered modern at the time. *(Photo: Dénes Simonyi)*

At the Zoltán Kodály School of Music, 1958. Even children wrote with fountain pens in those days. *(Photo: Dénes Simonyi)*

With my brother and sister at Copenhagen airport, 1962. Mother stands between Zsuzsi and me while a colleague's wife looks on. *(Photo: Dénes Simonyi)*

At the Bernadotte International School in Copenhagen, 1962. The masterpieces on the wall are the students' creations. *(Photo: Dénes Simonyi)*

Soviet cosmonaut Jurij Gagarin arrives in Copenhagen, 1962. Years later this photo would earn me a big hug from American astronaut John Glenn. *(Photo: Dénes Simonyi)*

With my brand-new Framus Golden Strato, December 1965. It meant the world to me. *(Photo: Dénes Simonyi)*

Péter Békés (right) and Gyuri at Dózsa György street, spring 1966. Péter and I would soon found our own band, the Purple Generator. *(Author's family archives)*

"It says here it's the George Washington Monument."

"Yes, the first president," I said.

The night before Father arrived back home, I couldn't sleep. Neither could I pay attention in class during that day. I kept looking out the window, wondering if the plane I saw flying above was my father's plane. I was so nervous that when the trolley got stuck two stops early, I got off and ran all the way home.

Father was sitting in the study when I got there, relaxing in his leather armchair, smoking his cigarettes—fancy L&Ms. There was an air of a foreign land about him. I threw down my bag and kissed him on both cheeks. (We did not hug in our family. It wasn't a Hungarian thing.)

"Where do you want me to start?" he asked.

"Start with New York."

"New York is crazy. Everything is big. It's full of skyscrapers. The Empire State Building is taller, much taller than I had imagined."

"Where did you stay?"

"At the Hilton."

"*The* Hilton?"

"Yes, the real Hilton."

"Did you see Broadway? Did you see a show? Did you see *Hair*?"

"I did see a show—it was called *Oh! Calcutta!* And then I was taken to the Playboy Club. Here, see this. The menu!"

"Really—*ojsztersz* and *shampane*! But what is this? Here is a woman dressed up like a rabbit?"

Father just laughed.

"What I really want to know is, how were your meetings with Levi's?"

"It's a big company. Just like ours, Hungarotex," he said. "We met at their headquarters. A fancy tall building. They were all there to greet me. Men in suits."

"They weren't wearing Levi's jeans?"

"No, they wore suits like mine." That surprised me. Disappointed me, even. "And Andris, some very good news: we agreed we will be making Levi's jeans in Hungary."

"Did you tell them I wear a pair?"

"Yes. They said, 'That's nice, and maybe now more Hungarians can wear them.'"

After telling me about American root beer, which he said isn't real beer and tastes terrible, like soap, and American roads and American cars, Father talked to me about capitalism.

"I saw both sides of it," he said. "The very rich and the very poor on a street called 42nd Street, which is a dangerous place. And the Bowery with the drunk men and the down-and-outs."

"So it's bad?" I asked. I didn't want it to be bad.

"No, it's not bad, it has extremes of both. But the Americans are nice, friendly people. They shake your hand when they meet you and they always treat you with respect. It's one big democracy." He paused for a second, took a sip from his cigarette as if revising his comment—but no, he reinforced it.

"Yes, it's a democracy."

We were all so happy that Father was home. Mother got her bottle of Chanel perfume. "And Zsuzsi, for you I bought something special," Father said, and handed over a bottle of dark-red Cutex nail polish.

"It's a very special Shake Well brand. You can read that

on the bottle," he said, teasing her for her obsession with fashion brands.

"A real Shake Well. Thank you, thank you!" And with that she disappeared, coming back some ten minutes later with her nails all covered in red.

"Ah, Zsuzsi," Mother said. "It's very beautiful, but now you will have to take that off. It is not allowed in school."

"I know," she said. "But I couldn't wait."

"Ah, but did you shake it well?" Gyuri asked. We laughed at that, happy to see my sister's red nails, happy that our father was back home.

"*Ez töh jó!*" I said, which, roughly translated, means "This is awesome."

"Sure is," Gyuri confirmed.

It was the next day that Father told me about the hippies.

"They are everywhere," he said. "Oh, I almost forgot." He handed me a Kodak envelope with snapshots showing young people dressed in tied-dyed T-shirts and frayed blue jeans, scarves tied around their necks. "Here are your hippies. On top of the stack."

I was holding pictures of real live hippies that Father had taken. "Is this San Francisco?" I asked.

"That is Central Park in New York. It's right there in the middle of the city. They told me not to go there at night. But during the day it's safe."

I was still thumbing through the photographs when Father reached into his brown leather briefcase and pulled out a magazine.

"Here is something special, Andris. *Life* magazine. It's all about the hippies. I have read it. It's interesting!"

"May I read it?"

"I brought it for you. Now you don't have to wonder what these people are really like," he said.

I was curious, really curious, as to what this magazine could tell me about hippies that I didn't already know. The article said that they were monogamous, which I found surprising. I thought communes exercised free love for all, but this article said otherwise. It also said that many communities banned the use of drugs, but I didn't believe that. I knew for sure that hippies all smoked pot.

The magazine carried page after page of photographs. My favorite was a large image of a blond woman washing a child's hair in the middle of a pond. It was very peaceful, very dignified, like a romantic painting from the nineteenth century. Other photos showed the hippies in the countryside or standing outside their tepees, holding hands and smiling. They looked like they were on holiday. They looked happy. Maybe there was something to this hippie way of life.

I was eager to share the magazine with my friends. There were so many rumors going around about the hippies and how bad they were. But now I had proof, reliable information from America proving that they were peaceful, friendly people. The next day I took the magazine to school, hiding it well in my bag so that the teacher wouldn't discover it. At break I stood with my friends in a circle, to shield this valuable artifact from prying eyes.

"My father brought this from America," I said as the magazine was passed around.

"Half naked. That is so cool."

"Those kids don't have to go to school?"

"These are Americans?"

"Yes, you moron, *Life* is an American magazine," someone responded. "Let András talk."

"Yeah, and he also saw some real ones in Central Park," I bragged, as if it had been me who had been there.

Then Péter Friedman, the redheaded Jewish boy, whom I just called Friedman, said, "I heard of a group of Hungarian hippies who got fed up with our great society and decided to do exactly the same as these Americans. They moved into the forest in the outskirts of Budapest and set up their tents."

"Do you know where they are?" I asked.

"Yes I do!" he said, but was a bit more hesitant as he continued. "Or at least I think I do."

"Then let's go!"

More than anything I wanted to find these heroic hippies. If they were considered subversive to Hungarian society—they could face punishment for being too American or for being *dangerous work avoiders*—they must be doing something right. I packed my old Czechoslovak-made blue rucksack with food, and of course the *Life* magazine, which I wrapped carefully in brown wrapping paper. The hippies might need help, and what better than fresh bread, some fruit and cheese, and proof of their brothers and sisters in America.

Friedman and I took the number 56 tram to the outskirts of Buda, walking the remaining half mile to the forest. He had a map on which he had marked our destination—what he thought was our destination. On the way we asked anyone we came across if they had heard of the commune, if they knew where "those people" were. That got us nowhere.

"I know these woods," a young bearded man said. We had hoped he was a hippie. "It's improper and dangerous for you to be out there. What is exactly your business?"

"We are collecting plants and frogs for biology class," Friedman said.

"Bullshit," the man said. He was smiling, now, warming to us a little. "What are you really here for?"

"We're actually looking for hippies, okay?" Friedman said. "They're camping somewhere out in the woods here. We want to meet them."

"We have food," I said, eager to be included.

"Well, I met a policeman a while back and he said that there are dangerous criminals out here. They don't have jobs," the man continued, "and they're stealing from people."

These were our hippies all right.

"Be careful, my young friends," he said with honest concern. "I don't want you to get hurt."

We followed a trail but found nothing. Friedman didn't give up, though. "This can't be. They must be here somewhere!"

"Maybe the whole story isn't true," I said.

"Maybe they're just smarter than us and will never be found," he countered.

"But then it was a stupid idea to come all the way out here."

Friedman turned serious. "Listen," he said, "these people deserve our fullest respect. They are the resistance."

"What resistance?"

"András, you don't get it. This isn't just about having fun or emulating America or wearing a crazy shirt. This is about telling the powers holding us in their grip to go fuck themselves. Yes, those are the right words. Go fuck themselves."

"But to what effect?" I asked. Not for the first time, I felt chastened.

"I'll tell you to what effect. For people like you and me to start thinking. Not to grow up like sheep. To have the courage to fight for what we think is right." I had never heard him speak like this before. "Because I don't want to be like sheep. I don't want to fucking live my whole life being scared like my old mother and father. Scared of the Nazis because they were Jews. Scared of the communists because they were capitalists for owning a shitty little store on the Garay Market. Scared of the interiors. Scared of their own shadows."

I understood I'd better not talk to him, as angry as he was. And I didn't really need to say anything, because I was thinking—about the resistance, about how Friedman did not want to grow up like sheep. I had always thought of him as a funny guy, a kid who would pull faces behind the teacher's back or make fun of your name. I had never thought of him as a deep thinker. Now here he was, telling me something really important. People change, I guessed. Time and circumstances can change them.

In the next issue of *Youth Magazine*, I read that the police had arrested a gang of hippies in the hills of Buda. The group consisted mostly of young people from an orphanage who had no work, the article said. They were taken in for antisocial behavior and for not having a registered workplace. The authorities said that they were copying the hippies in America, and accused them of practicing promiscuity, which was a crime in itself because "their careless conduct had endangered the mental stability and health of young people." These young people were the poster children of unacceptable behavior, and their arrest was to serve as an example for others. There would be a trial and they would be convicted.

I later learned that these hippies were, in fact, educated young people who had grown disgusted with convention and lack of opportunity, with the lies they had been fed day after day. They weren't violent in the least. They just wanted to show society the middle finger. The hippies of Budapest had not been allowed to step out of society like their American counterparts, to leave the city and their frustrations behind. I looked at them differently now.

Then came news of yet another so-called gang. This was the "Big Tree Gang," who took their name from a tree that served as a prime viewing spot for the events of Youth Park. Because of their long hair and the jeans they wore, they had been denied entrance by the director and his men.

Exactly a year after the Traffic concert, in the summer of 1969, they had marched through downtown Budapest, chanting songs to commemorate the death of Brian Jones. The members of this "threatening" gang wore badges emblazoned with MAKE LOVE, NOT WAR. This was unacceptable and provocative behavior in a peace-loving country, the police said. These youngsters were a threat to society. They would be tried and convicted like the hippies in the forest, the hippies Friedman and I had set out to meet.

It was clear to me now. These people—the hippies, the troublemakers, the "gangs"—were the real heroes. They were the resistance.

CHAPTER THIRTY-FIVE

It had been a year since Woodstock. When half a million young Americans gathered in Bethel, New York, I was glued to my transistor, listening closely in my own little room. And I wasn't the only one. All across Europe—East and West—young people had tuned in to their beloved rock stations to hear about the best musicians in the world play in front of this massive crowd at an unheard-of location in America. They really were the best: Janis Joplin, John Sebastian, Country Joe, Crosby, Stills, Nash & Young, Joe Cocker, Jefferson Airplane, the Who, Santana, and, of course, Jimi Hendrix.

"Look at all those people. Can you imagine?" Péter marveled at the photograph inside the sleeve of the Woodstock album. It was now the summer of 1970, and we were finally getting to listen to the concert ourselves.

"It must have been something when Jimi played 'The Star-Spangled Banner,'" Gyuri said.

"What's 'The Star-Spangled Banner'?" Péter asked.

"That's what Americans call their national anthem."

"Are you serious? This is what the American national anthem sounds like?"

"In Jimi's version."

We sensed that Jimi was honoring not just America, but the intense years in which rock-and-roll music came of age and was perhaps coming to an end. It was hard to put your finger on it, but a year after Woodstock it seemed as if the music that had started with the Beatles no longer knew which way to go. The high that came with *Sgt. Pepper* could not be sustained, nor could it be repeated. The *White Album* came out in late 1968, a few months after the invasion of Prague. We all sang "Back in the U.S.S.R." and "Blackbird," tracks which we felt contained a strong message. But "Ob-La-Di, Ob-La-Da" spoiled the whole album with its happy-go-lucky sound. No way could we even pretend that we lived in a world where everything made sense. Things were not okay, and now I resented our beloved Beatles. Sure, I got it. With this album they were getting back to their roots. But by the end of 1969, I was into Blind Faith, Colosseum, Yes, the Electric Flag, Led Zeppelin, and David Bowie. Soon the list would include groups like Ginger Baker's Air Force and artists like Neil Young. I wasn't shocked when the Beatles disbanded. It was the inevitable end of an era.

I had grown into rock and roll. I was just a kid when it all started, and the songs brightened my days. But as I grew older, the music helped me make sense of the world. Rock and roll was a philosophy, an outlook, a way of life. It was young and free, and it belonged to my generation. Without a doubt, this was the most accessible, most democratic, and least imperialist of any art form. It spoke to us, and it spoke for us. We were an indomitable force—rock made that clear.

My close friendship with Gabi, the satisfaction of playing in the Purple Generator, and the successful concert at the Omega Club gave me a lot of street cred among musicians, even if I was the youngest among them. Hungarian bands were following the trends in America and England even more closely, while adding their own indigenous inspiration. The lyrics, almost all in Hungarian, grew ever more exciting, more in-your-face political. Doublespeak was of great help in this. I now understood that if the hopeful message of freedom was to reach Hungarians, it all had to be in Hungarian, our mother tongue. A rock and roll purist, I once would have considered such a thing sacrilege. No longer.

The tremendous experimentation and innovation resulted in a burgeoning underground scene. Colosseum and King Crimson had a great influence on one of the best, called Syrius, which was fronted by Miklós Országszky, a great bass player with an incredible voice. Syrius played in the small, packed basement club of my neighborhood in Csanády Street; their smoke-and-booze-filled gigs were a meeting place for political radicals. I thought the locale could become the Speakeasy Club of Budapest, fashioned after the famed London rock Mecca. I was proud to be a regular.

If life was never easy for Hungarian rock music, no doubt it was because of the "Who's in charge?" message that was brought home repeatedly. Illés, the popular band I unfairly mocked when I was choosing my band's name, finally made it to London. That triumph was followed by the devastating news that they would be banned from playing in Budapest for six months because they had the audacity to give an interview to the BBC. Illés had said nothing of political significance but had "failed to clear the interview with the authorities." Control! Control! Control!

Another band, a favorite of mine called Kex, was a precursor to the punk movement a few years later. They called the shots for many of us. Their music, their performances, their lyrics were pure revolt. The concerts were spontaneous and radical. You'd never know what was going to happen when they hit that first note. State Security tried "refined" methods to silence Kex, like beating up the front man, János Baksa-Soós, or banning the concerts. János once came onstage with a bloodied head. He didn't say a word about the incident, but we could guess what happened. We all knew that Kex was followed and harassed on a regular basis, called in for "interviews"—laced with a few beatings for good measure.

I graduated from Stephen I with excellence, although I should have failed the final exam with the little amount of work I put into my studies. I left high school with mixed feelings and a lot of good memories. Soon I was accepted into the Karl Marx University of Economics. But first a year of military service that was due to start in September.

I was enjoying my summer off, the long hours of playing guitar and just hanging out with my friends. I spent a lot of time with Gabi, too. His fame had grown, and he was now considered to be something of a godfather of rock musicians, the Hungarian Paul McCartney. All this at just age twenty-two. Now that I was no longer a schoolboy,

I sensed our conversations had changed. He seemed to take me more seriously as a person and a musician. We talked almost as equals now.

Gabi had been working with filmmakers for a while, writing scores. He was fascinated by the interplay between music and film, so it was no big surprise when he called me up and asked if I wanted to go to the Film Studio with him.

"We're doing the sound track to a documentary," he told me. "It's called *Munkashow* (*Workshow*). György Dobray is the director."

"Sounds great. Do you want me to play?"

"Yes, of course. Bring your acoustic guitar. I don't have the music yet, just some ideas. We'll make it up as we go along."

"I don't know how he got this script through the censors," Gabi told me. "It's funny, but it's political, too. All in all, it's pretty courageous."

When I asked if he thought the film might be shown in public, I got a noncommittal "Maybe."

According to communist dogma, workers—in particular factory workers—were responsible, moral, and disciplined subjects. They were the proud pillars of socialist society, the fully employed men and women who carried out their eight-hour shifts with joy and dignity—unlike the exploited workers in the West.

Munkashow was in the "gray zone" of material barely tolerated. It told a different story. This film was about carelessness and lack of discipline, about poor quality of work and its disastrous results. It showed workers complaining of their low pay, standing by idly, taking long breaks, and, essentially, doing nothing for hours. The voiceover made ironic remarks about how "unemployment is just something that exists in capitalist societies" and is "unknown to socialism." It projected a grim picture of Hungary.

Dobray instructed us to sit in a circle facing one another, to play our guitars and sing along with appropriately sarcastic words. "The music is live," he said. "That's how it will go on the sound track." There were four musicians there that day: Gabi, Elephant from Omega, Béla Tolcsvay, and me. I felt so good about life. So confident. As we sang, we had to stop the takes several times because we would burst out laughing. Like during one scene that was showing workers sleeping sweetly during work, the lyrics would say "The dream of the worker is sacred." Like I said, *sarcastic*.

CHAPTER THIRTY-SIX

It was time to grow up. I had to care about more than myself and the latest records. Jimi died on September 18. A month later Janis was gone. I felt sorrow. Real sorrow. I felt like something had ended and something else was coming. I did what I could to avoid becoming a soldier of the People's Army. I pretended to have a chronic disease by eating tobacco and chalk before the military doctor's exams, which induced dangerously high blood pressure. I pretended to be deaf in one ear—inspired, perhaps, by my father's ruse some years before. Nothing worked. First I ran out of options. Then I ran into Master Sergeant Varjú.

"You are an asshole, do you understand?"

"Yes, Comrade Master Sergeant, I understand. I am an asshole."

"Good, because for the next year I will be your father. Yes?"

"Yes, Comrade Master Sergeant."

"What's your name?"

"Private Simonyi, Comrade Master Sergeant."

"No, your name is Private Asshole!"

An auspicious start to my military service, I'd say.

The master sergeant was a proud man. He told endless stories about the *real war*, which was how he referred to the invasion of Czechoslovakia. He had been part of an elite unit of Hungarian reconnaissance officers whose task it had been to build a bridgehead for the invading troops.

"The Czechoslovak population were scared of us and we were scared of them," he said. "But we did what we were told and we did it well. We are soldiers. We follow commands. *Why* is not our job. *How*—that is our job."

I was in the middle of nowhere, in a base near a small town called Kalocsa, which was inhabited by army officers and paprika farmers. It may have been only about ninety miles from the capital, but it seemed light-years away. When I picked up my uniform and other equipment upon arrival, I tried to spot a radio or at least some sign that we would not be cut off from the outside world. It seemed hopeless. This wasn't a music-friendly place, especially not to my kind of music. I wanted to talk to my brother. If I couldn't have music, at least talking to him might make me feel better.

"Comrade Master Sergeant, where is the telephone?"

"The telephone is locked away."

"So if we want to phone home?"

"You don't want to phone home."

"I don't?"

"The telephone is locked away. It's not there for you to complain to your mother." I was tempted to make a smart-ass joke about complaining to my brother—not my mother—but thought better of it. He continued: "When I grant you leave, you can go to the post office and use the phone. But that won't be anytime soon."

On our second day at the base we were met by the political commissar, who informed us that we were to be an ideologically well-prepared force. If it was up to him—and it was—we would accept and promote the superiority of communism. We were the defenders of the system, the stalwarts who would resist the encroachment of capitalism.

"Communism has conquered one-third of the world. The time is near when it will conquer one-fourth, even one-fifth of the world."

Mathematics was obviously not his forte.

Despite my haircut, despite the uniform, I didn't really feel like a soldier. That all changed when an angry-looking weapons master handed me a semiautomatic rifle.

"This AK-47 is now your best friend," he said. "And you will treat it that way!"

"Yes, Comrade Sergeant."

"It's like a Kalashnikov with a foldable butt. I will teach you how to take it apart and put it together and you will keep it clean. I don't want to see dust on your little baby."

"Yes, Comrade Sergeant."

"Here is the magazine, it holds thirty bullets. God forbid you lose one!"

"Yes, Comrade Sergeant."

"If you lose *one*, you will be court-martialed."

"Yes, Comrade Sergeant."

Soon we were out in the exercise range.

"You see that Italian mountain trooper," the training officer shouted as he stood behind me.

"No, I see a tree!" I shouted back.

"Imbecile. That's an Italian mountain trooper. Shoot him down!"

Shooting a weapon is a great responsibility. A grown-up thing. I had never used a murder weapon before—that's how I thought of it—and I certainly didn't want to use it on any Italians. Nevertheless, when my first shot hit the target I felt proud.

My room at home was decorated with psychedelic posters. The posters on the base took a sharp 180 from those mind-altering designs. (Or, if you were the commissar, a sharp 360.) Colored drawings of epaulets instructed us on the ranks of officers. We learned those fast. Others advised what to do in case of a nuclear strike and what to do should the dirty Americans decide to drop a bomb on our heads. One had photos of the mushroom cloud, another had instructions about how to wear the all-plastic outfit we had to pull on above our uniform in case of a nuclear or chemical attack. Yet another one was about decontamination.

There was one company, three platoons in each barrack, one room for each of them. Twenty-seven metal bunk beds in one room, plus a fire stove, the sole provider of heat in the winter. The bunk beds were uncomfortable, with old, tired mattresses. I was in a bottom bunk, below another boy from Budapest. In the bed next to me was Gábor, my friend from the neighborhood. We were surrounded by boys from the countryside, very different from us. I tried my best to adapt, as I knew I would only be allowed to begin university studies if I made it through the military service.

"Can I take a guitar with me, sir?" I had asked the officer at the recruiting office a few months prior.

"At your own risk, soldier. Cultural activity in the military is very important," he said.

I couldn't think of a year without the consolation of my dear acoustic guitar. I decided to risk it.

A few days into basic training, I met a kindred spirit.

"I saw you with your guitar on the train. Are you a musician?" he asked.

"A musician of a sort, I guess."

We were in the bathroom, one of the few places where soldiers felt comfortable talking. I was trying to get used to the long sink with ten faucets, which served about forty people at a time. There was always a bad smell of putrid water in the bathroom, probably from the rotting rag used to clean the floors.

Tibor was a pleasant surprise. I needed a friend.

"What is your favorite rock band?" Tibor inquired further. Knowing someone's favorite band, of course, was an important point of reference.

"Traffic. I am a big Steve Winwood fan. Do you like them? Did you make it to the concert at the Sports Stadium two years ago?"

This really got Tibor's eyes wide open. Mentioning Traffic and Winwood clearly impressed him.

"Of course I was there. Who would have missed that?" he answered. "I love Traffic. You know, basically I love them all, pop or rock. The louder the better."

With this we established our credentials. I was pleased

to have someone I could talk to, someone to share the hard times ahead, someone who had the same taste in music.

When Tibor and I moved on from talking about bands, he told me about Trudi, "the West German girl." The picture he showed me was of a pretty young woman with a big smile and curly brown hair. Tibor had been head over heels in love with Trudi, but unfortunately she left him for a famous Hungarian guitarist. He was heartbroken. And maybe a little relieved.

"If the officer in charge of counterespionage found out about Trudi he would be 'unhappy' to say the least," Tibor said. "A West German girlfriend could surely be considered a spy."

"Are you serious?"

"You bet. All Western contacts are looked upon with suspicion. These officers are desperate to catch someone. And that would be the end of my university studies before they even got started."

"Well, all we can hope for is that she will drop that other guy when she sees you in your uniform." We both laughed.

In the evenings we'd gather in the barracks and sit around the Sony tape recorder I had smuggled in. We'd make tea and eat cookies from the care packages our mothers sent us. On rare occasions we'd eat Russian caviar or Chatka, the crabmeat that sold for a fortune anywhere in the world—courtesy of the Russians.

There was a Soviet military base close to town that, we suspected, took care of the nuclear missiles that didn't officially exist on Hungarian soil. As a rule, the Russian soldiers weren't permitted to mix with their Hungarian allies, so it was a big surprise when one of our friends returned to the barracks with a little glass jar of Beluga caviar, a can of Chatka crabmeat, bottles of vodka, and a loaf of dark Russian bread.

"I met these Russian soldiers in town," he explained. "They worked at the officers' canteen on their base and they offered me all this for my two Yugoslav-made Beatles records. The Russians told me that they have supplies coming in regularly, so if we want, they can get us more caviar. Even more vodka They'd like a Rolling Stones record next time."

We talked about music all the time. But as much as I missed Voice of America and Radio Free Europe, I knew that being caught listening to an American radio station would have drawn severe punishment. It could mean prison or an extended stay at the penal military unit in the south. Only the bravest attempted to listen to Radio Free Europe, Voice of America, or the more innocent Radio Luxembourg. Informers were surely all around us. We'd never know who, when, why, or what they would report to the counterintelligence officer. This wasn't paranoia, it was reality.

And yet we were never far away from our beloved rock and roll. János, aka Johnny, one of the other soldiers, actually had a subscription to the *New Musical Express*. How he got it remained a secret; nevertheless, every Thursday, like clockwork, the latest issue arrived at the base, having taken a turn in Johnny's hometown, the little village of Kunszentmárton. His mother went to the post office each week and mailed the paper to her son, and a dozen or so other soldiers in the People's Army eagerly awaited it as well. Johnny read the paper first, of course. He'd take it to the base library where, equipped with his English-Hungarian dictionary, he'd stay until closing time. Once back in the barracks, he'd recount the latest musical news to his bunk mates after lights-out. Johnny was considered to be the professor of rock among the soldiers of the First Platoon of the First Company of the First Battalion of the Revolutionary Regiment. He was a good man.

I was glad I had brought my guitar, even though I dreaded something happening to it. But it was safe, locked away in a storage room. I'd find opportunities to play it a few times a week—sometimes for a couple of minutes, and sometimes for an hour. It gave me great comfort to close my eyes and play some familiar chords.

I'd shut myself up in this small supply room and there, amid the brooms, buckets, rags, and ladders, I'd start to play. I kept a little book with me in which I had noted the chords and the words to my favorite songs. Sometimes Tibor, Gábor, or Johnny would join in, sitting on an overturned bucket while I played.

One quiet evening after a victorious day in which we had "defeated the enemy," I was playing my guitar in the closet when suddenly there was a knock on the door. It was Major Péter, our company commander. Major Péter was something of a bully who took great satisfaction in intimidating the soldiers who reported to him. He used his booming voice with great skill to scare the hell out of the soldiers every morning. "Good morning, comrades," he'd shout. "It's exercise time! You have exactly six minutes to pull on your pants and boots, make your beds, and line up outside in the corridor. I will be checking the beds!"

It was a brutal way to start the day, so when he appeared in the doorway of the supply closet I was worried that he would take away my guitar. But to my great astonishment, he said: "I know you've been hiding in here playing your guitar. Please...continue. Maybe one day you can form a band and play at the officers' club. I would like that," he added with a smile. I had never seen him smile.

Perhaps if he had been born in a different place and time, Major Péter might have become a rocker, just like me.

CHAPTER THIRTY-SEVEN

Time spent in the army was like walking in lead boots. Month after month of monotony. Political course after political course. Exercise after exercise—including shooting the Italians.

Because we were the southern front of a possible confrontation with NATO, it would have been our duty to engage in combat with the Italians. I no more wanted to kill the *Fiamme Verdi*, or "Green Flames," as they were called, now than I did at the beginning of my service, but I did long to do something different, something to break the boredom. It didn't matter if it was against the rules, just as long as it was different. I wanted to do something exciting. Something out of the ordinary. Something stupid.

Much of the summer was spent away from the military base at a place called Box of Sand. It was a treeless desert of an outpost in the middle of nowhere. Bleak and hot without a hint of vegetation, it might as well have been the moon. I had, in fact, seen the moon landing live on

Hungarian television, watching rapt as Neil Armstrong uttered his famous words: "That's one small step for man, one giant leap for mankind." And here I was on my own private moonscape, and I did not like it one bit.

We worked like dogs at this lonely outpost, swatting the buzzing flies as we built a road that led nowhere and had no real purpose. Supplies were few, and our only pleasure was walking to a little hamlet where a local farmer would prepare fresh omelets and home-baked bread. His prices were exorbitant, but then he knew there were no restaurants or even stores in a ten-mile radius.

The food was good, and the grape brandy the farmer served with it was decent. It was moonshine distilled in the back of the house and it hit us hard in the scorching summer heat. We got drunk even before we could start on the enormous portion of eggs and bread. I don't remember how we got back to the base, but I was sick for a day after that with the worst hangover I'd had in my life.

Getting drunk wasn't cool. Getting high from real drugs—now, that was cool. So cool, in fact, that people often bragged about getting high, even if they hadn't. Pretending you used drugs was a way to play the part of someone you wanted to be, someone like Mick Jagger, Jimi Hendrix, or Keith Moon. But the truth was, hash or marijuana was very hard to come by. Hungary was outside the mainstream of the drug routes at the time. Smugglers thought it safer to go through Turkey, Greece, Italy, and then into Northern Europe, thereby avoiding communist countries.

I had some hash that I got from two Swiss guys who were traveling through Hungary. Stefan and Manuel were driving a 1938 Mercedes-Benz sports car, a convertible, with a Swiss license plate. Gyuri and I happened to be at the right place at the right time when they stopped at a traffic light and asked for directions. The guys introduced themselves and we talked for a bit. They told us they were on their way from Kabul to Zurich via Istanbul. Gyuri and I suspected what this meant.

"You have hashish in the Mercedes! Aren't you afraid you'll be caught?"

"It's well hidden," Manuel said. "Sure, it's risky. If the Afghanis or the Turks had caught us, they'd have thrown us into prison or cut off our hands or something, for sure. But this is really good stuff. Hard-hitting."

They surprised us with their openness. They could easily have spent what remained of their lives in some harsh prison in Turkey or Afghanistan. They could even have received a death sentence. They wouldn't have been the first.

The ebony-white Mercedes, a rare sight on the streets of Budapest, had red leather seats and a spare wheel attached to its left side. We helped the guys find a place to stay. Later that night they detached the spare tire, which was filled not with air but with bars of hash, carefully arranged and wrapped in silver foil, like bars of chocolate. It was "Black Afghan."

"This is some of the strongest and finest ever produced," Manuel explained. And they handed us over a good chunk, their way of thanking us for helping them get set up for the night.

After my last leave I'd brought a piece of that hash back to the base and hidden it in the metal pipes of the bunk bed. If I had been caught, I would have said that it was chocolate gone bad. But I wasn't caught, and I decided to share the hash with my friends. The time and place for the little experiment was admittedly strange: the barracks of the Hungarian People's Army, a stronghold of the Warsaw Pact. As usual, most officers were gone for the weekend and, as usual, the duty officer was drunk. The group, maybe five of us, Tibor, Janó, Gergely, and perhaps Gábor, gathered around my bunk bed watching in silence as I prepared everything. I had a small pipe to be used exclusively for the purpose and *John Barleycorn*, the new release from Traffic, in the Sony cassette.

I explained the process. "Look, here is the pipe. I will stuff it with a mix of tobacco and hash, light it, and we'll pass it around. Keep it in as long as you can. If you take it down properly, like cigarette smoke, you'll be able to feel the music with all your senses," I told them. "So lock the door and get ready."

"Haha, this is the end of the Warsaw Pact!" Tibor mused. "We are destroying it from within!"

I filled the little pipe, lit it slowly, and puffed a few times. A sweet smoke filled the room. The smell of cigarette smoke was heavy in those days, so it was unlikely that anyone would have been able to make the connection. That's what I told myself. But what if one of us passed out or had a bad trip and freaked out? What if Major Major, as we referred to Major Péter after the character in the novel *Catch-22*, showed up and started asking questions? We would be standing there like idiots, stoned and laughing, and he would have us taken away by the military police immediately. We would be court-martialed, imprisoned for years. That would be the end of our university studies, which hadn't even begun.

Never mind, they all said. They were in.

I wanted my friends to be impressed. However, as is often the case with first-time users, they felt no impact whatsoever. I wasn't a first-time user; I had tried it a few times with my friends at the Hellerup school. But for my friends it was just a funny-smelling pipe with an unfamiliar bad taste. They were truly disappointed. Tibor said he could feel something, but I wasn't convinced.

"What are you supposed to feel?" he asked.

"You should feel light, like you're floating."

"Yes, I feel something," he said hopefully.

"How about you, Gergely? Are you doing okay?" I asked my other friend.

"Maybe," he said. "But not what I expected."

"Okay, stay with it, it gets better. Now leave me alone." I didn't want to talk; I was the only one in the group who was getting high fast.

I took off after a few puffs. The music was beautiful. My senses were sharp. Suddenly little yellow airplanes appeared around my head and I had to move fast to avoid them. My pretty little yellow airplanes were, of course, just common flies. But I was hallucinating.

"Hey, Pilot, get out of my way, you'll hit me," I said, bucking to avoid the crash. "There's another one. The pilots are waving at me with their red caps."

Suddenly, as if lightning had struck, everything turned black. I got scared. Real scared. I was screaming for my life, in the midst of a terrifying panic attack. I passed out.

Tibor stayed with me to make sure I was still breathing, although he had no idea what to do if I wasn't. "Here, drink some water," he said, and held a cup to my mouth. "Sit up. And shut up. There are people coming."

"What happened? I don't remember a thing. Except for the little yellow airplanes."

When the other soldiers started coming in, they asked about the funny smell. Tibor just shrugged.

I woke up the next morning with an awful headache and a terrible thirst. That was the extent of the damage, though—thankfully, nobody reported me to the duty officer for almost destroying the Warsaw Pact and giving America and its allies an easy victory. I spent the rest of the week at Box of Sand, building the road to nowhere. I swore never to touch the stuff again.

CHAPTER THIRTY-EIGHT

Visitors from the countryside came to see the boys in the military. They came with big boxes of homemade food: breaded chicken, fried potatoes, and pickles. Péter visited me once. My family came twice. Otherwise, I was forgotten in this godforsaken place. Or so I thought. I was loafing in bed one Sunday morning, feeling sorry for myself because the other soldiers were welcoming friends and family members, when the duty officer announced that I, too, had a visitor. The officer had such a big smile on his face that I snapped out of my funk and followed him outside.

It was Gabi! And he brought some news.

"I quit Omega," he said, almost immediately. "I've been thinking about this decision for a long time now. So much is happening. The Beatles broke up. Cream and Blind Faith are gone. So is Hendrix. It's Led Zeppelin and the Allman Brothers, Black Sabbath, Santana, and Deep Purple. We have to keep up. We need something new," he said. "Blind Faith is the model. Handpick the best musicians you can find. Create a vision, work hard…and then we'll be the best fucking rock band east of the Wall."

The news was earth-shattering and so very bizarre. There I was, looking like some soldier boy with that awful haircut and that dumb uniform, listening to news that would change the face of rock music in Eastern Europe. I had so many questions, but my first was obvious.

"Gabi! What's the name of the band?"

"Locomotiv GT," he responded, beaming. "We'll be the new Hungarian super-group. We'll stir the waters of rock in this country and then we'll invade England and America! I've already lined up some of the best musicians in the country: Tamás Barta from Hungária will be our guitarist; József Laux from Omega will be our drummer; we'll have Károly Frenreisz from Metro on bass."

We talked for hours—about music, family, our future in the world. We talked about everything, really, while my friends looked on enviously. Here was their buddy András talking to Gábor Presser, one of the most famous rock musicians in all of Hungary! I knew they'd be excited to hear the news. Gabi's new band might not be significant in the global context of rock and roll, but in this little country in Central Europe it would be a very big deal indeed, a sign that we were keeping up with the West.

And yet, as much as I believed in Gabi, as much as I knew that his decision would have far-reaching consequences, he still had to prove that prog rock—a Hungarian-speaking American rock band—could succeed in a country with conservative tastes. He'd have to be ready to fight the censors and the narrow-minded bureaucrats, to exercise his artistic independence within the law. As far as I could tell, he was ready.

Then Gábor was gone and I was still here. And still miserable. But I was part of a *new* family now. Tamás, the super-talented and handsome guitarist, showed up at the base a few weeks later with a leave permit for me in his hand. He called on the base commander and an hour later we were on our way to a jazz festival at Székesfehérvár where John Surman, the tenor-saxophone player from England, was playing. We would meet Gabi there.

"How did you do that, get me out of there just like that?" I asked.

"Don't worry about the commander," Tamás said. "My uncle is a lieutenant colonel in the cardiology department at the military hospital in Budapest, and the commander is his patient. These guys all end up with heart attacks, so they want to be friends with my uncle."

Tamás picked me up outside the gates of the base in his Fiat 850 Coupé. Having the right car was all part of the way he wanted to be seen. Driving this little red Italian car and not an East German Wartburg or a Russian Lada, Tamás made a statement, as he did with his Gibson Les Paul Goldtop. It was great to get away for the day and to see this phenomenal concert. John Surman was amazing. Tamás, Gabi, and I even got to meet him backstage. A striking contrast with a day at the base. But all too soon I had to return to the dreary barracks, where the only music was the snoring of two dozen soldiers of the People's Army. Tamás saw my desperation.

"Our first concert will be in July. It's important to me and to Gabi that you come. I'll ask my uncle to get you out of the service for a while."

I could hardly believe my ears.

"Here's how we'll do it," he said. "You'll become *ill* on

your next home leave and report to the Military Hospital. We will make sure my uncle László is there to order a few weeks of examination. You'll get a good 'rest' in Budapest. It's no big deal. Nobody will go after him. As I said, all those generals and colonels are his patients."

Tamás drove me back to the base where, for the next weeks, I prepared for heart failure. Soon enough I found myself at the hospital, where I was told to skip the big military exercise for which my unit had been training for months. I didn't even feel guilty. How could I when I was having such a good time at the cardiac ward of the Military Hospital of the Hungarian People's Army, where the nurses treated me like a prince? They were all part of the conspiracy, of course, and they loved Tamás. Who didn't love the handsome twenty-three-year-old guitarist?

On the day of the first Locomotiv concert—the band's debut—the good doctor László arrived with a special permit. We drove together to Park Stage in Buda, where hundreds were waiting to see the Hungarian super group with their fresh, new sound. I was standing on the corner of the stage, almost next to Gabi, enjoying myself. Tamás occasionally glanced my way, perhaps letting me know that he considered me a colleague. That meant a lot to me after having been forced out of action for a whole year. I was grateful to my friends for not forgetting about me.

The guys were a little nervous—it was LGT's first concert, after all. They needn't have worried. The audience liked the new sound, even if it was different from what they had been used to from these great musicians. Locomotiv shook Hungary. And inadvertently—or maybe intentionally—created a greater space for others. But it wasn't easy, and their success would be laced with tragedy.

* * *

I spent the next months waiting for my military service to end so that I could once again be part of the circuit. I was planning to put together my own band and it was that, rather than any notion of a university career, that kept me going. Then came the day when we shed our uniforms. Freshly demobilized from the army, high on the freedom I was going to enjoy, I prepared to jump into the middle of Hungarian rock and roll.

I was still sporting that nasty military crew cut when I went to the studio of the State Recording Company to hear Locomotiv record its first album. I had grown close to the band during the past few months, so it was only natural that they would invite me to the big event.

The once private studio in Rottenbiller Street now belonged to the people. The dowdy building was gray on the outside and olive green on the inside, as were almost all factories and large-scale institutions. The guard defending this temple of music appeared indifferent and bored, just like every guard at every official building. Only when you entered the studio of the State Recording Company did you get a hint at the magic that was made there.

There were no private recording studios in Hungary. The music industry was strictly controlled by the state. He who controlled the soundboard, controlled the content—more or less. It was a privilege to record your music. And this privilege had to be earned. Popularity helped. Or simply, popularity with someone who was politically well positioned. Unless of course you had been marked as a dissident. Then you were disqualified, no matter what.

Rock and roll in Hungary had grown up. Five years earlier, if you had three guitars and a set of drums, you were part of a dynamic, ever-changing movement. And you were considered a radical who had better be watched carefully by the authorities. Rock and roll was a tool, a powerful instrument for those who wanted to change their lives, and the lives around them. Things were different now. Playing songs by the Beatles or the Stones, or even Jimi Hendrix, didn't mark you as a radical anymore. Rock had become a broadly accepted art form.

Or had it really?

The challenge for Locomotiv was to avoid being used by the authorities for their political purposes. The authorities favored some bands, even supported them, while subjecting them to tough control. Others were shut up and then shut down. Extreme innovation, experimentation, or radical thoughts were simply not welcome. Just when you might have thought there was all the freedom you needed, the authorities would let you know that you had trespassed into forbidden territory. Politics, doublespeak, wild music…none of it was allowed. With the exception, of course, of those activist musicians who were paid to promote propaganda under the veil of rock music. But what serious rock musician would have wanted to be openly supportive of the Party line, despised as it was? Sure there were some musicians who went along, but they quickly lost favor in the eyes of young people. It was a difficult process, navigating the space between freedom of expression and political control. Locomotiv did its best to walk that narrow line.

I had never before met the people in charge of making those big decisions, the people who determined if a band should be in the studio or not. I imagined those rulings took place in austere offices behind closed doors by men in gray suits who sat around a conference table looking through files. And now, in the studio of the State Recording Company, I saw one of those men, a certain Comrade Reich. A sleek, fox-faced guy with longish, graying hair, Comrade Reich wore jeans in an effort to be part of the scene. He commented on the lyrics and made suggestions to the band. He was proud to be part of the action, and to let us know what his real job was: to set limits.

Gábor, through hard work and his obvious talent as a composer, had made it to the top. He couldn't be discarded just like that. Not that he was allowed to do whatever he pleased; in the context of the studio he was at the mercy of Comrade Reich. But millions of people listened to his music—within Hungary, throughout the Soviet bloc, and even in America and England—which gave him some clout in negotiating with the authorities.

Tamás enjoyed himself in the studio. Here there was no Hungary, no politics, no Party, no censor. There was only his guitar and rock and roll. How can you censor a guitar riff? How can you say the slide guitar is an imperialistic tool? Onstage, Tamás was always great. He played fantastically and the crowd brought out the best in him. But this was different. When you're in a studio, you play for an unknown audience. There's no immediate feedback, so it feels as if you're playing for an eternity. But whether he was on a stage or in the studio, Tamás wanted to show off his talents. He was ready to be one of the best guitarists in the world. He had a mission.

I spent days and nights at the studio watching Locomotiv record their songs. They were recording "A Song for the Ones Who Are Not with Us Any Longer," which ended up as the opening track on the LP, when suddenly Gabi turned to me and said: "Would you want to play on this track? Tamás and I want you to help out."

I was blown away. I'd been waiting for this moment for a very long time. In secret, of course.

I brought my acoustic guitar the next day. I was nervous, but I did well. We had a few takes and my part was done with the recording. But I wasn't done inside my head. I was flying high, proud as hell. I played my part to myself again and again, as if there would be more. As we wrapped up the session and listened to the takes of the day, I felt as though the moment had come for me to talk to Gabi about something very personal, an idea I had been nurturing for months now. I found a quiet moment and told him that I wanted to talk to him, just the two of us. My heart was pounding as I started what turned out to be the defining conversation of my young life.

"I need your support. I don't think I want to go to university. I want to be a musician. That's what I really want. I want to be a guitarist. I want to have my own band, travel the world, make records," I told him with a clear determination.

Gabi looked at me terrified. His usually calm face turned white, then red.

"Have you lost it? Don't you see how devastating this whole business can be? Can't you see the struggles I have, the battles I have to engage in? Have you not understood all the things I have been telling you about for years? Do you think this is just about playing music? I'm not going to allow you to do this! You go do your university or else I'll beat the shit out of you!" As Gabi was talking, I felt like his towering body grew even taller. This was the outrage of a friend who really cared. I had never seen him so upset, ever. "It's not going to happen! You hear? It's not going to happen," Gabi shouted.

My dream had evaporated in a matter of minutes. I wouldn't play on the big stage in England or America. I didn't have the courage to go it alone, even if rock music was my life. I felt like I was sinking into a deep hole. This decision would force me in directions I might not have gone, had I become a musician. That night I could not sleep, tossing and turning, on the verge of crying. My most beautiful day in music turned into one of the saddest.

CHAPTER THIRTY-NINE

I had been standing in front of the pawnshop for a while, hesitating. The window was almost empty, as if the display had no purpose at all, as if the decorations and the products haphazardly arrayed had no role in the business inside. A badly designed sign over the window announced that this was the SATURN TRADE CO-OPERATIVE. Apparently, Soviet-made water pumps, random car parts, dusty electrical motors, used tape recorders, and a collection of dead flies constituted a "co-operative." I checked the piece of paper in my pocket. This was the address Gabi had given me, all right.

"I'm Simonyi," I said to the man standing in the middle of the store.

"I was expecting you. It's the guitar, right? The Framus Strato?"

He watched me lift the top of my guitar case with barely concealed curiosity. In a society of scarcity, men like Mr. Szabó were fixers, ready to find a buyer for someone who had something—anything—to sell. In this case it was a quality Western instrument. A rare find. When Mr. Szabó saw my Golden Strato—because at this stage the instrument was definitely still mine—he stared at it for a while. Then he lifted the guitar out of its box and held it to his chest, strumming it clumsily. It was obvious he couldn't play, but I could see that he, like millions, wished he could.

After the fateful conversation with Gábor, I had put my guitar back in its case. It was months before I could bear to pick it up again. I was still very much involved with Locomotiv, though, and when they opened their LGT Club at the University of Horticulture I was one of the disc jockeys. In less than a year Locomotiv's members had established themselves as the Uncrowned Kings of Hungarian Rock.

Tamás and I still talked a lot, and met up at concerts and recording sessions. He would get sad at times, complaining about all the idiots and the informants in the music industry, the difficulties in getting travel permits, the lengths to which they had to go to please intractable bureaucrats. Sometimes he'd just come to our home to say hi. He liked to sit on the carpet and fiddle with my acoustic guitar or just listen to music.

Tamás had never before hinted at leaving the country. That was beginning to change.

"I think America would be a good place for me," he said one day.

"You want to go to America? But you're famous here!" I couldn't believe that anyone would give up rock stardom for an uncertain future.

"I could be a musician there. Like Gábor Szabó, who plays with Santana. He made it!"

We talked for a while after that. I told him all the reasons he should stay. He told me all the reasons he should go.

"Don't worry," he reassured me. "I won't leave Locomotiv."

The last year had been something of an emotional roller coaster. After leaving the military and starting university, I had fallen head over heels for a beautiful girl. My relationship with Zsuzsa was passionate and overpowering. After all, it was my first serious relationship. We complemented each other. I gave her a reason to rebel against her ultra-conservative parents. She was attracted to my rock-and-roll world, and maybe my big mouth. I loved her intelligence, her wit, and her beauty.

We'd spend time in Budapest, hanging out and listening to music. Sometimes she'd take me to the village where her grandparents lived, a place so remote in its culture that it was like a foreign land to me. But a year into the relationship I was feeling the pressure. Zsuzsa lived under the strict scrutiny of her parents, who were conservative both in their communism and their Catholicism. I was happy to continue as we were, but Zsuzsa was keen to escape the confines of her strict family and suddenly saw marriage as a logical step. I was only twenty. Marriage was the last thing on my mind. But I didn't want to lose her, so—coward that I was—I went along with it. I guess I hoped that my father would put his foot down, or maybe my mother would try to talk me out of it. But they said the choice was mine. When they invited Zsuzsa's parents for a formal engagement lunch, I knew I was done for. I bought a ring and, after a stressful and awkward lunch, asked Colonel Otto for his daughter's hand in marriage.

I was now officially engaged.

Looking back on it now, I realize that I was trying to be something I wasn't. A man with a fiancée. A university student. I had convinced myself that things would work out with Zsuzsa, but I wasn't responding well to university life. I took some comfort in knowing that a couple of professors I admired seemed to quietly like my rebel ways—my outrageous clothes and long hair—but otherwise I didn't really belong. I had a nice connection with my statistics professor, Mr. Mundruczó, prompted by his respect for my English-language skills and our mutual fondness for L&M cigarettes. And I liked Professor Katalin Kovács, my economics professor, who urged me to write a study on big corporations: IBM, Honeywell Bull, Mitsubishi, and ICL. She instructed me to investigate the computer industry and to prove her hypothesis that there would be tremendous competition among these companies and that, over time, only a handful would survive. She was right, of course, and much as my father had years before, Professor Kovács taught me to look for clues and to read between the lines.

But things weren't going well for me at Karl Marx University. Apart from spending too much time with Zsuzsa, I didn't apply myself to subjects I wasn't interested in. I was bored by my classmates, who spent all their time at the library and in small groups studying. It was about this time that I turned toward politics. And I did so with an absolute devotion. I was interested in the relationship between economics and politics, between a market economy and a democracy.

Karl Marx University was a great place to study these associations because the university itself was at the center of ideological battles.

Economics was at the core of the constant fight between conservative communists and reformers, the Muscovites and the Westerners. The latter understood that the laws of economics could not be dismantled or explained away by some twisted political theory. The communists, on the other hand, tried to bend the laws of the market at every juncture. When John Kenneth Galbraith was invited to the university at the insistence of some reform-minded professors—including my favorite, Iván Berend—he left a very deep impression. He was a rock star among economists, a charming American who swept us off our feet. It was a truly amazing experience. He, of course, enjoyed talking to students in a communist country.

When the time came to select a major, I chose foreign trade because I wanted to follow in my father's footsteps. A capitalist at heart, my father would often joke about the system. "I made a lot of money today," he'd tell us. "Millions of dollars. Not for myself, though, but for the state. Too bad." Alas, I was rejected from my major on the grounds that I wasn't "reliable enough." Even Father's fame could not get me past the representatives of the Communist Youth League, who had a big say in admissions.

Before, I could only see the differences between East and West. Now I was starting to understand the root causes of these differences. I realized that those who shared my view of rock music, those who listened to the music I listened to, were the people with whom I shared political views. I was looking for the company of those who had the courage to stay away from the Communist Youth League—Gábor, Janó, Tibor, Géza, János—and looking to stay clear of the dreaded "Lenin Couple." These two young people considered themselves the defenders of the communist flame, and we knew they reported on us. The Lenin Couple kept me on the short list of those students who were considered unreliable, a state security liability. My appearance on that list would play a role in my future.

I flirted with the illegal political opposition, who were very much active at my university. They introduced me to the work of György Konrád, whose book *The Visitor* was a scathing criticism of the system, discussing issues of poverty and deprivation in a society that was supposed to be faultless.

The world was looking more promising. America and the Soviet Union started a slow rapprochement, something that would turn into what they called a détente and which, some twenty years later, would lead to the fall of communism. But for now, despite some optimism, there was the constant fear that Russian intervention would stop the painfully slow march toward more freedom.

Just as notions of freedom and economics dominated my studies, they also seeped into my personal life. That's what I thought when Zsuzsa asked me if I would buy her a bottle of Fidji perfume by Guy Laroche. It was the trendy new scent and all the women wanted it. I wanted Zsuzsa to be happy, so I said yes.

The perfume was available at the Luxus Warehouse on Vörösmarty Square, a luxury store that stocked Western goods. I figured the perfume would be pricey, but I didn't know how expensive it would be until the salesclerk took it out of the glass display case. It cost a fortune—which I didn't have. The only real asset I had was my Golden Strato. I hadn't played it much lately, not since Gabi had talked me out of my rock-star dreams. Which was how I came to be standing in the Saturn Trade Co-operative.

Mr. Szabó continued his scrutiny of the guitar. He examined the scratches on the back of the body caused by my belt buckle—as if they were something serious. Clearly he was assembling the ammunition for a tough negotiation. He put the guitar back in its case.

"I will give you 9,500 forints. I can't do better." He looked into my eyes, the old fox, and knew instinctively that I wasn't a good negotiator.

I had no idea how much the guitar was worth. It seemed like a lot of money, more than what I had paid for it six years earlier.

"All right," I said. "I'll take it."

He reached into his pocket, pulled out a stack of bills, and counted out the money in nerve-racking slow motion, all nine thousand, five hundred forints. It was the equivalent of six months' salary for a well-paid factory worker. I would regret the exchange many times over.

The irony of this episode was that Zsuzsa and I broke up after I bought her the outrageously expensive Fidji perfume. It was a tough but liberating decision. I wanted to be free again, free to explore new relationships. That afternoon I walked down to the Danube, stopped in the middle of Margaret Bridge, and threw the golden engagement ring into the river.

CHAPTER FORTY

When Father received Uncle Egon's letter advising us of his family's visit, I was more than happy to go along for the evening. It was always nice to see old friends, and I had been hoping for an opportunity to check out the newly opened InterContinental Hotel. I heard that it had plush wall-to-wall carpeting, glittering chandeliers, and well-dressed employees ready to cater to a guest's every whim. The hotel was very much a symbol of Western capitalism and I, for one, was all for it. Forbiddingly expensive for most Hungarians, nevertheless there it stood, a shining jewel on the shores of the Danube.

Auntie Else and Uncle Egon were waiting for us, with their daughters Susan, Lotte, and Jane.

"Hi, Andris!"

"Hi...Lotte?" The last time I saw her she was a child.

"Yes, it's me!" She was laughing as she said this.

I had thought of Lotte as Susan's annoying little sister. I wasn't expecting this striking young woman with long golden hair and warm blue eyes. Then I saw that she carried a stack of records in her arms. Oh my gosh! This was as good as it gets. While my parents caught up with Auntie and Uncle, Egon gave the two older girls some money and sent us to the Moonlight Bar on top of the hotel. We were clearly the youngest guests in this sophisticated room, but we had never been to a place with red leather seats and dim lighting.

"What's happening in Copenhagen?" Gyuri asked, in Danish of course. Suddenly we were all Danes again.

"So you haven't forgotten the language?" Susan was surprised.

"Sometimes we speak Danish at home, just to practice," I said, hoping to impress the girls.

"Look, we brought you some records," Lotte said as she spread out a few LPs on the coffee table. "This is my favorite, *Gasolin'*. Nobody knows them outside of Denmark, but they are the big hit now. And this one's *Grand Funk*. They are American."

"Thank you so much. We know Grand Funk Railroad but we don't have any of their records," Gyuri raved. "This is great. Really great!"

But I wasn't listening. I couldn't take my eyes off Lotte.

The waiter came and asked what we wanted to drink. "Cola, orange juice?" he suggested.

"Martinis, of course," Susan said.

"Martinis?" he asked, somewhat shocked. The legal drinking age was eighteen, but he could surely make some concessions for these wealthy Western kids. He didn't ask for IDs—a good thing, because Lotte was seventeen.

"Yes," Susan confirmed. "Martinis."

"We'll have the same," Gyuri said.

"Dry or sweet, *sir?*" He dragged out that last word,

wanting to be smart, wanting to prove that these four young people had no idea how to drink a martini.

"Dirty," Lotte replied, establishing her credentials. Then she went on to tell the waiter how to make a dirty martini, ending with "I like mine with a twist." This girl was cool.

She put a cigarette in her mouth from a tiny pack of King's, a Danish brand. Then she offered me one. I took a few puffs and she burst out laughing.

"Andris! But you are not inhaling. That's not smoking, my friend. That's pretending." I felt stupid, like a little boy. "How do you smoke dope, if you don't inhale?"

"That's different," I said. "Anyway, I don't smoke dope every day. In fact I have decided never to smoke dope again." I launched into the story of my bad trip in the People's Army, hoping again to impress her.

Toward midnight Egon showed up to remind the girls of their curfew. I wrote my phone number on a book of matches and slipped it to Lotte.

"I want to see you, too," she said, softly—the sweetest thing I had ever heard.

Lotte and I spent the next three days roaming the streets of Pest, climbing the hills of Buda, kissing on the beautiful Chain Bridge. We had to keep things secret; Lotte knew her parents wouldn't be happy about us getting so close. To them, she was very much a little girl.

"What did you tell your father?" I asked as we met on a side street by the hotel.

"I told him that I'd be with you and your sister and that we'd visit a museum."

"Ah, but we are going to Hotel Olimpia with the cogwheel."

"The cogwheel?" she asked.

"Yes. The tram goes up into the hills—it pulls itself up by a cogwheel that bites into a track with cogs. Pretty ingenious. Swiss."

"Wow, that sounds great. When we get into this Swiss tram of yours, you can tell me about the museum, about shiny swords and the hussars—"

"Ah yes," I chipped in. "Hungary's glorious past."

"That will be enough if Father asks. He won't ask, though. He trusts you." Hearing that, I felt bad, as if I was betraying Uncle. But then I looked at Lotte and all feelings of guilt fell away.

On the night before her departure I sat on the cobblestones beneath her hotel room. I was wearing the calfskin belt she had given me as we said goodbye. "Wear this every day . . . to remember me," she said, and we shared a long, sad kiss.

Now she was standing on the balcony on the fifth floor of the hotel, throwing air kisses, looking over her shoulder to see if her father had returned. There was no way she'd be able to visit me again soon. And there was no way I could visit her. When suddenly Lotte disappeared behind the balcony door, my heart shattered. I stayed there in the cool night air, thinking about how unfair life was. Then a policeman walked up and poked me with his baton. "What are you doing here, sitting in the streets like this?" the officer asked.

"She's leaving!" I blubbered, and pointed to the balcony.

"Sorry, son. But it happens," he said quite benevolently. "It happened to me!" Then we went through the formality of a routine ID check; I was used to them. I handed over my burgundy ID booklet, which he paged through.

"You're a student. And you've been in the army, I see. And you are a sergeant first class. That's my rank." I wasn't in the mood to talk, but he continued. "Soldiers don't cry, you know. Go home, son. You'll feel better in the morning."

I didn't feel better in the morning. When I woke the next day, still in my clothes, I looked at my watch and knew that Lotte was in the air. Gone. All I had of her was the calfskin belt and the records.

I called every day.

"Oh, it's you again, dear," the operator would say. "Let me try to connect you."

Our conversations were friendly, uncomplicated—variations of *How are you today? Have you heard this record? Have you seen this movie?* Nothing those listening in on every call made to the West would care about. I just needed to hear her voice, as she needed to hear mine. I racked up an enormous phone bill that my parents made me pay out of my own pocket. But it was worth it—every forint.

I was a young man in love, praying for a miracle. It came in the unlikely form of a poster put up by the Communist Youth League:

VOLUNTEERS NEEDED
The International Association
for the Exchange of Economics Students
is seeking English speaking volunteers
to assist in the preparation of
the upcoming AIESEC Conference
to be held in the Danish town of Elsinore
January 23–28, 1973

Elsinore. That's where Hamlet's castle stood. I had visited it dozens of times as a child when my father had taken Hungarian visitors there. Never mind that it was made famous by Shakespeare. Elsinore was less than fifteen minutes from Lotte's house.

So far I had pretty much avoided the offices of the Communist Youth League. In fact, just a few months prior I had been sanctioned for non-social behavior, meaning that I hadn't participated in the mandated activities and, worse, I was keeping company with people who themselves had been kicked out of the CYL. I wasn't normally one to trust in fate or the notion that things always work out for the best (no Hungarian believes that), but I took this as a sign.

My heart was pounding as I approached the comrade at the front desk of the CYL.

"My name is Simonyi," I said.

"I know who you are."

"You do?" This was a surprise.

"Yes, I do. You are with the Transportation Faculty. There are some people here who don't like you. Your name comes up frequently." I was convinced that was it, end of conversation. "But I don't care about that," he said, shocking me. "How's your English?"

"Pretty good. You can ask my English professor!"

"I don't need to, you'll prove yourself by writing all the letters and filling out the application forms for the conference. Come and see me tomorrow afternoon and we'll get started. We don't have much time."

"But what is this all about? I don't even know what this AIESEC is!"

"Ah..." he said with a smile, as if to say, *Does it really matter?* Then he put on his official hat and continued. "The AIESEC recruits students for an exchange program to multinational corporations in the West. It provides opportunities for young Hungarians to spend time at the headquarters of Western corporations." He spoke as if reading from a pamphlet. "Then students from these Western countries will in return spend months with our companies here in Hungary. We have already done it once and we have permission from above to continue." He pointed upward, an indication that somebody higher up was giving him cover. He mentioned a name, a certain László Kovács, who many years later would become the foreign minister of a democratic Hungary.

Just recently Galbraith had presented his theories on the "New Industrial State" to Karl Marx University. And now the AIESEC had launched activities in Hungary. There had to be a connection, a dotted line between the two. I had seen it myself: economic reforms to admit the role of the market; a (somewhat reluctant) opening to the West; and this—sending Hungarian students to learn Western practices. It was progress, all right. But these developments, wonderful as they were, didn't interest me then. I was just looking for a way to get to Lotte.

CHAPTER FORTY-ONE

The AIESEC offices were pretty much as expected: wooden desks and chairs, an ugly gladiolus on the windowsill, a door to another office that was off-limits. In these Kafkaesque settings there was almost always another office, and it was almost always off-limits.

Two young secretaries were pounding away on their East German Optima typewriters when I entered, but it was Ádám the "manager" who said, "Hello!" A tall guy with longish hair, he smiled at me from under his mustache. "Let's get going."

"What's my job?" I asked.

"Help me with these application forms. Some of them are okay, but some are pretty bad. I mean, look at this one. It's make-believe English. Even I can see that. Seems like she is trying hard, but it's tough to say whether or not she would understand the manager of an American corporation. Fix it, please. Or maybe we should throw her out altogether."

I thought of that young woman and the hope that she

would have poured into this application. "You're quite right," I agreed. "'If a student from Karl Marx University' doesn't make a good first impression...But maybe I can fix it."

I kind of liked Ádám. I mean, I wouldn't have wanted to hang out with him after work, but he was okay even if he was hard to please. But he was my boss now, and I made a good effort for him. When I found out later that there had been a big debate about my involvement, I was glad I had. Apparently some people on the committee made reference to my antisocialist attitudes, claiming *that* alone should disqualify me. Others argued that I was unreliable, that I couldn't be trusted with a project requiring such a high level of confidentiality. Still others—and Ádám was one of them—came to my defense. My language skills were needed, they argued. I was an important asset. They'd be fools to let me go. That was how I got my "job" at the AIESEC.

The next few weeks were taken up with administrative duties. There was nothing very interesting about what I was doing, but at least I didn't have to climb any trees. Using my language skills was empowering. These guys actually needed me, and that felt good.

As the date of the conference drew nearer, Ádám took me for a drink at the University Club, a large room full of guys playing table football and drinking vodka and beer in not-so-deep black and red faux-leather chairs.

"The program is under siege," he told me. He was four or five drinks in by this time.

"Under siege?" I repeated.

He put down his glass with the vodka and the orange flavor mix and leaned toward me, an indication of how serious this all was. "Some people in high places are attacking the program as too dangerous, too capitalistic." I thought of Father and how he had been trying to fight the hard-liners in his reforms. "Luckily," Ádám continued, "there are others fighting on our behalf."

"What do you mean?" I cast my mind back to my conversation at the CYL and how the comrade had pointed to the ceiling, indicating that everything had been cleared.

"They tried to torpedo the whole thing!" he continued. "But for now Comrade Kovács is with us."

"Who is this mysterious Kovács?"

"He is a good man. He drives a BMW, which he bought with his own money, believe it or not. He called me and said that he had heard that some people want to shut down the whole program because it's too liberal."

"But this is just an exchange program." I pretended I didn't understand what he was getting at. But of course I did.

"We are instilling capitalist attitudes here," he said, "so you know we have to be careful about how we handle this."

Of course we were instilling capitalist attitudes, I thought. That was the whole point.

Ádám continued. "They're going to look for a pretext to shut us down. Just watch what you're saying, okay? Watch your mouth. Watch your fucking mouth." He was clearly drunk, speaking slowly, wagging his middle finger. "And God forbid one of our exchange students forgets to come back from the West. Then I am doomed and you are doomed and Comrade Kovács is doomed! Get it, my little friend?"

For weeks after that I worried that I would be excluded from the delegation. I was a long-haired troublemaker, not to be trusted. And then two weeks before the travel date, I got the word: I had been approved!

"András, you're in," Ádám told me. "Fill out these papers. You'll need a passport and a Danish visa!"

Soon I was on my way to Copenhagen. There were three of us: me, Ádám, and Comrade Nagy, a corpulent little man with a thick mustache and small eyes. A standard accompaniment to any youth delegation, Comrade Nagy was always in propaganda mode, always trying to intimidate me. He was the type of person who would do anything for an opportunity to go to the West, but once there wouldn't stop criticizing what he saw. Comrade Nagy probably knew that his comments about the West were misguided, but he also knew, much better than I, what was expected of him if he wanted a political career in Hungary: to stand up for socialist values and principles, loud and clear. That he was a hard-liner might have been a benefit to us. Having a man like him support the program would appease the conservative camp and give the program cover. Politics, I was to learn, worked in mysterious ways.

CHAPTER FORTY-TWO

We were the darlings of the congress. It was ironic, but as the first representatives from an Eastern Bloc country to join the program, we were treated like royalty. A delegation from a communist country participating in an event designed to breed capitalists was a very big deal. Moscow noticed that we were breaking rank, and they weren't too pleased with our eagerness to bring capitalism to the young people of Hungary. But then, as Ádám told me, "We don't always open our umbrellas in Budapest just because it's raining in Moscow."

We were an odd little delegation, just the three of us, but we made it work. Ádám could get by with his broken English as long as he kept his conversations simple. But Comrade Nagy couldn't speak a word. I wasn't thrilled to be his de facto translator.

"Ask the waiter if they have goulash," he said.

"This is Denmark. Of course they don't have it."

"Just ask him. I want to see his face when you ask."

"Sir, we don't serve Hungarian goulash soup. But if

the gentleman so wishes, I will ask the chef if he would prepare it as an exception. If you would explain to him how to make it."

"Tell him I make the best goulash soup in my home-town!" He laughed at his own primitive joke.

I left Comrade Nagy to his own devices whenever I could, as I did that first morning when he and Ádám were sitting at the breakfast table eating *wienerbrød*. I walked up to the smorgasbord to refill my plate and to meet the people I hoped would become my contacts and colleagues. A sharp-looking American came up to me and studied my name tag. "Hi…Andrew?" I had noticed this guy before. He was wearing a fashionable suit and tie with super-polished shoes; his trousers were deliberately short, his black socks visible.

"András," I corrected. "I am from Budapest."

"Far out," he said. "I'm Bruce, head of the US delega-tion. We're so pleased to see you guys here."

"We sure are happy to be here," I said, pointing to the table where Comrade Nagy and Ádám were sitting. (Under the circumstances, I thought it best to use the communal *we*.)

"Welcome to the world of AIESEC, András. I really hope we can work together," he said, adding, "Long term." He led me away from the buffet line toward a small, diverse group of young people.

"This is Michiko from Japan. Here is Sarah from Israel. And this is Manuel from Spain. I asked him to help you Hungarians in particular. We all want you guys to get good jobs." Spain was responsible for helping Hungary, the newcomer. It was a curious buddy system, particularly as Spain was a fascist country under dictator Francisco Franco. But it was capitalist, and that's all that mattered to the AIESEC. Comrade Nagy wasn't thrilled with this partnership, but Manuel turned out to be a helpful guy. And he was no fascist. "We appreciate that," I said. "The expectations in Budapest are high. Everyone wants to understand how modern companies are run."

"Maybe you can also tell us a little about how companies are run and owned in Hungary. Are they public companies?" Bruce asked.

"Yes, all of them are public companies," I said. "They are owned by everybody, represented through the state." I didn't say the obvious: that maybe it would be better if they weren't.

"No, no," he said. "Not *that kind* of public company. I mean a company whose shares are owned by the public and traded on the stock exchange. But don't worry, we're here to make contacts, not discuss politics."

The word *politics* inserted an awkward note into the conversation. "Do you listen to music?" I asked, keen to get back on an equal footing. Music was the international language of youth. A safe topic, I thought.

"Yes, I do," he responded, less eagerly than I had hoped.

"I listen to American bands all the time." I named as many as I could in one breath, then asked the obvious question, "Who are your favorites?"

"Maybe Pat Boone?" he said. "I'm afraid I'm not big on rock music. Not my thing." I was very disappointed.

We got the job done—making a positive impression, matching our members with some really good companies. Hilton International and IBM in the United States.

Shell and Unilever in Holland. Siemens and Bosch in West Germany. All these years later I only vaguely recall who got what position. But I remember that Kati Veres, a fourth-year girl studying finance, landed a coveted position as assistant to one of the directors of Nestlé, the Swiss food giant. Everybody knew what Nestlé was—instant coffee and chocolate. They were impressive. I remembered Kati's application, which was also impressive. Actually, it was flawless. I didn't have to change a thing. I was proud to be part of that first delegation, and I worked hard during the day so that in the evenings I could break free. Lotte had recently turned eighteen, and every day she'd come get me in her father's Jaguar, stopping a few blocks away in the parking lot of Hamlet's castle so as not to raise the suspicions of the comrades. We visited clubs in downtown Copenhagen, where we'd drink beer and dance. We hung out on the waterfront, just talking and laughing—there was a lot of laughing. And we went shopping for the latest fashionable clothes.

"Let's go get a pair of pants for you," she said. "I'll take you to Buksesnedkeren, the Trouser-Carpenter, down by the Round Tower. They're wonderful."

This Trouser-Carpenter specialized in corduroy pants, which in those days were a serious competitor to blue jeans.

"I want a pair of grays," I said to the sales assistant. I loved this store. All those colorful pants hanging in neat rows, nicely arranged. The heavy smell of dyed cotton.

"He wants a pair of *light* grays," Lotte said. "And also a pair of dark grays." I tried to signal that I found the store expensive, that I could barely afford one pair of trousers, never mind two.

"I'll pay for the dark grays," she said. "It will be a present from me, so shut up and try them on." The sales assistant had come back from the stockroom by this time with two pairs of cords draped over her arm. I tried them on.

"Well, what do you think?" I asked, wanting her approval on the dark grays.

"They're great!" Lotte said "Such a pity your ass is missing. Go for a size down." I liked hearing her talk about my ass, but I didn't like taking her money.

"Don't you worry. I have money. My own money," she said. "Later, you'll have your own money, too." I would have asked her what she was smoking, but I knew.

We went to a Gasolin' concert and screamed together with the other kids when they played my favorite, "Langebro," a melancholy song about Copenhagen. Then, full of joy, we went to her little home. Lotte had moved out of her parents' house by this time. Egon and Else were at a safe distance. It was quite amazing that an eighteen-year-old girl would have her own apartment, as small as it was, but she wanted to be independent and she could afford it, so why not? It was very peaceful, romantic even. We stayed up all night, every night, talking and listening to music. She smoked dope and drank red wine. I stuck to my Carlsberg beer. Every morning she'd drive me back to the hotel before dawn in the big car, so that I could take a catnap before breakfast and pretend to the delegation that I'd had a good night's sleep.

Back home in Budapest I had counted the days, hours, and minutes to my arrival in Elsinore. And now that I was here, as much as I tried not to, I started what I thought of as the countdown to the end, almost on my very first day. Maybe it was Hungarian pessimism—that notion of *don't get too comfortable, don't expect too much*—but I was very much aware of the limitations on my happiness.

Five days seemed like an eternity at first. I had five whole days—five whole evenings and five whole nights with my girl. On the second day, I thought, *Well, four days, that's still a very long time. You can pack a lot into four days.* But on the third day, I realized that I was halfway through my visit. That hurt. On the fourth day, I panicked. Where did the days go? Could the world just stop turning? Could time not stand still—or at least slow down a little?

On the very last evening Lotte took me to dinner at Hviids Vinstue. "I want to reciprocate the great meal we had at the Hotel Olimpia in Budapest," she said.

Hviids Vinstue was the oldest restaurant in Copenhagen. It was crowded that night, but we found a table in the back.

"Where would you live if you were to stay here?" she asked, lighting a cigarette, taking a sip from her bottle of Tuborg beer.

"If I were to stay here?" I repeated, as if the thought had never occurred to me. "In Hellerup, down by the sea."

"House or apartment?"

"Apartment. A big one, two thousand square feet! Four bedrooms. Three bathrooms. Room for the kids. Large kitchen. Like the one Else and Egon built. That would be at the heart of it all."

"Which floor?"

"Top floor. No neighbors!"

"You have big demands, my friend. And what if you couldn't afford it?"

"As long as I'm dreaming, might as well dream big." Her face turned serious. She was leading up to something.

"Would you consider staying in Denmark?" she asked. Then, "With me?" She looked at me straight. She wasn't joking. "I know you've been considering it."

Yes, I had been thinking about it. But vaguely, the way you'd wonder what your life would be like if you were taller or you'd been born in a different time. Now that I was confronted with the reality of it, I didn't know how to respond.

"How do you know?" I asked.

"Different things," she said. "You've been hinting at it for five days now."

"I have?" This was a surprise to me, but I guess it was my unconscious working its tricks. I thought I had kept things to myself.

"I see the way you look at things. The way you swear under your breath when you have to go back to your comrades. Andris, everything you look at, you look at it like it's going to be the last time. You think I am blind? Even this flounder!" she said, pointing to the remains of my meal. "I've never seen anyone look at a piece of fish with so much affection."

I didn't know whether to laugh or cry. "But, but—"

"Guess what," she continued. "I am a girl. I sense things you stupid men can't even imagine."

"So what if I stay? What can I become? Would I even be able to finish university?"

"Of course you would. You would enroll at the University of Copenhagen. It wouldn't be a big issue. They'd honor your studies in Budapest so you wouldn't have to start from scratch. I've checked." That surprised me. She came well prepared to this "meeting."

"Okay...and then what? Become a capitalist, like your father?"

"Would that be such a bad thing?"

"No, as a matter of fact. I would really like to become a capitalist. I want to make a lot of money. Money is—"

"Yes, Andris, I know. Money is power. You've said that before." I had never seen her like this.

"But it's just not realistic," I said softly.

It was a tough conversation. It wasn't just about her. This was that proverbial fork in the road: to the left was Hungary, to the right, the West. If I stayed here I would never be able to go home. Never see my mother and father again. Never see Zsuzsi and Gyuri. And what about Lotte? I loved her, but she was young. We were young. Such things mattered.

"You can become anything you want to. You could even maybe run Egon's factory when you are older. Your Danish is almost like that of a native. In a year they won't be able to tell you weren't born here. You are smart, you can do it."

"Yes, get married, have children..." I was thinking out loud now. Who knows how serious I was. "Or I could become a Danish diplomat? Maybe ambassador to Hungary." I was, of course, joking.

She didn't think this was funny at all.

I could think of nothing else. How would I tell my parents? Mother was the one I should talk to. She was the stalwart in the family, the one to hold us all together, the most likely to understand how I felt. But how would I tell her? I played the conversation over in my head.

Hello, Mother, I'm calling from Copenhagen, the train station, I've decided not to come home, I'm staying with Lotte, I would tell her as quickly as I could. Better to be fast, to rip the bandage off in one swift motion.

Andris, no. How could this be? she would say. *When did you decide this?*

I considered some other options. *What a wonderful idea. You are a courageous boy and I wish you good luck.* Not very likely.

Or maybe a more sober response: *You don't know what you are doing, son, you will be on your own and so far I've had to do everything for you. How are you going to survive? Oh, you are in love? You're twenty and you have your whole life ahead of you. Fill the bathtub with cold water, sit in it for a while, and if you are still in love after fifteen minutes go ahead and stay.* But she wouldn't be that vulgar.

Or maybe she would make a scene worthy of a silent-movie star, pressing the back of her hand to her forehead, her head tilted back a bit and tears running down her cheek.

The fact is, I had no idea how she would react. Maybe she wouldn't be home at all, even if I had the guts to call her in the first place.

I made my decision. I would stay. I had a plan, and I was determined to carry it out. I would travel with the other Hungarians to Copenhagen Central Station, and I would settle on the train with them. At the very last moment I'd make a casual comment about wanting to buy a magazine, and would get up from my seat and leave the train to make the call to my mother. Then I'd run as fast and far as I could. It might have been childish. It might have been naive. But it was my plan. And that was exactly what happened.

Almost.

We arrived at the station together—Ádám, Comrade Nagy, and me. They were both happy that we had ensured good jobs for every Hungarian applicant, as well as filling the Hungarian slots for candidates from other countries. Not to mention stuffing their suitcases with goods unavailable at home. Ádám and Comrade Nagy had substantially more luggage than they did on their way here, although neither would reveal to the other how they had the money to buy all the things they did—jeans, makeup, bars of soap. Comrade Nagy was most proud of the *Playboy* magazine with the centerfold.

We boarded the train about fifteen minutes prior to departure.

"Oh, hey. I'm just going to run and get a newspaper for my dad," I suddenly told them.

Ádám looked at me sharply. "Don't be late," he said.

I was dizzy, my heart beating hard. I ran like crazy across the platform, asking bystanders where I could find the post office to call long distance.

"It's in the left corner of the main entrance to the main hall. You can't miss it," a conductor told me.

The line at the counter was long when I got there, with people waiting to make their own long-distance calls. I couldn't wait. I walked right up to the counter and asked the telephone lady to get me through to Budapest real fast. "It's an emergency."

"If it's an emergency I'll ask these good people to let me take you first," she said. "It will be about twenty-five kroner for five minutes. You pay at the end. What's the number?"

I was praying for Mother to be home, for her to answer the phone. What would I do if Gyuri or Zsuzsi picked up? Or, God forbid, Father? I opened the door to the booth halfway and nervously told the lady at the counter, "No one's picking up!"

"Shall I try again?"

"Yes, please, could you?" Finally, after some nerve-racking moments, I heard something other than the ringing of the phone.

"Hallo..." Mother's voice.

"Hallo, it's Andris."

"Andriska? I knew it was you, it rang like long distance. How are you?" Andriska was my nickname in the family. Only Mother and Father, Gyuri and Zsuzsi were allowed to call me that.

"Very well, thank you." Considering the circumstances, I was very formal.

"You will be on your way home shortly, yes?"

"Mother, I have something to tell you." I took a deep breath. "I am not coming home. I am going to stay here. In Denmark. I am defecting." Had I really said those words?

No response.

"Hallo, Mother, are you there?"

Then she broke the silence.

"My Holy Lord, Andris! What is this you are saying? Please tell me you are joking. Please tell me that this is just a very bad joke."

I tried to stand my ground. "Mother, you see—"

A moment ago she couldn't speak. Now she couldn't stop talking. "You can't do this, Andris. You can't you can't you can't. Think of the consequences."

"Mother, yes, of course, this is not a decision I have made lightly."

"Do you know what will happen to your father—to his job? Your brother and sister, too. They will be tarnished. You know that we will not see you for a very long time? Please don't do this, please, please, please..." She was crying now. Deep heavy sobs.

I was standing there in the dimly lit wooden telephone booth, looking at the clock on the wall through the half-glass door, and seeing the precious minutes disappearing. Time was running out. I knew there would be drama. I knew there would be consequences. I had even considered that I might break my mother's heart. But I didn't think that she would break mine.

I had no choice. I paid for the phone call, ran to the kiosk, bought a magazine for show, and got back on the train with just a few minutes to spare. The comrades were happy, mostly due to the Johnnie Walker that had been passed around in my absence. As the train pulled away from the station, I looked out the window so they could not see the tears streaming down my face.

CHAPTER FORTY-THREE

It was a relief to be back in my room, the window wide open despite the winter cold. The sky was bright with stars. No one was home. I emptied my suitcase. A new shirt; a pair of red-and-blue Kickers boots. The prized records—Colosseum and Blodwyn Pig. A pair of support stockings for Mother. A copy of Solzhenitsyn's *Cancer Ward* for Father. Red candy caramel sticks for Gyuri. Mary Quant makeup for Zsuzsi. Two pairs of Buksesnedkeren corduroys, both gray.

I pinned the John Mayall and Gasolin' concert tickets on the wall, next to the funny poster I had picked up on the last day, the one of Sigmund Freud whose head turns into a naked woman if you look carefully. I tried hard to be romantic about it all, to pretend that each piece told a story. But that wasn't how I felt. I was empty. Numb. I felt like I had lost my way. I had given everything to my all-consuming affair with Lotte, and now it had come to a screeching halt. Yet as much as I was in distress, I knew that I had to move on, to get over this episode of my life one way or another. It wasn't going to be easy. But what other choice did I have?

I had to get out of the house. I walked up Fürst Sándor Street to Margaret Bridge and got on the number 2 tram to Vigadó Square. It was late and the tram was almost empty as it rode past Parliament and along the Danube quay. Looking out the tram window, I could see the royal castle on the Buda side, a boat sailing downstream loaded with coal, people hurrying by as if they were all on their way to somewhere important.

I walked past the old Thonet House where Károly Frenreisz the bassist lived. I stood outside the casino building, the art deco office building of the MAHART Shipping Company, and the InterContinental Hotel, where everything had started. The park on Vigadó Square, once dilapidated, was now nicely groomed. Roses were pushing up through the flower beds.

At last I made my way through Vörösmarty Square and Váci Street to the Paris Passage, the turn-of-the-century beauty with the stunning art nouveau design and the original old Belgian Villeroy & Boch tiles. I was heading for the espresso bar hidden in the back. That's where my friend Kati worked.

"Hey lovely, how have you been?" she asked.

"I just got back from Copenhagen."

"Wait a minute while I serve some customers and you can tell me all about it."

She made her rounds, then sat with me as I drank my coffee.

I started with the headline. "I almost defected."

"András!"

"I couldn't do it." That was all that mattered. I didn't want to go into details.

"I didn't do it, either, when I had the chance. I guess this is our destiny."

I tried hard to find some way to disagree with her. In the end, I just changed the subject.

"How's Gabi?"

"Locomotiv is touring England."

"Really? He never told me!"

"Because you were absent."

She was right. For almost a year I had neglected my friends: Gabi, Péter, Tamás. I'd stopped hanging out with them, hardly went to any of their concerts. I had gone AWOL. I had been disrespectful to the people who loved me, the ones who had supported me when I needed them most. It was time to reconnect. Time to grow up.

I looked around and couldn't resist the temptation to compare Copenhagen and Budapest. Not quite Copenhagen, I thought, but people were much better dressed than they had been just five years ago. They looked more confident, happier even, as if life was not quite such a heavy burden. Was that real, or just another illusion? Maybe in my desperation I was seeing something that wasn't actually there. Hope could do strange things to a person. I knew that now.

CHAPTER FORTY-FOUR

The Party was right to be worried about AIESEC. The experience of that first conference produced long-lasting relationships and provided opportunities for all who participated. It certainly took up a lot of my time and attention. In 1973 my first AIESEC "clients" arrived, opening another window to the West. I did my best to give these Swedes, West Germans, Spaniards, and Americans a good impression of Hungary. The AIESEC had a tremendous impact on my future. It raised my expectations of what was possible in the world and introduced me to international relations. We fought hard to keep the AIESEC going; it soon became an important feature of the Karl Marx University of Economics. We were fortunate enough to have the blessings of a number of professors. More fortunate still that they didn't shut it down when one of our exchange students "forgot" to return from the West.

Of all the students who came to Hungary, Michelle Berkowitz was my favorite. The daughter of a wealthy and influential New York family, she was one of the most modest and down-to-earth people I'd ever met. A young Republican, Michelle was nevertheless disgusted with American politics, especially President Nixon. She gave me an incredibly detailed report of how Nixon—"Tricky Dicky," she called him—orchestrated a break-in at the Democratic National Committee headquarters at the Watergate office complex in Washington, DC. She knew her stuff, right down to the last detail—that the Watergate compound was built by a Hungarian, Nicholas Salgo. She believed that Nixon would have to be impeached. It was, she assured me, "democracy at work."

Then darkness fell again. I remember the moment clearly. I was walking in the main hall of Karl Marx University. I'd just passed the statue of The Old Man (as we thought of him) when I noticed people talking in small groups. I didn't pay much attention; I was on my way to the cafeteria where my friends hung out. I ordered a cup of coffee at the counter. It was cheap despite being served in a small espresso glass, a small but welcome elegance. I was about to sit down when I saw my friend János Nemes waving at me from a distance, holding a copy of *Népszabadság* in his hand. His wife, Kati Mayer, was by his side.

"Goddamnit, they're back," he said. "The bastards are back."

"Who's back?" I asked.

"Béla Biszku and his henchmen."

This couldn't be true. Béla Biszku, member of the Politburo, was the terror of everyone who wanted to be released from Moscow's tight grip. Known as the Butcher of Budapest, Biszku was the man who mercilessly crushed pockets of resistance after the failed 1956 revolution, and who orchestrated the hanging of Imre Nagy, the leader of the revolution. A lackey of the Russians, a lapdog of Leonid Brezhnev, he had been held at bay for the last few years. And now this.

"That bastard of a murderer is back? How bad is it?"

"It's bad, András. This is the end of the road for people like your father and his friends. It's the end of the opening to the West. Just watch: soon our reform-minded prime minister and his supporters will be gone and his place will be filled by some idiot bureaucrat," he continued.

What now? How to go forward?

This was a grim reminder of our realities, of the dictatorship, of the presence of the Russians. We wouldn't escape the sorry fate of the Czechoslovaks. Moscow wouldn't let us gravitate toward the West. The Soviets wouldn't allow Hungary to flee the Soviet sphere of influence. There would also be Hungarian traitors to support them, to sell out the country for their individual gains.

Our immediate worry was losing the small freedoms we had gained, which were perhaps minor by Western standards, but to those of us living in a dictatorship, important nonetheless.

Perhaps the turn in the political atmosphere was the last straw for Tamás Barta. On a tour with Locomotiv in the United States, he turned his back on Hungary and defected. He left all his fans, his mother, and his girlfriend behind. He left the burgundy-red Gibson SG, and my little Dynacord amp, as well.

Not for the last time, cold winds were blowing in from the East. But the values instilled in me by my father, my years in Denmark, and my readings remained a reliable compass as I began my adult life. Our progress toward democracy was suffering a heavy blow; in fact, it was coming to a standstill. But the wheels of history did not stop turning. Our quest for freedom could not be denied.

Illegal concerts were taking place. Inspired by Woodstock, in the remote town of Miskolc, the first independent rock festival was spontaneously held. Many of the young people who wanted to attend were put in prison overnight. One of the musicians, János Bródy, thanked the police for their "hospitality" from the big stage. He, too, was arrested. It was a warning to us all.

Soon our amplifiers got louder, our bands got more courageous, the songs ever more political. Rock-and-roll music remained the music of hope in desperation. No one was able to shut it down. The more the authorities tried to suppress the sound of that electric guitar, the louder it got. It took exactly fifteen years before the Berlin Wall fell in 1989 and Hungary and the other captive nations of Central and Eastern Europe walked free. For all of those difficult years, rock and roll had been our inspiration, our stubborn friend, and our most faithful ally. We were euphoric. But as with all the historic disasters, the setbacks and lost causes were imprinted on our spirit, and our joy was mixed with a sense of caution: never to take our newfound freedom and our chance for democracy for granted.

ACKNOWLEDGMENTS

Writing this book has been a long process, one that has given me the immense satisfaction of repaying, in part, the debt I owe to my musical heroes: the Beatles, Traffic, Locomotiv GT, Jimi Hendrix, and Jimmy Page, as well as other great musicians and bands. I have tried to do justice to them all. Still, some musicians who have had a major impact on me are not mentioned, for which I apologize.

A very special thanks to two friends who have inspired me more than any others: Gábor Presser, my mentor; and Steve Winwood, my role model as a young boy. And then there is my very best friend for life, Péter Békés. I can't thank him enough for bearing with me as we ventured into playing rock music, as we experienced life's joys and hardships together.

I owe my positive curiosity for and outlook on life to my father and mother, who gave me more than any child could wish for. My thanks to my brother, Gyuri, and my sister, Zsuzsi, for whom I have always felt only love and affection.

Nada, my wife—my love of forty-five years—is my strongest supporter and fiercest critic. She is the one who holds the string on the ground, the other end tied to my ankle, and who tugs on it when I'm flying above the clouds, about to lose my way. She is also the one who has imposed a strict limit on the number of guitars I can own. I am lucky to have the best children, Sonja and Daniel, and the most remarkable grandchildren: Olivia, Jens, Ben, and Nico. I could not have wished for a better son-in-law than Niels or a better daughter-in-law than Kim. They all keep hoping I'll turn my amp down a bit.

This book would not have happened without my friend Barry Krost; the strong encouragement from Danielle Frum; my agents at Folio, Steve Troha and Jamie Chambliss; my editors, Rachel Kambury and Katherine Stopa; and Editor-in-Chief Karen Kosztolnyik. A big thank-you to cover designer Brigid Pearson and the rest of the team at Grand Central: Jordan Rubinstein, Alana Spendley, Brian McLendon, Jeff Holt, Carolyn Levin, Laura Jorstad, and Elece Green. At the very end, but never the very last, I want to express my utmost gratitude to my book doctor, Brenda Copeland. An angel on my shoulder, Brenda worked with me faithfully throughout the process of writing this book and taught me that inspiration is never a substitute for hard work.

Budapest–Washington, DC.
March 2019

ABOUT THE AUTHOR

András Simonyi is a former diplomat who has served as Hungary's first ambassador to NATO and as ambassador to the United States. An economist by trade, he holds a PhD in international affairs and is a specialist in multilateral diplomacy, transatlantic security, the use of "soft-power" as a foreign policy tool, and the Nordic countries. He has had a lifelong love for rock and roll and has been playing the electric guitar since the age of thirteen. Today he plays in his band, the Coalition of the Willing. András has two children and four grandchildren and lives with his wife in Washington, DC.